THE ART OF MUSIC

BY

C. HUBERT H. PARRY, M.A. Oxon

MUS. DOC. OXON., CANTAB., AND DUBLIN

FIFTH EDITION

LONDON
KEGAN PAUL, TRENCH, TRÜBNER, & CO. Lᵗᵈ
PATERNOSTER HOUSE, CHARING CROSS ROAD
1894

CONTENTS.

CHAPTER I.

PRELIMINARIES.

CHAPTER II.

SCALES.

CHAPTER III.

FOLK-MUSIC.

CHAPTER IV.

INCIPIENT HARMONY.

PAGE

Music and religion—Music of early Christian Church—Doubling melodies—Organum or diaphony—Counterpoint or descant—Singing several tunes at once—Motets—Influence of diaphony —Canons—Cadences—Indefiniteness of early artistic Music— Influence of the Church 83

CHAPTER V.

PURE CHORAL MUSIC.

Universality of choral music—Aiming at beauty of choral effect —Contrapuntal effect—Harmonic effect—Secular forms of choral music—Madrigals—Influence of modes—Accidentals —Early experiments in instrumental music — Imitations of choral forms — Viols — Lutes — Harpsichords — Organ— Methods—Homogeneity 112

CHAPTER VI.

THE RISE OF SECULAR MUSIC.

Reforming idealists—First experiments in ópera, oratorio, and cantata — Recitative — Beginnings indefinite — Expression— Tendency towards definition — Melody — Arias — Realism— Tendency of instrumental music towards independence . 137

CHAPTER VII.

COMBINATION OF OLD METHODS AND NEW PRINCIPLES.

Renewed cultivation of contrapuntal methods—Influence of Italian taste and style upon Handel—His operas—His oratorios—J. S. Bach—Influences which formed his musical character—Difference of Italian and Teutonic attitudes towards music — Instrumentation — Choral effect — Italian oratorio—Passion music—Public career of Handel—Bach's isolation—Ultimate influence of their work 171

CHAPTER XIII.

MODERN TENDENCIES.

CHAPTER XIV.

MODERN PHASES OF OPERA.

THE ART OF MUSIC.

CHAPTER I.

PRELIMINARIES.

THERE are probably but few people in the world so morose
as to find no pleasure either in the exercise or the receipt
of sympathy. It is the natural outcome of the state of
mutual dependence upon one another which is the lot and
the good fortune of human creatures; and though there
is no need to extol it at the expense of self-dependence,
it is not a thing society can dispense with or afford to
look down upon as a mere weakness. Human creatures
naturally vary to an immense extent in the character and
amount of their sympathetic impulses; and apart from
the mere commonplace everyday circumstances which call
them into play, most people have some special lines and
subjects which excite their sympathetic instincts and make
them specially conscious of the delight of fellowship in
tastes and interests, whether it be politics, science, literature, art, or sport. But of all types of humanity, those
who are possessed with artistic dispositions are notoriously
most liable to an absorbing thirst for sympathy, which is
sometimes interpreted by those who are not artistic as
a love of approbation or notoriety; and though it does
sometimes degenerate into that unhappy weakness, its
source at least is not unworthy of respect. The reason
that the sympathetic instincts are so specially character-

A

istic of the artistic type of human creature appears to
lie in the fact that the artistic nature is specially susceptible to beauty of some kind, whether it be the obvious
external kind of beauty, or the beauty of thought and
human circumstance; and the various arts of painting,
sculpture, music, literature, and the rest are the outcome
of the instinctive desire to convey impressions and en-
joyments to others, and to represent in the most attractive and permanent forms the ideas, thoughts, circumstances, scenes, or emotions which have powerfully stirred
the artists' own natures. It is the intensity of the pleasure or interest the artist feels in what is actually seen or
present to his imagination that drives him to utterance.
The instinct of utterance makes it a necessity to find
terms which will be understood by other beings in whom
his appeal can strike a sympathetic chord. And the
stronger the delight in the thought or feeling, the greater
is the desire to make the terms in which it is conveyed
unmistakably clear, and the pleasure to be obtained from
the contemplation of the work of art permanent; and
this instinctive desire is one of the main incitements to
the development of design.

Design has different aspects in different arts, but in
all it is the equivalent of organisation in the ordinary
affairs of life. It is the putting of the various factors of
effect in the right places to make them tell. In some
arts design seems the very essence and first necessity of
existence. The impression produced by vague sounds is
vague, and soon passes away altogether. They take no
permanent hold on the mind till they are made definite
in relation to one another, and are disposed in some sort
of order by the distribution of their up and down motion,
or by the regularity of their rhythmic recurrence. Then
the impression becomes permanent, and design itself
begins to take phases more like other arts. In most

arts, it is the permanence of the enjoyment rather than that of the artistic object itself which is dependent on design. In sculpture, for instance, the very materials seem to ensure permanence; but undoubtedly a piece of sculpture which is seriously imperfect in design soon becomes intolerable, and is willingly abandoned by its possessor to the disintegrating powers of rain and frost, or to some corner where it can be conveniently forgotten. Painting does not seem, at first sight, to require so much skill in designing, because the things which move the artist to express himself are so obvious to all men; but nevertheless the most permanent works of the painting art are not those which are mere skilful imitations of nature, but those into which some fine scheme of design is introduced to enhance the beauty or inherent interest of the artist's thought.

In music, form and design are most obviously necessary, because the very source and reason of existence of the art is so obscure. To some people beauty of form in melody or structure seems the chief reasons of the art's existence. At any rate, it seems on a different footing from all the other arts. Even the most unsophisticated dullard can see what inspired the painter or the sculptor to express himself, but he cannot understand what music means, nor what it is meant to express; and many practical people look upon it as altogether inferior to other arts, because it seems to have no obviously useful application or reason for existence. Painting, on the other hand, appears to the average mind to be an imitative art; and drawing a conclusion from two premises which are both equally false, some people have gone on to suppose that the only possible basis of all arts, including music, is imitation, and to invent the childish theory that the latter began by imitating birds' songs. There is no objection to such a theory if considered as a pretty poetical myth, and instances of people imitating birds can of course be substantiated; but as a serious explanation of the origin of music it is both too trivial and too incompatible with fact to be worth discussing. In reality both arts are much on the same footing, for painting is no more a purely imitative art than music. People deliberately copy nature chiefly to develop the technique which is necessary to enable them in higher flights to idealise it, and present their imaginings in the terms of design which are their highest sanction. It is just when a painter deliberately sets himself to imitate what he sees that he least deserves the name of an artist. The devices for imitating nature and throwing the unsophisticated into ecstasies, because the results are so like what they themselves have seen, are the tricks of the trade, and till they are put to their proper uses are on no other footing than the work of a good joiner or a good ploughman. It is only when they are used to convey the concentrated ideals of the mind of the artist in terms of beautiful or characteristic design that they become worthy of the name of art. Music is really much on the same footing, for the history of both arts is equally that of the development of mastery of design and of the technique of expression. The only real difference is that the artist formulates impressions received through the eyes, and the musician formulates the direct expression of man's innermost feelings and sensibilities. In fact, the arts of painting and sculpture and their kindred are the expression of the outer surroundings of man, and music of what is within him; and consequently the former began with imitation and the latter with direct expression.

The story of music has been that of a slow building up and extension of artistic means of formulating utterances which in their raw state are direct expressions of feeling and sensibility. Utterances and actions which illustrate the raw material of music are common to all sentient beings, even to those which the complacency of man describes as dumb. A dog reiterating short barks of joy on a single note at the sight of a beloved friend or master is as near making music as the small human baby vigorously banging a rattle or drum and crowing with exuberant happiness. The impulse to make a noise as an expression of feeling is universally admitted, and it may also be noticed that it has a tendency to arouse sympathy in an auditor of any kind, and an excitement analogous to that felt by the maker of the noise. A hound that has picked up the scent soon starts the responsive sympathy of the chorus of the pack; a cow wailing the loss of her calf often attracts the attention and response of her sisters in neighbouring fields; and the uproarious meetings of cats at night afford familiar instances of the effect such incipient music is capable of exerting upon the feline disposition.

Human beings are quite equally sensitive to all forms of expression. Even tricks of manner, and nervous gestures and facial distortions, are infectious; and very sensitive and sympathetic people are particularly liable to imitate unintentional grimaces and fidgets. But sounds which are uttered with genuine feeling are particularly exciting to human creatures. The excitement of a mob grows under the influence of the shouts its members utter; and takes up with equal readiness the tone of joy, rage, and defiance. Boys in the street drive one another to extravagances by like means; and, as Cicero long ago observed, the power of a great speaker often depends not so much on what he says, as upon the skill with which he uses the expressive tones of his voice. All such utterances are music in the rough, and out of such elements the art of music has grown; just as the elaborate arts of human speech must have grown out of the grunts and whinings of primeval savages. But neither art nor speech begins till something definite appears in the texture of its material. Some intellectual process must be brought to bear upon

both to make them capable of being retained in the mind;
and the early steps of both are very similar. Just as among
the early ancestors of our species, speech would begin
when the indefinite noises which they first used to com-
municate with one another, like animals, passed into some
definite sound which conveyed to the savage ear some
definite and constant meaning; so the indefinite cries and
shouts which expressed their feelings began to pass into
music when a few definite notes were made to take the
place of vague irregular shouting. And as speech grows
more copious in resources when the delicate muscles
of the mouth and throat are trained to obedience in the
utterance of more and more varied inflections, and the
ear is trained to distinguish niceties which have distinct
varieties of meaning, so the resources of music increased
as the relations of more and more definite notes were
established, in obedience to the development of musical
instinct, and as the ear learnt to appreciate the intervals
and the mind to retain the simple fragments of tune
which resulted.

The examination of the music of savages shows that they
hardly ever succeed in making orderly and well-balanced
tunes, but either express themselves in a kind of vague
wail or howl, which is on the borderland between music
and informal expression of feeling, or else contrive little
fragmentary figures of two or three notes which they
reiterate incessantly over and over again. Sometimes a
single figure suffices. When they are clever enough to
devise two, they alternate them, but without much sense
of orderliness; and it takes a long period of human development before the irregular haphazard alternation of a
few figures becomes systematic enough to have the aspect
of any sort of artistic unity. Through such crude attempts
at music, scales began to grow; but they developed extremely slowly, and it was not till mankind had arrived

at an advanced state of intellectuality that men began to take note of the relations of notes to one another at all, or to notice that such abstractions could exist apart from the music. And it has even sometimes happened that people of advanced intellectuality have not succeeded in systematising more than a very limited range of sounds.

But complete musical art has to be made definite in its horizontal as well as its vertical aspects—in the forward as well as the up and down motion; and this was first made possible by the element of rhythm.

All musical expression may be broadly distributed into two great orders. On the one hand, there is the rhythmic part, which represents action of the nature of dance motions; and on the other, all that melodic part which represents some kind of singing or vocal utterance. Rhythm and vocal expression are by nature distinct, and in very primitive states of music are often found so. In that state the rhythmic music is defined only by the pulses, and has no change of pitch, while purely melodic music has change of pitch but no definition or regularity of impulse. The latter is frequently met with among savage races, and even as near the homes of highest art as the out-of-the-way corners of the British Isles. Pure unalloyed rhythmic music is found in most parts of the uncivilised globe, and the degree of excitement to which it can give rise, when the mere beating of a drum or tom-tom is accompanied by dancing, is well known to all the world. It is also a familiar fact that dancing originates under almost the same conditions as song or any other kind of vocal utterance; and therefore the rhythmic elements and the cantabile elements are only different forms in which the same class of feelings and emotions are expressed.

All dancing is ultimately derived from expressive gestures which have become rhythmic through the balanced

arrangement of the human body, which makes it difficult
for similar actions to be frequently repeated irregularly. The evidence of careful observers from all parts
of the globe agrees in describing barbarous dances as
being obvious in their intention in proportion to the
low standard of intelligence of the dancers. Savages
of the lowest class almost always express clearly in their
dance gestures the states of mind or the circumstances
of their lives which rouse them to excitement. The
exact gestures of fighting and love-making are reproduced, not only so as to make clear to the spectator
what is meant by the rhythmic pantomime, but even
in certain cases to produce a frenzy in the mind of both
spectators and performers, which drives them to deeds
of wildness and ferocity fully on a par with what they
would do in the real circumstances of which the dancing
is an expressive reminiscence.

In these respects, dancing, in its earlier stages, is an
exact counterpart of song. Both express emotions in
their respective ways, and both convey the excitement
of the performers to sympathetic listeners. And both
lose the obvious traces of their origin in the development
of artistic devices. As the ruder kinds of rhythmic
dancing advance and take more of the forms of an art,
the significance of the gestures ceases to be so obvious,
and the excitement accompanying the performance tones
down. An acute observer still can trace the gestures
and actions to their sources when the conventions that
have grown up have obscured their expressive meaning,
and when the performers have often lost sight of them;
and the tendency of more refined dancing is obviously to
disguise the original meaning of the performance more
and more, and merely to indulge in the pleasure of various
forms of rhythmic motion and graceful gesture. But
even in modern times occasional reversions to animalism

in depraved states of society revive the grosser forms
of dancing, and forcibly recall the primitive source of
the art.

In melodic or vocal music the process has been
exactly analogous. The expressive cries soon began to
lose their direct significance when they were formalised
into distinct musical intervals. It is still possible to find
among lowly organised savages examples of almost undisguised expression which are on the border-line when
the cry or howl is barely disguised by the intervals used;
but even the first stages of artistic definition are of a
nature to put an end to untrammelled expression of
feeling. The establishment of a definite interval of any
sort puts the performer under restrictions, and every
step that is made in advance hides the original meaning of the utterance more and more away under the
necessities of artistic convention. And when little fragments of melody become stereotyped, as they do in
every savage community sufficiently advanced to perceive
and remember, the excitement of sympathy with an
expressive cry is merged in a crudely artistic pleasure
in something like a pattern.

It is obvious that the rhythmic principle and the
melodic principle begin very early to react upon one
another. Savages all over the world combine their singing and their dancing, and they not only sing rhythmically
when regular set dances are going on, but when they
are walking, reaping, sowing, rowing, or doing any other
of their daily labours and exercises which admit of such
accompaniment. By such means the rhythmic and the
melodic were combined, and it is no reckless inference
that from some such form of combination sprung the
original rhythmic organisation of poetry.

But the tendency to revert to primitive conditions is
frequently to be met with even in the most advanced

stages of art; and an antagonism, which it is one of the
problems of the art to overcome, is persistent throughout
its history. In very quick music the rhythmic principle
has an inevitable tendency to predominate, and in very
slow music the melodic principle most frequently becomes
prominent. But it must be remembered that the principle which represents vocal expression applies equally to
instrumental and to vocal music, and that rhythmic dance
music can be sung. The difference of principle between
melodic quality and rhythmic quality runs through the
whole art from polka to symphony; and, paradoxical as it
may seem, the fascination which some modern sensuous
valses exercise is derived from a distinctly cantabile treatment of the tune, which appeals to the dance instinct
through the languorous, sensuous, and self-indulgent side
of people's natures.

The antagonism shows itself as much in men as in
the art itself. Dreamers and sentimentalists tend to
lose their hold upon rhythmic energy, while men of
energetic and vigorous habits of mind set little store
by expressive cantabile. Composers of a reflective and
romantic turn of mind like Schumann excel most in
music which demands cantabile expression, and men
like Scarlatti in rhythmic effect. This rule applies even
to nations. Certain branches of the Latin race have
had a very exceptional ability for singing, and have often
shown themselves very negligent of rhythmic definiteness;
while the Hungarians manifest a truly marvellous instinct
for what is rhythmic; and the French, being a nation particularly given to expressing themselves by gesticulation,
have shown a most singular predilection for dance rhythm
in all branches of art. In the very highest natures the
mastery of both forms of expression is equally combined,
and it is under such conditions that music rises to its
highest perfection, as the use of the two principles

supplies the basis of the widest contrast of which the art is capable.

In this respect the two contrasting principles of expression are types of a system of contrasts which is the basis of all mature musical design; and when the ultimate origin of all music, as direct expression of feeling and an appeal to sympathetic feeling in others, is considered, it is easy to see that the nature of the human creature makes contrast universally inevitable. Fatigue and lassitude are just as certain to follow from the exercise of mental and emotional faculties as from the exercise of the muscles; and fatigue puts an end to the full enjoyment of the thing which causes it. It is absolutely indispensable in art to provide against it. Even the most subtle shades of such things count for a good deal; and it is the instinct of the artist who gauges human sensibilities most justly in such respects that enables him to reach the highest artistic perfection in design. The mind first wearies and then suffers pain from over-much reiteration of a single chord, or of an identical rhythm, or of a special colour, or of a special fragment of melody; and even of a thing so abstract as a principle. In some of these respects the reason is easily found in some obvious physiological fact, such as exhaustion of nervous force or waste of tissue; but it appears certain that the only reason why a similar law cannot be explained in more intangible departments is that the more refined and subtle properties of organised matter are not yet perfectly understood. But it holds good, as a mere matter of observation, that the laws which apply in cases where the physiological reasons are clear apply also in more apparently abstract cases. It is perfectly obvious that when any part of the organism is exhausted, its energy can only be renewed by rest. But rest does not necessarily imply complete lassitude of all the faculties.

It is a very familiar experience of hard-worked men that the best way to recover from the exhaustion of a prolonged strain is to change entirely the character of their work. Many of the phenomena of art are explicable on this principle. Up to a certain point the human creature is capable of being more and more excited by a particular sound or a particular colour, but the excitement must be succeeded by exhaustion, and exhaustion by pain if the exciting cause is continued. If the general excitement of the whole being is to be maintained, it must be by rousing the excitable faculties of other parts or centres of the organism; and it is while these other faculties or nerve centres are being worked upon that the faculties which have been exhausted can recover their tone. From this point of view a perfectly balanced musical work of art may be described as one in which the faculties or sensibilities are brought up to a certain pitch of excitation by one method of procedure, and when exhaustion is in danger of supervening, the general excitation of the organism is maintained by adopting a different method, which gives opportunity to the faculties which were getting jaded to recover; and when that has been effected, the natural instinct is to revert to that which first gave pleasure; and the renewal of the first form of excitation is enhanced by the consciousness of memory, together with that sense of renewal of a power to feel and enjoy which is of itself a peculiar and a very natural satisfaction to a sentient being.

In the earlier stages of the art the struggle to arrive at a solution of the problem this proposes is dimly seen. As man had only instinct to find his way with it is not surprising that he was long in finding out means of defining such contrasts. In the middle period of musical history the method and use of such contrasts is offensively obvious; and in the modern period they are disguised by infinite variety of musical and æsthetical devices, and are made to recur with extraordinary frequency. In mature art the systematisation of such contrasts is vital, and in immature art it is incipient; and this fact is the most essential difference between the two.

Of such types of contrast that of principle between the rhythmic and the melodic on one hand, and of emotional and intellectual on the other, are the widest. The manner in which they are applied in the highest works of absolute music, such as symphonies and sonatas, will hereafter come under consideration.

In the earliest stage of musical evolution these respective principles show themselves, especially in the manner in which definition is obtained, since, as has been pointed out, definiteness is the first necessity of art. From melodic utterance came the development of the scale, from dancing the distribution of pulses. The former is the result of man's instinct to express by vocal sounds, the latter of his instinct to express by gestures and actions; and in the gradual evolution of the art the former supplies the element of sensibility, and the latter that of energy; and when the nature of both is considered it will be felt that these characteristics are in accordance with the nature of their sources.

To sum up. The raw material of music is found in the expressive noises and cries which human beings as well as animals give vent to under excitement of any kind; and their contagious power is shown, even in the incipient stage, by the sympathy which they evoke in other sentient beings. Such cries pass within the range of art when they take any definite form, just as speech begins when vague signals of sound give place to words; and scales begin to be formed when musical figures become definite enough to be remembered. In the necessary process of making the material intelligible by definition, the rhythmic gestures of dancing played an important part, for by their means the succession of impulses was regulated. Both vocal music and dancing actually originate in the same way; as they are different ways of manifesting similar types of feeling. But they are in their nature contrasted, for in the one case it is the sound which forms the means of expression and in the other it is a muscular action, and the music which springs from these two sources is marked by a contrast of character in conformity with them. This contrast presents itself as the widest example of that law of contrasts which runs through the whole art, and forms next to the definition of material, its most essential feature.

The law of contrasts forms the basis of all the important forms of the art for a most obvious and natural reason. The principle of sympathetic excitement upon which the art rests necessarily induces exhaustion, and if there was no means of sustaining the interest in some way which allowed repose to the faculties that had been brought into exhausting activity, the work of art could go no further than the point at which exhaustion began. It is therefore a part of the business of art to maintain interest when one group of faculties is in danger of becoming wearied by calling into play fresh powers of sensibility or thought, and giving the first centres time to recover tone. And as there would be no point in such a device if the first group of faculties were not called into exercise again when they had revived, the balance and rationale of the process is shown in mature periods of art by a return to the first principle of excitation or source of interest after the establishment of the first distinct departure from it, which embodied this inevitable principle of contrast.

Taking the most comprehensive view of the story of musical evolution, it may be said that in the earlier stages, while the actual resources were being developed and principles of design were being organised, the art passed more and more away from the direct expression of human feeling. But after a very important crisis in modern art, when abstract beauty was specially emphasised and cultivated to the highest degree of perfection, the balance swung over in the direction of expression again; and in recent times music has aimed at characteristic illustration of things which are interesting and attractive on other grounds than mere beauty of design or of texture.

CHAPTER II.

SCALES.

THE first indispensable requirement of music is a series of
notes which stand in some recognisable relation to one
another in respect of pitch; for there is nothing which the
mind can lay hold of and retain in a succession of sounds
if the relations in which they stand to one another are
not appreciably definite. People who live in countries
where an established scale is perpetually being instilled
into every one's ears from the cradle till the grave, can
hardly bring themselves to realise the state of things
before any scales were invented at all. And the familiar
habit of average humanity of thinking that what they are
accustomed to is the only thing that can be right, has
commonly led people to think that what is called the
modern European scale is the only proper and natural one.
But it is quite certain that human creatures did exist for a
very long time without the advantage of a scale of any sort;
and that they did have to begin by deciding on a couple
of notes or so which seemed satisfactory and agreeable
when heard one after the other, and that they did have
to be satisfied with a scale of the most limited description for a very long period. What interval the primitive
savage chose was probably very much a matter of accident.
And inasmuch as scales used for melody are much less
stable than those which are used for harmony, it is quite
certain that the reiteration of a given interval was only
approximate, and that only in course of time did instinctive consensus of opinion, possibly with the help of some

primitive instrument, fasten definitely upon an interval which to modern musicians would be clearly recognisable as a fourth or a fifth, or any other acoustically explicable pair of notes.

It is advisable to guard at the outset against the familiar misconception that scales are made first and music afterwards. Scales are made in the process of endeavouring to make music, and continue to be altered and modified, generation after generation, even till the art has arrived at a high degree of maturity. The scale of modern harmonic music, which European peoples use, only arrived at its present condition in the last century, after having been under a gradual process of modification from an accepted nucleus for nearly a thousand years. Primeval savages were even worse off than mediæval Europeans. They did not know that they wanted a scale; and if they had known it they would have had neither acoustical theory or practical experience to guide them, nor even examples to show them how things ought not to be done. But it is extremely probable that in the end they selected an interval which would approve itself to the acoustical theorist as well as to the unsophisticated ear of a modern lover of art. It is extremely difficult to guess what that interval would be, and pure theoretic speculation is almost certain to be at fault; but examination of the numerous varieties of scales existent in the world, and of such as are recorded approximately by ancient wind instruments, with the help of theory, may ultimately come very near to solving the problem.

With reference to this point, it may be as well to recognise that in the great number of scales which have developed up to a fair state of maturity, there are no two notes whatever that invariably stand in exactly the same relation to one another throughout all systems. It might well be thought that the octave could be excluded from

B

consideration, as if it were not part of a scale, but only the beginning of a new series. But even the octave is said to be a little out of tune in accordance with the authorised theory of Chinese music. However, this is clearly only a characteristic instance of the relation between theory and art, for no Chinese musician would be able to hit an exact interval, in singing, which was just not a true octave, even if he was perverse enough to try. Of other familiar intervals the varieties are infinite. In our own system the fifth is less in tune than in many other systems, and in the Siamese scale there is nothing like a perfect fifth at all. The fourth is an interval which is curiously universal in its appearance, but that again does not appear in the true Siamese scale, or in one of the Javese systems. An agreement in such intervals as thirds and sixths is not to be expected. They are known to be difficult intervals to learn and difficult to place exactly in theoretic schemes; and the result is that they are infinitely variable in different scales. Some systems have major thirds and some minor; and some have thirds that are between the two. Sixths are proportionately variable, and are often curiously dependent upon the fifth for any status at all; and of such intervals as the second and seventh, and more extreme ones, it must be confessed that they are so obviously artificial that even in everyday practice in countries habituated to one scale, they are inclined to vary in accordance with individual taste and the lack of it.

Of all these intervals there are two which to a musician seem obviously certain to have been the alternatives in the choice of a nucleus. As has been pointed out, sixths, thirds, sevenths, and seconds are all almost inconceivable. They are all difficult to hit certainly without education, and are unstable and variable in their qualities. There remain only the intervals of the fourth and the fifth; and evidence as well as theory proves almost conclusively that one of these two formed the nucleus upon which almost all scales were based; and one of the two was probably the interval which primitive savages endeavoured to hit in their first attempts at music.

But at the outset there comes in a very curious consideration which must of necessity be discussed before going further. If a modern musician, saturated in the habits of harmonic music, was asked for an opinion, he would say instantly that it was impossible that any beings could have chosen the fourth as their first interval; for that seems as hard to hit as thirds and sixths, and is even more inconclusive and unsatisfying to our ears. But nevertheless the fact remains that it is oftener met with than the fifth in barbarous scales, and if modern habits of musical thought can be put aside the reason is intelligible. Our modern harmonic system is an elaborately artificial product which has so far inverted the aspect of things that in order to get back to the understanding of ancient and barbarous systems we have almost to set our usual preconceptions upside down. The modern European system is the only one in which harmony distinctly plays a vital part in the scheme of artistic design. Our scale has had to be transformed entirely from the ancient modes in order to make the harmonic scheme of æsthetics possible, and in this process the manner in which the cultivators of other systems regard their scales has become almost a lost sense. All other schemes in the world are purely melodic. They only admit of a single line of tune at a time, and their scheme of æsthetics is totally alien to such a highly artificial and intellectual development as that of modern European music. In melodic systems the influence of vocal music is infinitely paramount; in modern European art the instrumental element is strongest. The sum of these considerations is, that whereas in modern music people count their intervals from the bass, and habitually think of scales as if they were built upwards, in melodic systems it is, in most cases, the reverse. The most intelligent observers of Oriental systems notice that those who use them think of these scales as tending downwards; and in certain particulars it is undoubtedly provable that the practice of the ancients also was exactly contrary to ours. To take one consideration out of many as illustration. The leading note of modern music always tends upwards; in other words, the note which lies nearest to the most essential note of the scale, which is always heard in the final cadence, and is its most characteristic melodic feature, is below the final and rises to it. But this is exactly the reverse of the natural instinct in vocal matters, and contrary to the meaning of the word cadence.

Most of the natural cadences of the voice in speaking tend downwards. When a man raises his voice at the end of a sentence he is either asking a question or expressing astonishment, and these are expressions of feeling which are in a minority. Pure vocal art follows the rule of the inflections in speaking; and in melodic systems, which are so much influenced by the voice, cadences which rise to the final sound are almost inconceivable. They might be possible as expressing great exaltation of feeling and power, but in most cases a cadence means, artistically, a point of repose, and it is only in very exceptional cases that a point of repose can be imagined on a high note; for the sustainment of a high note implies tension of vocal chords and effort, and such sustained effort can scarcely be regarded as a point of repose. In modern music the cadence is a harmonic process and not a melodic one; and the rising of the leading note to the tonic in cadences becomes intelligible as a movement of upper portions of the harmonies which happen to coincide with æsthetic requirements of melody when supported by harmony.

In melodic systems the majority of cadences are, as the word implies, made downwards; and undoubtedly in a majority of cases the scale was developed downwards. This view puts quite a different complexion on the difficulty of accounting for the more frequent appearance of the fourth in scales used only for melodic purposes. For, going downwards, it is perfectly natural and easy to hit the interval of the fourth, and a curious peculiarity in the construction of many and various scales corroborates the likelihood of the fourth having been first chosen downwards. It is an indubitable fact that scales are developed by adding ornamental notes to the more essential notes which have been first established; that is, notes which lie close to the essential notes and to which the voice can waver indefinitely to and fro. A note of this kind would not at first be very exact in relative position. Mere uncertainty of voice would both suggest it and make it variable; and undoubtedly it became a conspicuous feature of the cadences very early. If the fourth below was chosen by a musical people in developing the melodic scale downwards, it is likely to be verified by the frequent appearance of a note a semitone above it, as this would be the first addition made to the scale, and the downward tending leading note of the system.

There are many proofs of this theory of the development of the scale, notably the ancient Greek scale, and the modern Japanese and the aboriginal Australian scale, such as it is. The first scale which history records as used by the Greeks is indeed absolutely nothing more than a group of three notes, of which those which are furthest apart make the interval of the fourth, and the remaining note is a semitone above the lower note. This is precisely the scale which analogy and argument alike lead us to expect as the second stage of scale-making under melodic influences, and a proof that the first interval

chosen was the downward fourth. The Japanese system
had nothing whatever to do with the Greek system, but
the same group of notes is extremely characteristic, and
is undoubtedly used with persistent reiteration in their
music. A modern European can get the effect for himself
by playing C, and the A♭ and G below it one after another,
and reiterating them in any order he pleases so long as
he makes A♭ the last note but one and G the final. The
result is a curious reversal of our theories of musical
æsthetics, for G seems to become the tonic, and C the
note of secondary importance—a state of things which
is only conceivable if we think of the scale as tending
downwards instead of upwards.

But it is not to be denied that some races seem to have
chosen a rising fifth as the nucleus of the scale, though it
is much less common. The voice has to rise in singing
as well as to fall, and it is conceivable that some races
should have thought more of the rise which comes early
in the musical phrase, than of the fall which naturally
comes at the end. One of the most astute and ingenious
analysts of musical scales, Mr. Ellis, thought that early
experimenters in music found out the fifth as the corresponding note to the fourth on the other side of the
note from which the fourth was first calculated. The
proof of the fifth's being recognised early—beyond its
inherent likelihood—lies in the fact that some barbarous scales comprise the interval of an augmented
fourth, such as C to F♯, which is only intelligible
in a melodic system on the ground of the F♯ being
an ornamental note appended to the G above it.
The original choice of a fifth or a fourth as the basis
or starting-point may have had something to do with
the fact that nearly all known scales which have arrived
at any degree of completeness can be grouped under
two well-contrasted heads. The scales of China, Japan,

Java, and the Pacific Islands are all pentatonic in their recognised structure. That is, they theoretically comprise only five notes within the limits of the octave, which are at various distances from one another. But in this group the fifth from the lowest note is a prominent and almost invariable item. The rest of the most notable scales of the world are structurally heptatonic, and comprise seven essential notes in the octave. Such are the scales of India, Persia, Arabia, probably Egypt, certainly ancient Greece and modern Europe. And in these the fourth was the interval which seems to have been first recognised. To avoid misconception, it is necessary to point out that all these scales have been subjected to modifications in practice, and their true nature has been obscured. But the situation becomes intelligible by the analogy of our own use of the modern scales. Ours are undoubtedly seven-note scales, as even children who practise them are painfully aware; but in actual use a number of other notes, called accidentals, are admitted, both as modifications and as ornaments. The key of C is clearly represented to every one by the white keys of a pianoforte, but there is not a single black note which every composer cannot use either as an ornament or as a modification without leaving the key of C. Similarly nearly all the pentatonic scales have been filled in, and the natives that use them are familiar with other notes besides the curious and characteristic formula of five, but in the background of their musical feelings the original foundation of their system remains distinct; just as the scheme of the key of C remains distinct in the mind of an intelligent musical person even when a player sounds all the black notes in a couple of bars which are nominally in that key.

It undoubtedly made a great difference whether the fifth or fourth was chosen, for it is noticeable that small intervals like semitones are rare in five-note systems and

common in seven-note systems; and this peculiarity has
a very marked effect in the music, for those which lend
themselves readily to the addition of semitones have
proved the most capable of higher development. It is
unnecessary to speculate on the way in which savages
gradually built their scales by adding note to note, as
the historical records of Greek music go so far back into
primitive conditions that the actual process of enlargement
can be followed up to the state which for ancient days
must be considered mature. It is tolerably clear that
the artistic standard of the music of the Greeks was very
far behind their standard of observation and general intelligence. They spent much ingenious thought upon the
analysis of their scales, and theorised a good deal upon
the nature of combinations which they did not use; but
their account of their music itself is so vague that it is
difficult to get any clear idea of what it was really like.
And it still seems possible that a large portion of what
has passed into the domain of "well authenticated fact"
is complete misapprehension, as Greek scholars have not
time for a thorough study of music up to the standard
required to judge securely of the matters in question, and
musicians as a rule are not extremely intimate with Greek.
But certain things may fairly be accepted as trustworthy.
Among them is of course the enthusiasm with which the
Greeks speak of music, and their belief in the marvellous power of its effects. The stories of Orpheus and
Amphion and others testify to this belief strongly, and
mislead modern people into supposing that their music
was a great art lost, when the very fact and style of their
evidence tends to prove the contrary. It is not in times
when art is mature that people are likely to tell stories
of overturning town walls or taming savage animals with
it; but rather when it is in the elementary stages in
which the personal character of the performer adds so

much to the effect. It is a sufficiently familiar fact that in our own times a performer of genius can move people more and make more genuine effect upon them with an extremely simple piece than a brilliant *virtuoso* of the highest technical powers can produce with the utmost elaboration of modern ingenuity. A crowd of people of moderate intelligence go almost out of their minds with delight when a famous singer flatters them with songs which to musicians appear the baldest, emptiest, and most inartistic triviality. The moderns who are under such a spell cannot tell what it is that moves them, and neither could the Greeks. They would both confess to the power of music, and the manner of their confession would seem to imply that they had not arrived at any high degree of artistic intelligence or perception. The Greeks, moreover, were much nearer the beginning of musical things, and may be naturally expected to have been more under the spell of the individual sympathetic magnetism of the performer than even uneducated modern people; and the accounts we have of their system tend to confirm these views. Its limitations are such as do not encourage a belief in high artistic development, for at no time did the scheme extend much beyond what could be reproduced upon the white keys of the pianoforte and an occasional B♭ and C♯; and all the notes used were comprised within the limits of the low A in the bass stave and the E at the top of the treble stave. The first records indicate the time when the relations of three notes only were understood, which stood in much the same relation to one another that A F E do in our modern system.

This clearly does not represent the interval of a third with a semitone below it, but the interval of a fourth looking downwards with F as a downward leading note to E. This was called the tetrachord of Olympos. In time the note between A and

F was added, which gave a natural flow down from A to E.
This was well recognised as the first nucleus of the Greek system, and was called the Doric tetrachord. It was enlarged by the simple process of adding another group of notes which corresponded exactly to the first, such as E, D, C, B, below or above, thereby making a balance to the other tetrachord. It is possible that their musical sense developed sufficiently to make use of the artistic effects which such a balance suggests; and it is even likely that the desire for such effects was the immediate cause of the enlargement of the scale. In course of time similar groups of notes, called tetrachords, were added one after another till the whole range of sounds which the Greeks considered suitable for use by the human voice was mapped out. The whole extent of this scale being only from B in the bass stave to A in the treble indicates that the Greeks preferred only to hear the middle portion of the voice, and disliked both the high and low extremes, which could only be produced with effort; and it proves also that their music could not have been of a passionate or excitable cast, because the use of notes which imply any degree of agitation are excluded. The last note which is said to have been added in the matter of range was an A below the lowest B, which was attributed to a lyre-player of the name of Phrynis in B.C. 456. But this note was considered to stand outside the set of tetrachords, and was not used in singing, but only to enable the harp-player to execute certain modulations.

The Greek musical system being a purely melodic one, it was natural that in course of time a characteristic feature of higher melodic systems should make its appearance. For the purposes of harmony but few arrangements of notes are necessary, but for the development of effect in melodic systems it is very important to have scales in which the order of arrangement of differing intervals vary. In the earliest Greek nucleus of a scale, the Doric, there was a semitone between the bottom note and the next above it in each tetrachord—as between C and B, or F and E. In course of time the positions of the semitones were altered to make different scales, and then the tetrachord stood as B, C♯, D, E, or as in our modern minor scale D, E, F, G. This was called the Phrygian, and was considered the second oldest. Another arrangement with the semitone again shifted, as B, C♯, D♯, E, resembles the lower part of our modern major scale, and was known as the "Lydian." When the tetrachords were linked together at first they overlapped, as in the Doric form if the lower tetrachord was B, C, D, E, the one added above it would be E, F, G, A, the E being common to both tetrachords. This was ultimately found unsatisfactory, and a scheme of tetrachords which did not overlap was adopted about the time of Pythagoras. Thus the Doric mode stood as E F G A B C D E, the semitones coming between first and second and fifth and sixth; the Phrygian mode became like a scale played on the white notes of the pianoforte beginning on D; and the Lydian like our ordinary major scale; and more were added, such as the Æolic, which is like a scale of white notes beginning on A, the Hypolydian like one beginning on F, and so forth.

The restrictions of melodies to these modes secured a strong variety of character, to which the Greeks were keenly alive; and they expressed their views of these diversities both in writing and in practice. The Spartan boys were exclusively taught the Doric mode because it was considered to breathe dignity, manliness, and self-dependence; the Phrygian mode was considered to have been nobly inspiring also, but in different ways; and the Lydian, which corresponded to our modern major mode, to be voluptuous and orgiastic, probably from the fact that the semitones lay in the upper part of the tetrachords, which in melodic music with a downward tendency would have a very different aspect from that of our familiar scale under the influence of harmony. But this mode was not in great favour either in ancient times or in mediæval times, when attempts were made to revive the Greek system.

In this manner a series of the notes which were supposed to be fit for human beings to sing were mapped out into distinct and well-defined positions. But one of the most important developments of the scale still remained to be done. In modern times the scale has become so highly organised that the function of each note and the particular office each fulfils in the design of compositions is fairly well understood even by people of moderate musical intelligence. What is called the tonic, which is the note by which any key is named, is the most essential note in the scale, and the one on which every one instinctively expects a melody or a piece of music in that key to conclude; if it stops elsewhere every one feels that a fair conclusion has not been reached; and all other notes are related to it in different degrees—the semitone below as leading to it, the dominant as the note most strongly contrasted to it, and so forth. But to judge from the absence of remarks upon such functions in Greek writers, and the obscurity of Aristotle's remarks on the subject, it must be assumed that the ideas of the Greeks on such a head were not strongly developed. In the beginning, when there were only three notes to work with, it seems as if their musical reason for existence necessarily defined their functions; but it is probable, as frequently happens in similar cases outside the range of music, that composers speculated in arrangements of the

notes which ignored the purposes which brought them
into existence, and that, as the scale grew larger and
larger, people ceased to recognise that any particular
note was more important than another It is true they
had distinct names for every note in a mode, and two
are specially singled out as important, namely, the
" middle " note and the " highest," which all modern
writers agree was what we should call the lowest. If
anything can be gathered from the writings on the
subject at all, it seems to imply that the middle note,
the " mese," was something like our dominant, and the
" hypate," which we should call the lowest, was the note
to close upon. If this was so, the original functions
described on page 21 were still recognised in theory;
but the wisest writers on the subject in modern times
think that matters got so confused that a Greek musician
would end upon any note that suited his humour. This
vagueness coincides with the state of the scales of all
other melodic systems; and though the Greeks were more
intelligent than any other people that have used a melodic
system, it is very likely that without the help of a system
of harmony it is almost impossible to systematise a scale
completely.

The Greek system was subjected to various modifications in the course of history. It was very natural that
such intellectualists as they were should try experiments
to enhance the opportunities of the composer for effect.
One experiment was made very early, which was to add
a note like C♯, but less than a semitone above the C,
which stood next above the lowest note of the old Doric
tetrachord. This was called the chromatic genus, and
other experiments were tried in subdividing into yet
smaller intervals; but the various writers who describe
these systems indicate that they were not altogether
successful, as the chromatic genus was regarded as

mawkish and insipid, and the enharmonic genus as too artificial.

The Greek system may therefore be considered to have arrived at its complete maturity in the state in which a range of sounds extending only for two octaves was mapped out into a series of seven modes, which can be fairly imitated on a modern pianoforte by playing the several scales which begin respectively on E, F, G, A, B, C, D, without using any of the black keys. The difference between one and another obviously lies in the way in which the tones and semitones are grouped, and the device affords a considerable opportunity for melodic variety. But it appears improbable that the Greeks arrived at any clear perception of the functions of the notes of the scale in the manner in which we regard our tonic and dominant: the full development of this phase of scale-making had to wait till after the attempt to systematise ecclesiastical music on what was supposed to be the ancient Greek system in the early middle ages, when the new awakening of the sense of harmony soon caused scales to take entirely new aspects.

But this being the highest artificial development of the scale element of music in connection with harmony must be considered later, as there are many other melodic systems like the ancient Greek in their application but different in their order of arrangement. In the many and various melodic systems of the world scales are found of various structure, but in all the process of building has evidently been similar. Races show their average characteristics in their scales as much as they do in other departments of human energy and contrivance. Such as are gifted with any degree of intellectual activity have always expended a singular amount of it on their scales; and the result has been pedantically minute, or theoretic, or extravagantly fanci-

ful in proportion to their inclinations in that direction.
The Chinese, as might be expected, have been at once
minutely exact in theory and bombastically complacent
in fancy. The races of the great Indian peninsula have
been wildly fanciful in their imagery and equally ex-
travagant in ingenious grouping of notes into modes;
while the Persians and Arabs have been remarkable for
their high development of instinct in threading the
difficult and thorny ways of acoustical theory in such
a way as to obtain a very perfect system of intonation.
The Persian system is probably the most elaborate scale
system in the world. Nothing appears to be known
of early Persian music, and the earliest records give
examples of scales which are already very complete,
implying a very long period of antecedent cultivation
of the art. In the tenth century they had already
developed a scale which looks singularly complete, as
it comprises the intervals which are characteristic of
both our major and minor modes, except the major
seventh, which is our upward tending leading note.
That is, it appears as the scale of C with both E flat
and E natural, and both A flat and A natural, but
B flat only instead of our familiar leading note B.
This shows that they certainly did not at that time
attempt cadences like our European ones, and kept to
the natural system; but they did not rest satisfied with
this scale. By the time of Tamerlane and Bajazet the
series of notes had been enlarged by the addition of
several more semitones, and the series had been sys-
tematised into twelve modes, on the same principle of
selection and for the same purposes of melodic variety
as had been adopted by the Greeks. In fact the first
three agree exactly with the ancient Ionic, Phrygian, and
Mixolydian modes of the Greeks, but go by the very different names of Octrag, Nawa, and Bousilik. But even

this did not go far enough for the subtle minds of the Persians and Arabians. A famous lute-player adopted a system of tuning which gave intervals that are quite unknown to our ears; as, for instance, one note which would lie between E♭ and E, and another between A♭ and A, in the scale of C. The former is described as a neutral third, neither distinctly major nor minor, which probably had a pleasant effect in melodic music; and the latter as a neutral sixth.

Going still further, they applied mathematical treatment of a high theoretical kind to the further development of the scale. They evidently discovered the curiously paradoxical facts of acoustics which make an ideally perfect scale impossible, and, to obviate the difficulties which every acoustical theory of tuning presents, they subdivided the octave into no less than seventeen notes. Their object was, not to have so many notes as that to make melodies with, or to employ quarter tones, but to have so many to select from as alternatives. The arrangement of these notes was quite systematic, and gave two notes instead of the one familiar semitone between each degree of the scale and the one next to it. That is to say, between D and C there would be two notes, one a shade less than a semitone (making the interval known as the Pythagorean limma 243 : 256), and another a little less than a quarter tone from D (making the interval known as the comma of Pythagoras 524288 : 531441). And the same arrangement came between D and E, and so on through the scale. By this ingenious arrangement they secured absolutely true fifths and fourths, a major third and a major sixth that were only about a fiftieth of a semitone (that is, a skisma) short of true third and sixth; and a true minor seventh. Theoretically this is the most perfect scale ever devised. Whether it really was used exactly in practice is another matter. Even under harmonic conditions, when notes are sounded together, it is impossible for the most expert tuners to make absolutely sure of intervals within such narrow limits as the fiftieth of a semitone, and it is well known that in melodic systems the successions of notes used by the performers are only approximately exact; for the finest ear in the world can hardly make sure of a true third or a true sixth when they are only sounded one after the other. In modern times this remarkable system has been changed still further, though on less delicately subtle lines, by the adoption of twenty-four equal quarter tones in the octave. But this, though it looks a larger choice, will not give such absolutely true intervals as the earlier scheme. With all this wonderful ingenuity in dividing off the range of sounds for use and defining the units exactly, it appears that the Persians and Arabians have but an uncertain sense of what we call a tonic, and as far as can be gathered, stop short of classifying the notes in accordance with their artistic functions just as the Greeks seem to have done.

In strong contrast to the Persians the inhabitants of the great Indian peninsula appear to have sedulously avoided applying mathematics to their scale. And though the Indian scales are even more complicated and numerous than the Persian, they were handed down purely by aural tradition. Unfortunately this avoidance of mathematics has caused the subject of Indian scales to be extremely obscure, and the extraordinarily high-flown imagery which is used in Indian treatises on music renders the unravelling of their system the more difficult. The method used for arriving at the actual scales used by musicians is to test the notes produced by the subdivisions of a length of string which are indicated by the actual positions of the frets upon the lute-like instrument called the vina, which has been in universal use for many hundreds of years. The

C

frets are supposed to mark the points at which the string
should be stopped with the finger to get the different
notes of the scale; but in practice a native player can
always modify the pitch by making his finger overlap
the fret more or less, and thereby regulate the fret to the
interval which tradition taught him to be the right one.
In fact the frets on different instruments vary to a considerable degree—even the octave is sometimes too low
and sometimes too high; but through examining a number
of specimens a rude average has been obtained, which
seems to indicate a system curiously like our own system
of twelve semitones. But it is clear that this can be only
a rough approximate scheme upon which more delicate
variations of relative pitch are to be grafted, for the actual
system of Indian scales is far more complicated than a
mere arrangement of twelve equal semitones can provide
for.

As in the case of the Persian and Arabic system, the
Indian scale does not come within the range of intelligible
record till it was tolerably mature and complete from
octave to octave. In order to get a variety of major and
minor tones and semitones the scale was in ancient times
divided into twenty-two small intervals called s'rutis,
which were a little larger than quarter tones. A whole
tone contained four s'rutis, a three-quarter tone three, and
a semitone two. By this system a very fair scale was
obtained, in which the fourth and fifth were very nearly
true, and the sixth high (Pythagorean). In what order
the tones and semitones were arranged seems to be
doubtful; and in modern music the system of twenty-two
s'rutis has disappeared, and a system of the most extraordinary complexity has taken its place. The actual series
of notes approximates as nearly as possible to our arrangement of twelve semitones; the peculiarity of the system
lies in the way in which it has been developed into modes.

The virtue of the system of modes has already been pointed out, as has the adoption of a few diverse ones by the Greeks. The Indians went so far as to devise seventy-two, by grouping the various degrees of the scale differently in respect of their flats and sharps. This can be made intelligible by a few examples out of this enormous number. Our familiar major mode of course forms one of them, and goes by the name of Dèhraśankârabhárna. Our harmonic minor scale also appears under the name of Kyravâni, the Greek modes also make their appearance, and every other combination which is possible to get out of the semitones, but always so that each degree is somehow represented. The extremes to which the process leads may be illustrated by the following. Tânarupi corresponds to the following succession—

C, Db, Ebb, F, G, A♯, B, C.

Gavambódi to

C, Db, Eb, F♯, G, Ab, Bbb, C.

This obviously carries the modal system as far as it can go.

But besides these modes the Indians have developed a further principle of restriction in the "ragas," which are a number of formulas regulating the order in which the notes are to succeed each other. The rule appears to be that when a performer sings or plays a particular raga he must conform to a particular melodic outline both in ascending and descending. He may play fast or slow, or stop on any note and repeat it, or vary the rhythm at his pleasure; it even appears from the illustrations given that he may put in ornamental notes and little scale passages, and interpolate here and there notes that do not belong to the system, so long as the essential notes of the tune conform to the rule of progression.—Just

as in modern harmonic music certain discords must be
resolved in a particular way, but several subordinate notes
may be interpolated between the discord and the resolution.—An example may make the system clearer. The
formula given for the raga called Nâda-nâmakrýa is
C, Db, F, G, Ab, C in ascending, and C, B, Ab, G, F, E,
Db, C in descending. In practice it is evident that the
performers are not restricted to the whole plan at once.
G may go either to F descending or to Ab ascending, and
Ab may either go to C or back to G, and so on; but the
movement from any given note must be in accordance with
the laws of the raga, up or down. The example of this raga
given in Captain Day's Music of Southern India helps to
make the system clear.

In the mode of Máya-mâlavagaula, and the raga Nâda-nâmakrýa.

By this means the freedom of the performer is restricted,
but curious special effects are obtained. For instance, the
ascending scheme of Mohànna is C, D, E, G, A, C, which
produces precisely the effect of Chinese or any other pentatonic music, though the Indian music belongs to the other
group of systems; and close as the restrictions seem to
be, it may be confessed that judging from the examples
given a good deal of variety can be obtained. A similar
device to that of the ragas is very commonly met with
even in modern European music, when a composer restricts
a melody to a particular group of notes in order to give

it more definite character. Pursuing their love of cate-
gorising still further, the Indians restrict particular ragas
to particular hours of the day, and they used also to be
restricted to particular seasons of the year. As was the
case with the Greeks and their modes, the different ragas
have different attributes, and respectively inspire fear,
wonder, anger, kindness, and so forth. And moreover
they are all personified as divine beings, and have wives,
and histories, and are the subjects of elaborate pictures
and apparently also of fanciful poems. This all points to
a very long period of development, and to a considerable
antiquity in the established system; for even people who
luxuriate in imagery and fancifulness like the Indians, do
not attribute divine qualities to a scheme which they
themselves have only devised in comparatively recent
times. The whole story also points to a considerable
feeling for the organisation of artistic material, but it is
recorded that the Indians have little feeling for anything
like a tonic, or for relative degrees of importance in the
notes that compose the scale; and there seems little
restriction as to which note in the scale may be used for
the final close.

The ancient Greek, and the Persian and Indian systems,
are the most important of the heptatonic systems; all of
which appear to have been developed from the basis of
the fourth, and they certainly have served for the highest
developments of pure melodic music. Some of the pentatonic systems (with modes of five notes) have also
admitted of very elaborate and artistic music, but the
standard is generally lower, both in the development of
the scale and of the art for which it serves.

The system which is usually taken as the type of the pentatonic group is the Chinese, which stands in most marked
contrast to the Persian and Indian systems in every way.
The passion for making ordinances about everything, and

the obstinate adherence to schemes which have received the
approval of authority, which characterise the Chinese, make
themselves felt in their scale system as everywhere else.
According to authorised Chinese history, their music is
of marvellous antiquity, and copious details are given
about the surpassing wonders of the ancient music, and
of the great emperors from nearly 3000 B.C. onwards,
who composed music and ordinances for its regulation;
but the account is so overwhelmed by grandiose and absurd
myths and extravagances that it is impossible to trace
the development of the scale. It has been altered several
times, but the alterations are by no means of the nature
of developments. About B.C. 1300 the scale is said to
have corresponded to C, D, E, G, A,
which may be taken to be the old pentatonic formula.
About 1100 B.C. it was amplified to C, D, E, F♯, G, A, B, C.
Later still, when a
great Mongol invasion occurred, the Mongols changed
the F♯ to F, and made the scale like our major mode.
But then some of the musicians wanted to use F and
some F♯, and Kubla Khan, founder of the Mogul
dynasty, ordained that there should be both F and F♯
in the scale, which accordingly became C, D, E, F, F♯, G,
A, B, C. About a couple of hundreds of years later the F♯
was abolished again, and soon after that the late form
of the pentatonic scale was adopted, which stands as
C, D, F, G, A. But meanwhile the
Chinese had from early ages a complete set of twelve semitones just as we have, but arrived at, as their history tells,
in a singular semi-scientific manner. According to the
very careful and conscientious treatise of Van Aalst, the

Chinese say that there is perfect harmony between heaven and earth, and that as the number 3 is the symbol of heaven and 2 of earth, any sounds that are in the relation of 3 to 2 must be in perfect harmony. They accordingly cut two tubes, one of which is two-thirds the length of the other, and took the sounds which they produced as the basis of their musical system. Fanciful as the story is, it points to the germ of truth, that the interval of the fifth, which is produced by such a pair of tubes, was really the nucleus of the pentatonic system. And according to their story they went on to find out other notes by cutting a series of twelve such tubes, each of which was either two-thirds of the next longer, or gave the octave below the note obtained by that measurement. To all appearance this gave them a complete series of semitones. The tubes so cut were the sacred regulators of the national scale, and were called the "lus." They were also held to be the twelve moons, and also the twelve hours of the day, and other strange things; and the fact that they were all these wonderful things at once made it indubitable that the scale was perfect and not to be meddled with. But in fact nearly all the intervals were out of tune. The fifth tube would ostensibly give a note a third above the lowest tube—as, if the lowest was C the second would give G, the third D, the fourth A, and the fifth E. But that note would really be too high, and the intervals would go on getting worse till they arrived at the octave, which would be the worst of all. But the matter is ordained so. The "lus" were made in accordance with the sacred principles of nature, and therefore though the scale does not sound agreeable it is right, and so it must remain. In order to keep the scale in accordance with these sacred principles the "lus" were made of such durable materials as copper and jade; and though it appears that the "lus" are no longer in use, the system on which they were constructed still regulates the Chinese scale. But this must not be taken to imply that all these twelve semitones were to be used in the same piece of music. Their only service was to enable the characteristic pentatonic series to be made to start from different pitches. Practically the Chinese only use one mode at a time. In early times they only used a series corresponding to the notes produced by the first five "lu" pipes; that is, C, D, E, G, A, which is their old pentatonic form. The modern series is theoretically that which corresponds to C, D, F, G, A. The use of the semitones is to enable the series to be transposed, which does not alter the mode, except by varying the degree in which the notes are out of tune. On great ceremonial occasions the hymns have to be sung in the "lu" which is called after the moon in which it is celebrated. So if in a ceremony which took place in the first moon the pentatonic series began on C, the hymn would be sung a semitone higher each successive moon, till at a ceremony in the twelfth moon it would begin on B, a seventh higher than the first; and then at the next performance the hymn would drop a whole major seventh, and be sung in notes belonging to the scale of C again. To be hedged in with such conditions as these cannot be expected to be encouraging to art, and it is not to be wondered at that the Chinese system is the most crudely backward and incapable of development of any of the great melodic systems. But at the same time it must not be ignored that notwithstanding such obstacles, and the fact that musicians are looked down upon as an inferior caste in China, the Chinese do manage to produce good and effective tunes; and it cannot be denied that the pure pentatonic system lends itself peculiarly to characteristic effects, and to the production of impressions which are more or less permanent. Its very restrictions give it an

appearance of strangeness and definiteness which attract
notice, and with some people liking.

Nations which have not been so tied and bound by
ordinances and dogmatic regulations have managed to
develop pentatonic systems to a much higher degree of
artistic elasticity, and the result has naturally been in
some cases to destroy the characteristic pentatonic effect.
The Japanese were among the foremost to expand their
system in every way they could think of. They have
nominally a complete series of twelve semitones just as we
have in Europe, but like all other employers of melodic
music they only use them to select from. Authorities
differ, but their type seems to be pentatonic in origin,
like the Chinese; though, unlike them, they distribute
their intervals so as to obtain twelve different modes of
five notes each. For instance, one mode of five notes,
called Hiradioschi, corresponds to C, D, E♭, G, A♭;
another, Kumoi, to C, D♭, F,[1] G, A♭; another, Iwato,
to C, D♭, F, G♭, B;[2] from which it is to be observed
that they fully appreciate the artistic value of semitones;
which again distinguishes them from the Chinese, who
rarely use such intervals. They are said to make use of
the octave, the fifth, and the fourth in tuning, and to tune
their thirds and sixths by guesswork, and not by any
means scientifically. The thirds are said to be often more
like the "neutral thirds" described in connection with
Persian music, which are neither major or minor, but
between the two. A Japanese musician, who seems fully
competent to form an opinion, has expressed doubts as
to whether their scale was true pentatonic or not. In
face of the distinct grouping of five notes which is
almost invariable this seems rather paradoxical; but the
frequent occurrence of a fourth with a semitone above the

---

[1] Mr. Pigott gives a note equivalent to E.
[2] Mr. Pigott gives a note equivalent to B♭.

lower note is so like the early tetrachord of the Greeks,
with a sensitive downward tending leading note (see p. 25),
that the doubt is not without some grounds.	The mode
Kumoi, quoted above, would in that sense represent two
tetrachords, C, Db, F—G, Ab, C, like those of Olympos
put one above another; and the effect of them may be
gauged by the process suggested on p. 22.

There are two other important systems of melodic
music which are most probably true pentatonic, but
quite different from either Chinese or Japanese.	The
oldest of them is the Javese.	In this case there is no
possibility of unravelling the process of development;
we can only take the results as examined by Mr. Ellis
and Mr. Hipkins, whose methods seem thoroughly trust-
worthy, and gather what we can from the facts.	The
Javese have two plans of tuning, one called Gamelan
Salendro, and the other Gamelan Pelog, which differ so
much that they cannot be played together.	In the
Gamelan Salendro scale there are five notes, which are
fairly equidistant from one another, and each of them
exceeds our whole major tones, as C and D, by a con-
siderable interval.	To our European ideas such a scale
seems almost inconceivable.	To compare it with our
major scale of C, the first degree would be from C to
a note half way between D and Eb, the next degree
would be between E and F but nearer to F, the next
would be a quarter of a tone higher than G, and the
next about half way between A and Bb, and the next
move would be to the octave C above the starting-point.
How such a scale could be tuned by ear almost passes
comprehension, and implies a very remarkable artificial
development of scale-sense in the musicians who use it.
The Gamelan Pelog is a very different mode, and almost
as singular.	The first step would be from C to a note a
little higher than E, the second to a note a little below F♯,

the third note would be just below G, the next a little
below B, and the remaining step would reach the octave
C. This is evidently a very elaborate artificial development of some simpler pentatonic formula that has long
passed out of record. The Siamese system is almost as
extraordinary. It is not now pentatonic, though supposed
to be derived originally from Javese. The scale consists
of seven notes, which should by rights be exactly equidistant from one another; that is, each step is a little less
than a semitone and three-quarters. So that they have
neither a perfect fourth nor a true fifth in their system,
and both their thirds and sixths are between major and
minor; and not a single note between a starting note
and its octave agrees with any of ours. The difficulty of
ascertaining the scale used in practice lay in the fact that
when the wooden harmonicon, which seemed the most
trustworthy basis of analysis, was made out of tune, the
Siamese set it right by putting pieces of wax on the bars.
which easily dropped off. Their sense of the right relations of the notes of the scale is so highly developed
that their musicians can tell by ear directly a note is not
true to the singular theory. Moreover, with this scale
they have developed a kind of musical art in the highest
degree complicated and extensive.

This survey would not be complete without reference
to the scale of the Scotch bagpipe. This again is a
highly artificial product, and no historical materials seem
available to help to the unravelling of its development.
Though often described as pentatonic, the scale comprises
a whole diatonic series of notes, from which modes may
be selected. These notes do not agree with our ordinary
system, and their relations are merely traditional and
chosen by ear. Taking A as a starting-point, the next
note is a little below B; the next is not C, but almost a
neutral third (p. 32) from A; the next very nearly a true

fourth above A, that is, a little below our D; the next
almost exactly a true fifth from A, that is, very near E;
the next a neutral sixth from A (p. 32), between E and F;
and the remaining note a shade below G. The type is
more like the ancient Arabic than any other, and not
really the least like the Chinese, though the impression
conveyed by the absence of the leading note misleads
people into supposing they are akin. Whether it is really
a pentatonic scale, as some have thought, is therefore
extremely doubtful. Even if the modes were really of
five notes, that is not a proof that its constitution is of
the pentatonic order, as has been indicated in connection
with the Indian and Japanese system; both the fifth and
the fourth are very nearly true, and as it seems based on
the old Arabic system, which was not pentatonic, the argument would tend to class it with the Indo-European and
Persian seven-note systems.

The above summary is sufficient to show the marvellous
variety of the scales developed by different nations for
purely melodic purposes. The simple diatonic system of
the Greeks, the subtly ingenious mathematical subdivisions
of the Persians and Arabs, the excessive modal elabora-
tions of the Hindus, the narrow and constricted stiffness
of the Chinese, the ambiguous elasticity of the Japanese,
and the truly marvellous artificiality of the Javese and
Siamese systems, are all the products of human artistic
ingenuity working instinctively for artistic ends. Simi-
larity of racial type seems to have caused men to produce
scales which are akin. They are all devised as means to
ends, and when the artistic feeling of the races who
devised the scales has been similar the result has been
so too. The seven-note systems are mostly characteristic
of Caucasian races, and the five-note scales of the somewhat
mixed but probably kindred races of Eastern Asia. And
this does not so much indicate that they borrowed from

each other as that the same types of mind working under artistic impulse produced similar results. One important defect they have in common. Though in most of them the relations of the notes are actually defined with the utmost clearness, in none have they arrived at the artistic completeness of maturity which is implied by classification. This remained to be done under the influence of harmony.

It is quite clear that the early Christians adopted the principles and some of the formulas of melody of the ancient Greek system—in the state it had arrived at about the beginning of our era—for as much music as their simple ritual required. But none of it was written down, and in those centuries of general disorganisation in which the collapse of the Roman Empire was going on, the traditions became obscure and probably conflicting in different centres. To remedy this state of things efforts were made, especially by Ambrose, Bishop of Milan, and one of the Popes named Gregory, to establish uniformity by restoring the system of the Greek modes and making the music they used conform to it. Knowledge of every kind was at that time at a very low ebb, and the authorities who moved in the matter had very limited and indefinite ideas of what Greek music had been. But between them they contrived to organise an intelligible arrangement of various modes, and it was of no great consequence that they got most of the names wrong. Ambrose authorised four modes, the (1) Dorian, (2) Phrygian, (3) Lydian, and (4) Mixolydian—corresponding more or less to the ancient Greek (1) Phrygian, (2) Doric, (3) Syntono-Lydian, and (4) Ionic. These were called the authentic modes. Gregory nominally added four more, which were not really new modes, but a shifting of the component notes of the modes of Ambrose; for as by Ambrose's regulations musicians were only allowed to use the scale of D between D and its octave, by Gregory's arrangement they might use the notes *a, b, c* below the lower D instead of in the higher part of the scale. And similarly with the other three. Gregory's group were called plagal modes. In later days four more modes were added; the mode beginning on C, and that beginning on A and their plagals; and two hypothetical modes which were not supposed to be used, namely, that beginning on B and its plagal. The total amounted therefore to fourteen modes, of which two were not actually used. It was very soon after this organisation of modes that attempts at harmony began to be made; either by doubling an ecclesiastical tune at another pitch, such as the fourth or the fifth, or by really trying to get two tunes to go together. The idea of harmony in the modern sense did not develop into clearness for centuries; but musicians got more and more expert in contriving to make various melodies go together without ugly combinations, and by degrees the meaning of chords and their possible functions in a scheme of art began to dawn upon men's intelligence. Meanwhile human instinct soon led composers to modify the ecclesiastical modes. Even when they were only used melodically, certain imperfections soon made themselves felt. The mediæval musicians had quite an intense detestation of the interval of the augmented fourth, such as appears between F and B; and singers were allowed to take the note a semitone lower than B, that is, B♭, wherever the notes forming the objectionable interval occurred close together in a passage of melody. This was not at first dictated by a feeling for the ugliness of the harmonic effect of the notes, but for that of their melodic effect; it was not till their sense for harmony began to grow and expand that the ugliness of the interval in harmony became equally apparent. Then one modification led to another. The adoption of B♭ got rid of the ugly interval between F and B, but it created a new one between B♭ and E; and to obviate this, a new flat had to be introduced for E. Then as their harmonic sense developed a still further step began to attract them strongly. At first the principal melody of the plain song had been generally in the bass, and had been doubled in the higher parts; then it was transferred to the middle parts, and other melodies called counterpoints were written round it; and then, finally, a totally new aspect of things for art was reached when men began to feel that the tune was at the top. As long as their feeling for the pure melodic side of music predominated, they regarded the passage of the last note but one of the principal melody one step downwards to the tonic as the principal feature of the cadence. When they began to accompany this passage by harmony their attention was soon drawn away from this part in the combination to the notes that accompanied it in other parts. At first it was common to accompany the last note but one with the third below or the sixth above, and pass to the unison or the octave for the conclusion. And as long as nothing else was added this did very well, though in the favourite modes the accompanying part moved up a whole tone instead of a semitone. The aspect of things was changed when men found out that it sounded well to accompany the penultimate step of the plain song by the fifth below as well as the third or sixth, as E and C by A, or A and F by D;

then the effect of the minor

third created by the system of most of the modes began to appear objectionable; because the artistic sense of musicians made them long for definite finality at the conclusion of a piece of music, and this was not produced by such a process as the progression of the chord of A minor to the chord of D minor. To obviate this a sharp was added by musicians to the third of the penultimate chord, as to C in example (*a*) above, and to F in example (*b*), thus creating the upward tending leading note, and giving a better effect of finality to the progression. The move was opposed by ecclesiastical authority, but in vain; the artistic instinct of musicians was too strong, and the major penultimate chord with its sensitive leading note became an established fact in music. It is not possible here to trace the gradual transformation of the modes through every detail. Step by step in analogous ways to the above the modes were subjected to further modifications by the addition of more sharps and flats. Men's sense of the need for particular chords in particular relations to one another drove them on in spite of themselves; and the most humorous part of the story is, that after centuries of gradual and cautious progress they ultimately completed a scale which they had known all along, but had rather looked down upon as an inferior specimen of its kind. This simply proves what is now quite obvious, that for melodic purposes such modes as the Doric (beginning on D) and the Phrygian (beginning on E) were infinitely preferable to the Ionic (beginning on C), and that when they began to add harmonies they had not the least notion where their course was going to lead them. They first attempted harmony in connection with the melodic modes which they thought most estimable, under the familiar misconception that what was best in one system would be best in all, and only found out that they were wrong by the gradual development of their artistic sense for harmony in the course of many centuries. At last, in the seventeenth century, men began to have a distinct sense of an artistic classification of the notes of the scale. The name note or tonic of a scale arrived finally at its decisive position as the starting-point and the resting-place of an artistic work. The establishment of the major chord on the dominant note—the fifth above the

tonic—gave that note the position of being the centre
of contrast to the tonic; and upon the principle of
progress to contrast, and back to the initial starting-
point, the whole fabric of modern harmonic music is
built. The other notes fell into their places by degrees.
The mediant (as E in C) chiefly as the defining note
for major or minor mode; the subdominant (as F in C)
as a subordinate centre of contrast in the harmonical
system of design, and as the sensitive downward tending
leading note to that very important note the third of the
final chord in the cadence. The leading note (as B in
the key of C) had a melodic function in strengthening
the cadence, and served as the major third of the dominant
chord; the supertonic (as D in the key of C) served as
fifth of the dominant chord, and as the basis of the harmony which stands in the same relation to the dominant
of the key as that stands to its tonic. And the remaining
diatonic note (the submediant, as A in C) appears chiefly
as the tonic of the relative minor mode, and otherwise
as the most indefinite note in the system. This does
not of course exhaust the functions of the various notes.
To give them all would require a treatise on modern
composition. They are always being expanded and
identified with fresh manipulations of the principles of
design by able composers. The fact is worth noting that
the complete classification of the functions of the various
items of the scale is one which puts our harmonic system
of music—as a principle suited for the highest artistic development—eight centuries ahead of all melodic systems.
For it took musicians fully that time to arrive at it from
the basis of the old melodic system of the Church.

The last stage of refinement in the development of
our scale system was the assimilation of all the keys—as
they are called—to one another. That is, the tuning of
the twelve semitones so that exactly the same modes

can be started from any note as tonic. But it took men long to face this, and the actual adoption of the principle implied a further modification of the scale.

As long as people could remain content with approximately diatonic music, and a range of few keys, they did not become painfully aware of the difficulties which acoustical facts throw in the way of perfect tuning. Till the end of the sixteenth century musicians did not want more accidentals than B♭, E♭, F♯, C♯, and G♯. But as their sense for harmony developed they began to make A♭ stand for G♯, and D♭ for C♯, and D♯ for E♭, and endeavoured to get new chords and new artistic effects thereby. Then they began to find out the artistic value of modulation as a means of contrast and variety, and by degrees they came to want to use all the keys. But under the old system of tuning B♭ was by no means the same thing as A♯, and any one who played the old G♯, C, and E♭ under the impression that it was the same chord as C, E, and G transposed, was rudely undeceived by an unpleasant discordance. The spirits whose instinct was genuinely and energetically artistic insisted that our system must accept a little imperfection in all the intervals for the sake of being able to use all keys on equal terms. The struggle was long, and various alternatives were proposed by those who clung to the ideal of perfectly tuned chords—such as splitting up the semitones as the Persians had done. But in the end the partisans of the thoroughly practical and serviceable system of equal temperament won the day. The first great expression of faith was J. S. Bach's best-known work, the two books of Preludes and Fugues in all the keys, called by him the "well-tempered clavier." An ideally tuned scale is as much of a dream as the philosopher's stone, and no one who clearly understands the meaning of art wants it. The scale as we now have it is as perfect as

our system requires. It is completely organised for an
infinite variety of contrast, both in the matter of direct
expression—by discord and concord—and for the purposes
of formal design. The instincts of human creatures for
thousands of years have, as it were, sifted it and tested
it till they have got a thing which is most subtly adapted
to the purposes of artistic expression. It has afforded
Bach, Beethoven, Schubert, Wagner, and Brahms ample
opportunities to produce works which in their respective
lines are as wonderful as it is conceivable for any artistic
works to be. A scale system may fairly be tested by what
can be done with it. It will probably be a good many centuries before any new system is justified by such a mass
of great artistic works as the one which the instincts of
our ancestors have gradually evolved for our advantage.

CHAPTER III.

FOLK-MUSIC.

THE basis of all music and the very first steps in the long
story of musical development are to be found in the
musical utterances of the most undeveloped and unconscious types of humanity, such as unadulterated savages
and inhabitants of lonely isolated districts well removed
from any of the influences of education and culture. Such
savages are in the same position in relation to music as
the remote ancestors of the race before the story of the
artistic development of music began; and through study of
the ways in which they contrive their primitive fragments
of tune and rhythm, and of the way they string these
together, the first steps of musical development may be
traced. True folk-music begins a step higher when these
fragments of tune are strung together upon any principles
which give the whole an appearance of orderliness and
completeness; and power to organise materials in such a
manner does not come to human creatures till a long way
above the savage stage. In such things a savage lacks
the power to think consecutively, or hold the relations of
different factors in his mind at once. His phrases are
necessarily very short, and the order in which they are
given is unsystematic. It would be quite a feat for the
aboriginal brain to keep enough factors under control at
once to get even two phrases to balance in an orderly
manner. The standard of completeness in design depends
upon the standard of intelligence of the makers of the product; and it cannot therefore be expected to be definite

or systematic when it represents the intellectual standard of savages. Nevertheless the crudest efforts of savages throw light upon the nature of musical design, and upon the manner in which human beings endeavoured to grapple with it. The very futility of the arrangement of the musical figures in their tunes is most instructive, and the gradual development of power to arrange them in an intelligible order, is clearly seen to proceed parallel to the general development of capacities of all kinds in the human race.

At the very bottom of the process of development are those savage howls which have hardly any distinct notes in them at all. Many travellers record such things, and try to represent them in the European musical stave. For instance, the natives of Australia are described by a French traveller as beginning a howl on a high note and descending a full octave in semitones; and the Caribs are described by an English traveller as doing the same thing.

Every one who knows anything about music is aware that the stave notation cannot in this case represent the reality, as a downward scale of correct semitones is beyond the powers of any but very highly trained singers even in advanced stages of musical development. Another traveller quotes some Polynesian cannibals as gloating over their living victims, shortly to be devoured, and singing gruesomely suggestive passages of rising quarter

* Compare the following Hungarian tune for the same type of expression made into music :—

tones. In all such cases the process must have been a
gliding of the voice up or down, without notes that were
strictly defined either in relation to one another or to any
general principle. This process of gliding is familiar in
every stage of art, even the most advanced, and always
implies direct human expression in the action, for it is
obviously out of the range of any scale. But in advanced
stages of art it is a mere accessory which the performers
use for expressive purposes at their own discretion, and it
is not often indicated in the actual writing of the musical
material of compositions. With the savage it is pure
human expression no further advanced than the verge of
formulation into musical terms.

The first step beyond this is the achievement of a single
musical figure which is reiterated over and over again.
Of this form the aborigines of Australia are recorded to
afford the following example :—

These simple figures they are said to have gone on singing
over and over again for hours. It seems to represent
a melancholy gliding of the voice downwards—the first
artistic articulation of the typical whine above described—
and as far as it represents any scale, it indicates the use of
the downward fourth as the essential characteristic interval, with a downward tending leading note (see page 21).
A similar example of the reiteration of a single figure is
quoted by a traveller from Tongataboo, which is also
described as being reiterated endlessly over and over
again :—

et cet.

It is extremely difficult to make sure what intervals
savages intend to utter, as they are very irregular in
hitting anything like exact notes till they have advanced
enough to have instruments with regular relations of
notes more or less fixed upon them. But if the latter
illustration can be trusted it represents the nucleus of
the pentatonic system (page 23), with a sort of ornamental glide round one of the essential notes.

From a very different and distant group of natives, the
Macusi Indians of Guiana in South America, comes a
formula of repetition which is one step further advanced,
as there is a contrast of two melodic formulas, A and B.

The design is obviously unsymmetrical, and the real impulse of the singers seems to have been to derive pleasure
from the mere sense of contrast of the two little musical
figures, and, like children, to reiterate the first phrase till
they were tired of it, and then to sing the second a little
for a change, and then to go back to A for a little, and
then sometimes to reiterate B till they were tired of that,
and then to go back to A again, and so on. They are said
to have gone on doing this for hours.

As we rise in the human scale the phrases get longer
and more varied; and the relation of phrase to phrase
becomes more intelligible, and the order in which they
occur becomes more symmetrical. The relative lack of
mental power shows itself in weakness and indefiniteness
of design. A sort of music will go on for a long time,
but be totally devoid of systematic coherence; indeed

resembling nothing so much as attempts at stories made
by excitable children or people of weak intellect, who
forget their point before they are half way through,
and string incidents together which have in reality nothing to do with one another. There is a most remarkable example of this kind of helplessness in a long
Trouvère song in an English manuscript of the thirteenth century. It tells the story of Samson, and begins
by reiterating a very genial little fragment of tune,

Sam-son dux for-tis - si - me   vic - tor po - ten-tis - si - me.

which rambles on pleasantly for some time, and then—as
if there had been enough of it—is replaced by another
phrase of similar type, which in turn gives place to
another, without any attempt at system or balance or
co-ordination of the musical material. It is as if the
singer went on with a little phrase till he was tired of it,
and then tried another till he was tired of that, and so
on as long as the words required.

A type of this sort, with a little more sense of system,
is quoted from Mozambique :—

It must be confessed that this must either have been

improved upon in the recording, or else it is not pure
native music. But by reading between the lines it is
easy to see that the music had organisation enough to
start from a high point and end on the low point of repose,
and that three different types of fairly well-defined figures
were successively alternated without further attempt at
balance than the repetition of the first phrase.

As the standard of human organisation improves the
capacity to balance things more regularly becomes evident;
and the power to alternate simple figures systematically
immediately produces the most primitive form of the
rondo.

The following example of Feejee music illustrates the
type with very fair regularity :—

This type of design persists through the whole story
of musical art with different degrees of extension in
the phrases which are alternated. The familiar aria
form of the middle period of opera is merely an alternation of characteristic material and contrasting keys, and
the more highly organised rondo of symphonic art is a
constant alternation of one special musical passage with

others which contrast with it. In the Feejee tune there
are only two figures which are alternated.

As an extraordinarily compact example of reiteration
with different phrases alternating with the recurrences of
the principal figure, the following Russian tune is worth
examination, and it certainly puts the type in almost the
closest limits conceivable:—

The tune is specially interesting because it reverses the
familiar order of the rondos, and puts the essential characteristic figure second to the contrasting figures each
time. And this rather emphasises the universality of the
general principle of knitting a whole movement together
by the reiteration of a characteristic feature. In this case
the tonal form is obscure, for the tune begins on D and
ends on C, so the curious little figure indicated by the
asterisk is apparently the only thing that holds the tune
together; but the management of the alternations shows
a skill and subtlety which enhances the effect of the whole.
For the little figure is approached first from D, next from
C, next from A, and last from E; and in the last case the
figure itself is neatly varied by raising the pitch of its
initial note.

The principle of constant reiteration of a figure or a
rhythm to unify a movement is of familiar occurrence.
It is illustrated in the reiteration of a figure of accompaniment to long passages of free melody, as in the slow
movement of Bach's Italian concerto, and in the organ

fantasia in C; it is also illustrated in the familiar form of
the ground bass so often used by Lulli, Purcell, Stradella,
Bach, and others, which consists of the incessant repetition
of a short formula in the bass with the utmost variety of
melody, figure, harmony, and rhythm that the composer
can contrive in the upper parts. The device of reiteration
is also happily used to give a characteristic expression to
the whole of a movement, as in the first chorus of Dvorak's
"Spectre's Bride," and in the Nibelung music in Wagner's
"Ring;" and carrying implication to the utmost, the
same principle is the basis of the "variations" form, which
is simply the reiteration of a recognisable formula of
melody or harmony in various disguises.

Of the ways in which such reiteration may be managed
there are many examples in folk-music. One that indicates a certain advance in artistic perception is the
reiteration of the same phrase at different levels, which
corresponds to the type known in more advanced music as
a sequence; which indeed is one of the most important
devices known to composers for giving unity and intelligibility to progressions, and is used constantly by every composer of any mark from Lasso and Palestrina to Wagner.

The two following tunes from different parts of the
globe will serve to illustrate the primitive type.

The first is a Russian peasant tune quoted in a book of
the last century :—

The second is English of the Elizabethan era :—

This last represents a much higher standard of musical perception, as unity is maintained without strict uniformity of one principle of procedure. Indeed there are a considerable number of devices which imply design in this tune which should not be overlooked. The closeness of the first half to the central note C, and the wide range of the second half, give an excellent principle of contrast; and the consistency of the principle of contrast is maintained by making the levels of the sequence close in the first half and wide in the second; further, the ends of each half are ingenious extensions of the principal figure, and as each of them breaks the regularity of the repetitions it throws the essential points of the structure into relief; and as the first half ends on C, and the second on the tonic F, the principle of contrast is carried out with comprehensive variety; and, what is of highest importance in such a case, the tune is knit into complete unity by the definiteness of the tonality.

The feature of defining design by tonality marks a considerable advance in musical intelligence, as it implies a capacity to recognise special notes as of central importance in the scheme, and others as subordinate. In the above example the C at the end of the first half has the feeling of being a point of rest, though not a final point; but the F at the end is an absolute point of repose, and is felt to round off the design completely. If the last note had been G or E instead of F, the whole thing would have sounded hazy and incomplete. This impression of finality is produced solely by the feeling for the key, which is a result of long human experience of certain types of progression and melody. In this individual instance the key is understood through the harmonic implications of the melody; for the end implies what is called a regular dominant-tonic cadence, and would probably not give the effect of finality at all to musicians only accustomed to melodic music. Indeed, the melodic systems are not well adapted to such forms, since they have none of them any strong definition of a tonic such as is characteristic of harmonic music. The modern European system rests upon a systematisation of the scale which recognises certain notes as being final, and all the other notes as having relative degrees of importance, while all have their special functions in determining design; and this system is perfectly invaluable for establishing the unity of a piece of music. But it is purely the result of harmonic development, for in all melodic systems the notes are more on an equality. Their functions are not decisively fixed, and a tune can begin or end with any note of the scale. This makes it much more difficult to establish the unity of a piece of music, and the possibilities of variety in intelligible designs are thereby limited. Indeed, long consistent development of a single movement is impossible in pure melodic music; the resources of art are not various enough to admit of it; and even in short tunes, if the music is to be fully intelligible in design, it has to be so without the resource of a well-defined pair of contrasting points like tonic and dominant. But on the other hand, melodic systems admit of an arbitrary choice of any particular note, which can be emphasised so persistently that it takes rank as a sort of tonic. The pentatonic systems are happy in this respect, because the definiteness of difference in the relation between one pair of notes and another helps the mind to fasten on special notes with ease, and to accept them as of vital importance to the design.

The following Chinese tune will serve to illustrate this device, as it is all threaded upon the single note D :—

It will also serve to illustrate again the same principles
as those illustrated by the Russian tune quoted on p. 58,
as it is practically little more than a series of variations
on the figure of the first two bars.

A similar use of a note like a tonic is to be observed in
the following Indian tune, which will also be useful as
illustrating at once a capacity for contriving a longer sweep
of melody, and a higher sense for clear and decisive
balancing of contrasting phrases, and also the Oriental
love of ornamentation :—

The Indians of the Orient contrive to make long passages of melody; but the order of the recurrence of the characteristic figures is very frequently incoherent. The rondo type is, however, fairly common. But it must be acknowledged that many of the tunes are not true examples of folk-music, but rather of a conventional art-music, which represents the skill of more or less cultivated musicians. The ornamental qualities are characteristic features of nearly all Oriental music, and demand more than passing consideration.

With genuine Orientals the love of unmeaning decorative ornamentation is excessive in every department of mental activity, whether literature, art, or music. This is generally a sign that the technical or manipulatory skill is far in excess of the power of intellectual concentration. When mental development and powers of intellect and perception are too backward to grasp a design of any intricacy or a conception that is not obvious and commonplace, the human creature who is blessed with facility of execution expends his powers in profusion of superfluous flourishes. In European countries the type is most commonly met with among popular operatic singers; but it is also plentiful among showy pianists, violinists, and other virtuosi, who rejoice the hearts of those members of the general public who are as unintelligent as themselves. Indeed the truth is of much wider application than merely to music; for it is noticeable that people who delight in excess of ornament and decoration are almost always of inferior intellectual power and organisation. Ornament is the part of anything which makes for superficial effect. It may co-exist with a great deal of force and fire, as in what is called Hungarian music, which is really a gipsy development of Hungarian substance; and it may be used as an additional means of expression, as it is in some Scotch and Irish tunes; but

when it is purely a matter of display, it generally implies either undeveloped mental powers or great excess
of dexterity.   The Siamese are among the most musical
nations, and most skilful in performance; but their mental
development has only begun in comparatively recent
times, and the masses of the people are still childlike in
intellectual matters.   A thoroughly competent observer
says that their vocal performances seem to be made of
nothing but trills and runs and shakes, and it is certainly
much the same with their instrumental music.   The florid
character of Egyptian music is also notorious; but the
most curious example of the sort is what is familiarly
known as Hungarian music.   The original Hungarian
music is extraordinarily characteristic in rhythm and
vigorous in melody, but devoid of ornament.   The
recognised musicians of Hungary are gipsies, who are of
Oriental descent, and are well known for their taste for
finery and ornamentation all the world over; and in their
hands Hungarian music has become the most ornamental
thing of its kind that Europeans are acquainted with.   The
ornaments are perfectly meaningless, except as implying
singular dexterity of manipulation and an extraordinary
aptitude for purely superficial invention in the decorative
direction.   The following is an example of parts of a
Hungarian tune, and of the version with the ornamentation
added by the gipsy performers.   The beginning stands as
follows :—

And the close :—

Nearly all the music of South-Eastern Europe exhibits the same traits. The Roumanian folk-music and dance-music is very vivid in neatness of phraseology; full of little trills and jerks, and characterised also by quaint and rather plaintive intervals, such as are very familiar in many Eastern quarters. The following fragment is unusually simple in part, but very characteristic as a whole :—

Similar peculiarities, both of intervals and of ornaments, are shown in the tunes of Smyrna and the islands of the Hellespont. And even in Spain, in the southern districts, where traces of Oriental influence are still to be met with in other lines besides music, a type like the tunes of Eastern Europe is met with in combination with higher qualities of design.

Racial differences, which imply different degrees of emotionalism and imaginativeness, and different degrees of the power of self-control in relation to exciting influences, are shown very strongly in the folk-music of different

E

countries. No people attempt folk-tunes mechanically without musical impulse. The very fact of musical utterance implies a genuine expression of the nature of the human being; and is, in varying degrees, the revelation of what the particular likings and tastes and sensibilities of that being or group of beings really are. The natural music of a demonstrative people is rhythmic and lively; of a saturnine people, gloomy; of a melancholy and poetical people, pathetic; of a matter of fact people, simple, direct, and unelaborated; of a savage people, wild and fierce; of a lively people, merry and light; of an earnest people, dignified and noble. It remains so through all the history of art; and though the interchange of national products has more or less assimilated the arts of certain countries, the nature of man still governs his predilections, as is easily seen by the average differences of tastes in art in such countries as Italy, France, and Germany.

Before discussing folk-music in general, certain circumstances have to be taken into consideration. A large proportion of the tunes came into existence in connection with poems and ballads which told some story or tragic event of local interest, and each tune was made to fit all the verses, whether they were cheerful or tragical. Such a tune is likely to be little more than a mere design, which might be very pleasant and complete as design in itself, but would leave it to the singer to put the necessary expression corresponding to the varying sentiment of the words, by giving to a rise in the melody the character of exultant happiness or poignant anguish, and to a fall either reposeful satisfaction or hopeless despair. Any attempt to infuse strong expression into music makes the systematic management of design more difficult, because it is liable to break through the limitations which make design possible, and to force the composer into climaxes and crises at moments

which are difficult to adapt to the general conventional
rules of orderliness. The greater part of the history of
music turns upon this very point; for composers have
been constantly attempting to enlarge their resources so
as to be able to bring more and more expression into
use without spoiling the consistency of the design. For,
as has been indicated in connection with the English
sequence tune (page 59), different principles of design
can be set off against one another; and when the terms
of one principle of order are broken for any purpose,
such as expression or variety, they can, in advanced
states of art, be supplemented by some other principle
of form or expression.

The difficulty of introducing expression without spoiling the design was felt as much by the makers of folk-
tunes as by composers of more advanced music; and the
way in which nations looked at expression and design is
the source of the most deep-seated differences between
the different national products. Indeed the whole of the
folk-music of the world may be broadly classified into
two comprehensive divisions. On the one hand there are
all those tunes whose ostensible basis of intelligibility
is the arrangement of characteristic figures in patterns;
and on the other all those which by very prominent
treatment of climaxes imply a certain excitement and
an emotional origin. The various national groups of
folk-music may be classified by the way they incline to
one or other of these types. No nation is restricted
entirely to one or the other, but the preponderance
with some nations is decisively in favour of emotional
tunes, and with others of formal tunes. The formal
tunes are the most primitive types, and also undoubtedly
the least interesting and beautiful.

Before proceeding, therefore, to the highest type of
folk-tune, it will be well to consider the universality of

certain simple principles of design in all branches of folk-
music. The simplest arrangement is the alternation of
two characteristic figures in various patterns. The crude
attempt of savages to make some sort of pattern out of
two figures has been illustrated from the Macusis and
Feejees. A primitive but more successful pattern is the
following Russian peasant's tune :—

Here are only two figures, as in the Macusi tune, but
the treatment implies an immense difference of artistic
sense; for four principles of design are combined to give
the tune variety and unity—rhythmic contrast, melodic
contrast, and contrast of pitch, all held together by unity
of tonality. The tune centres on A, starting from it and
returning to it. The first half represents the part of the
scale which lies above A, and the second half the part
that lies below it. The rhythmic system is consistent,
but inverted; so that the characteristic anapæst comes
at the beginning of the phrases in the first half, and
at the end in the second. And a very neat little subtlety
is that the high note which completes the balance of
the two contrasting halves of the scale is obtained by a
slight variation of the principal figure.

To shorten the discussion of the principles upon which
such patterns are contrived it will be of service to take
the letter A to represent the figure or complete phrase
with which the tune begins, and B to represent the
second, and if there is a third to call it C, and so on.
The greater portion of the folk-tunes of the world are
simple patterns, based upon all possible interchanges of
strongly characteristic figures similar to the possible
combinations of A, B, or A, B, C, in symmetrical order.

It is truly extraordinary what an amount of variety proves
to be possible. The simplest type of all is A, B, A, without disguise. And of this there are literally thousands
of examples, ranging from very short phrases to long
passages like the arias of the old Italian operas. As
types of the most compact kind with slight variations
the following will serve :—

Hungarian.

Poitevin.

Welsh.

From the mountains of Galicia in N.W. of Spain.

Every possible order that can give the impression of balance is adopted; and special types of character are often emphasised by the way in which particular figures are insisted upon. The plaintiveness of the following old Servian tune is intensified by harping on the phrase that contains the curious augmented interval, and by the ingenuity with which the accent is shifted in different repetitions :—

As the sense for design grows stronger and skill in putting things to effective issues improves, the repetitions are varied to enhance the interest. The following for its size is very comprehensive. It comes from Bas Quercy :—

Each clause ends on a different note except the first

and last, and this gives a very strong impression of variety in unity.

The device of repeating two different phrases successively (as A, A, B, B) is very familiar, and so is the alternation ending with the second phrase (A, B, A, B). Both of these necessitate a feeling for tonality, as, without that the unity would not be complete. In other words, the tonality supplies the impression of unity, and the successive alternations the contrast. When the tonality is not decisive the effect is quaintly incoherent, as in the following Russian tune :—

Of the same A, A, B, B, with a little coda to strengthen the close and give the impression of unity, the old form of the tune " In dulci jubilo " is a good instance :—

MS. of A.D. 1305.

An illustration of A, B, A, B, with a variation of B to strengthen the close, is the following Slavonic tune :—

In the more highly organised types the simplicity of
such methods of procedure is very much disguised. Very
often the figures are not repeated in their entirety, but
only characteristic portions of them, especially those portions which occupy the most prominent positions, such as
the first part of the phrase or the figures of the cadence.

In the most highly organised examples also the phrases
become much longer, and are subject to variations which
strengthen the design to a remarkable degree. A fine
instance is the following Scotch tune:—

In this the effect of contrast between A and B is mainly
achieved by difference of position in the scale, as B is

almost entirely composed of fragments and variations of
fragments of A; so that the whole tune is knit together
with the utmost closeness. Tonality, relation of pitch,
rhythm, and characteristic figures of melody are all used
with remarkable skill to attain the end of variety of contrast within unity. A tune of this sort indicates a great
power of mental concentration in the nation which produces it; but the elaborate ingenuity with which it is
knit together is by no means rare. Nearly all strong and
responsible races possess tunes of this kind, which will
bear a very careful analysis in every detail.

But by way of contrast it will be well to take a passing
glance at the tunes of advanced but less concentrated races.
In southern countries the impulse is neither towards concentration of design nor often towards any degree of expression. Very simple forms are met with, such as the Galician
tune on page 69. But in the more highly organised tunes
there is often but little consistency. The song is a sort
of wild utterance of impulse by the type of creatures
who do not criticise but only enjoy. The Basques have
extraordinarily long rambling tunes, which in a sort of
vague way suggest disposition of materials like those
above described (A, B, A, &c.). But there is no closeness
of texture as in the Scotch tune, nor is any concentration
of mind shown by any feature of form or idea. In some
Spanish tunes there is a sort of luxury of irregularity
which may be illustrated in a small space in the following
example from the neighbourhood of Barcelona :—

When analysed at close quarters there are some interesting

and subtle principles of cohesion even in. this tune, but
the general effect produced is a sort of careless abandonment to impulse. A characteristic feature of Spanish
folk-tunes is a curious jerk which commonly occurs at
the end of phrases; and this not only appears in tunes
from various districts of Spain, but has crossed the seas
and continues to appear in places where the Spaniards
were once masters, as in Sicily and in South America.
A very characteristic example of this very feature comes
from Vera Cruz in Mexico:—

There is very little of close-knit orderliness about this
tune, but it is a good illustration of an impulsive type,
and the sequence in the second half illustrates the same
principle of cohesion as in the Russian and English tunes
on page 59. As an illustration of the Spanish jerk from
Sicily a small fragment will suffice:—

The Italians also possess this jerk; possibly it remains
as a relic of former Spanish occupation. The indolent
insouciance of their tunes is familiar. They are some-

times cast on very simple lines, but a highly organised
and closely knit example would be harder to find in Italian
than in almost any branch of national folk-music.

Passing on to more reserved and self-contained but
highly reflective races, folk-music is found to become
more and more simple and plain. There is an enormous
quantity of genuine early German folk-music; but it is
quite singularly deficient in vividness of any kind, and of
marked characteristics in the way of eccentric intervals
or striking rhythms. Expression is sometimes aimed at,
but always in a self-contained manner; that is, in such a
manner that both the outline of the melody and the general
distribution of its phrases adapt themselves to closely coherent and intelligible principles of design ; and the designs
themselves are on an average of a higher order and represent higher powers of intelligence than the tunes of
other nations which in actual material are more attractive.
There are certain obvious features which show an inclination for coherence and completeness of design. In a
very large majority of tunes the first couple of phrases—
making, as it were, the first complete musical sentence—
is repeated, thereby giving the strong sense of structural
stability. The middle portion of the tune often provides
contrast to the stability of the first portion by being
broken up into shorter lengths, or by being poised upon
different centres and notes of the scale; and the final
portion is very frequently marked by a singular melisma
or grave flourish in the final cadence, which serves to
give weight and firmness to the return to the most
important note of the song, which clinches the design into
completeness. This melismatic device is one of the most
characteristic features of old German songs, and is of
course an ornamental process ; but it is generally applied
with great sense of expressive effect, and never gives the
impression of being introduced for the sake of display.

A tune, which was printed at least as early as 1535, will serve to illustrate most of these points :—

Besides the points above mentioned, the tune indicates a fine sense for knitting things together, by presenting a formula of melody and rhythm successively in different phases. The portion of the second phrase marked C is derived from B (by imitating its diatonic upward motion); and in its turn it serves as the basis for the whole of the middle part E and F, by appearing in successive repetitions in a rising sequence. Again, the passage marked H, and the whole of the final cadence K, are successive variations of the last bar but four, G, which is in itself a kind of mixture of A and D. And it is most noteworthy that in the course of the repetition the figure G grows more like D, till at K it gives the impression of being a perfect counterpart to the cadence of the first half of the tune; and the impression is enhanced by the introduction of the little parenthesis I, which at the same time neatly defers the last recurrence of the highest note of the song, so that it shall not come three times running in the same rhythmic position.

Other points which are characteristic of German folk-music are the irregularity of the rhythm, in mixing up threes and fours, the diatonic and serious nature of the tunes, and the absence of any obvious sense of vivid rhythm. The impression produced by a large range of these tunes is far more intellectual and responsible than is the case with southern tunes, and they admit of closer analysis. This implies a race that takes things more seriously, and instinctively makes for something that will stand the test of close and frequent scrutiny and endure. The light-heartedness and excitability of southern races makes them care less for the element of permanence, which is one of the essential objects of art (see p. 2), and they place themselves in an attitude of receptivity to the pleasures which appeal to them most quickly, and rather resent the attitude of instinctive reserve which makes men hesitate to abandon themselves to an impression before they have to a certain extent tested its soundness.

Permanence in a work of art depends to a great extent on its being able to stand the test of frequent scrutiny without betraying serious flaws; and this is only obtained by considerable concentration of faculty and self-restraint. Folk-music is often most successful in abandonment to impulse, but the type of human being which takes even its folk-songs seriously is likely to succeed best in higher ranges of pure art work; and it may be confessed that the relative standards of later art in various countries are the natural result of qualities which betray themselves in genuine folk-music. With regard to principles of design in general, it may be said that Germans rarely adopt the plan of consecutively reiterating short phrases, either simply or with variations, like the Russian and Oriental examples quoted. When they repeat phrases it is either to re-establish a balance after contrast, as in the rondo form, or to make essential parts of the structure correspond, as in the tune above quoted. The close of the whole often corresponds to the close of the first half, and sometimes the whole of the first half is repeated at the conclusion of the tune; and at times the tune appears to have very high qualities of design which defy anything but a very close analysis. As an example of this type the following especially beautiful tune is worth quoting :—

Von ed - ler art, auch rein und zart, bist du ein kron, der ich mich hon er - ge-ben gar, glaub' mir für war das hertz in mir krenkt sich nach dir dar-umb ich gern auff all dein er hilff mir, ich hab' nit tros - - - - tes mer.

This is obviously a strong emotional utterance, and the chief basis of form is the alternation of implied tonics— alternately F and D—as if the keys were major and relative minor; which is an alternation very often met with in folk-music, specially amongst northern peoples, such as the Scandinavians. Then there is the contrast of long sweeping phrases and short broken ones; the variety of the closing notes of each phrase; the long sweep of the opening and closing phrases, which are thereby made to match; and the subtle balance of the curves which constitute the melody.

Characteristic formulas are rather rare in German folk-music. The most noticeable in old folk-tunes is a curious pathetic rise up to the minor seventh of the scale through the fifth. Many tunes begin in this way, as—

And again:—

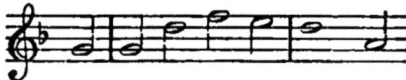

The same interval occurs in Scandinavian tunes, as in the following from Upland:—

In more modern German folk-music the influence of harmony becomes strongly apparent. Harmony represents the higher standard of intellectuality in mankind, and the Germans have always had more feeling for it than southern races. In folk-music the harmonic basis is of course very simple and obvious, but it is very apparent, and shows itself even in a strong inclination to construct melodies on the basis of arpeggios. The Tyrolese adopt arpeggios for their singular jodels, which are the most ornamental forms of vocal music in Teutonic countries. In their case, however, the excess of decoration does not so much imply low organisation or superficial character, but rather the very exuberance and joy of life in the echoing mountains; and the physical

effect which mountain life has upon them is shown by
the extraordinarily wide compass of their songs. The
arpeggio form of melody was found out very early in
pastoral districts of Germany through the help of the
horn. The following is part of a "cow-horn" tune of
the fourteenth century, from Salzburg:—

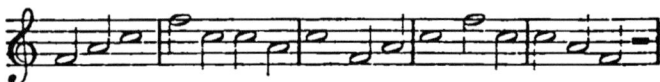

The folk-tunes of England present much the same
features as the German tunes. There is next to no
superfluous ornamentation about them, but a simple
directness, such as characterises most northern folk-
tunes. As in the German tunes, there is an absence
both of eccentric intervals and of striking and energetic
rhythms. There are plenty of dance tunes, but like the
German and Dutch and Scandinavian tunes, they rather
imply an equal flow of contented and joyous spirits than
the vehement gestures, the stamping, and the concentration of muscular energy which are represented by the
dance tunes of many southern races and of savages. In
a very large proportion of the tunes there are clear evi-
dences of a liking for simple and definite design, which
is shown in the orderly arrangement of characteristic
phrases. The most familiar form is singularly like a
form prevalent in German tunes, which consists of the
repetition of the first phrase for balance and stability,
then a contrasting phrase, and finally a return to the first
phrase, or a part of it, to conclude with; and this principle of design underlies many in which it is just shaded
off so as to conceal its obviousness. The following is a
concise example to the point:—

A

It is worth noting that the final repetition of A is effectively varied by the interruption of the parenthesis C, just in the same manner and in the same place that the recurrence of the high note is deferred at I in the German tune on page 76. There are far more instances of reiteration of short figures in English than in German tunes, and a single figure varied or given at different positions in the scale sometimes does duty for the whole tune. An extremely characteristic example, in which there is a large quantity of such reiteration, is the well-known "Carman's Whistle:"—

Features of these kinds make the tunes rather more human than a large proportion of German tunes, but, as might be expected, there is very little of strong emotional

F

expression in English folk-music, except in such rare
examples as "The Poor Soul sat sighing," and "Willow
willow;" there is, however, a good deal of expression
of a less powerful kind—gaiety, humour, tenderness, and
playfulness; but pathos is rare, and morbid or feverish
passion is entirely absent. The more genuinely English
the folk-music, the more it breathes the genuine love of
country, of freedom, of action and heartiness. From the
wonderful early tune "Sumer is icumen in" to the few
uncontaminated examples of the present day the same
qualities of style are apparent—a style which gay nations
would call too plain and matter of fact, but infused with
much more character and showing more genuine taste,
freshness, and variety than almost any but those of the
very highest standard.

So far the process of development is very easily followed.
The savage stage indicates a taste for design, but an
incapacity for making the designs consistent and logical;
in the lowest intelligent stage the capacity for disposing
short contrasting figures in an orderly and intelligent
way is shown; in the highest phase of the pattern-type of
folk-tune the instinct for knitting things closely together
is shown to be very remarkable; and the organisation of
the tunes becomes completely consistent from every point
of view. A higher phase still is that in which the skill in
distributing the figures in symmetrical patterns is applied
to the ends of emotional expression.

The tunes which imply an emotional impulse indicate
it by the manner in which the rise to a high note is made
the conspicuous feature of the tune. The difference
between high and low organisation is shown in much the
same way as in pattern-tunes. In the low standards of
pattern-tunes there are but few principles of cohesion; in
the highly organised ones (such as the Scotch tune on
page 72) there are many interlaced. Similarly in emo-

tional tunes of the lowest grade there is only one climax,
in the most highly organised tunes there are many, and
in the best there is a steady gradation of climaxes; so
that the higher points succeed one another in such a way
as to make the emotional expression of the tune stronger
at successive moments.

It is very common, even in tunes which have the general
character belonging to the pattern order, to make a special
rise to the highest point in the middle, or early in the
latter part of the tune (*e.g.,* " Weel may the keel row ").
Hungarian tunes illustrate both types very happily; and
of course the finest tunes in the world combine the emotional aspect with the finest adjustment of design. With
the Hungarians both the dance tunes and vocal tunes
are so full of energetic intervals and rhythms that even
when there are no crises the impression produced is often
emotional. Many Scotch tunes are in the same category.
The latter branch of folk-music affords many examples of
fine emotional tunes. Indeed, for the simple type of tune
combining emotional crises with very distinct and simple
form, it would be difficult to find anything better than
the following :—

The successive sweeps up to the high note in the first
half lead beautifully to the pathetic F natural in the
second half, and the expression is finely intensified by
the rise to the highest crisis on G immediately after.

As a very characteristic example from a different part
of the world, the following from Murcia, in the south of
Spain, is worth examining:—

The rises and falls are singularly systematic, and the
relations of the different points are admirably diversified,
and always well calculated both for relative contrast and
human expression.

Irish folk-music — probably the most human, most
varied, most poetical, and most imaginative in the world
—is particularly rich in tunes which imply considerable
sympathetic sensitiveness; and the Anglo-Scotch border
folk-music is not far behind. In many tunes of these
districts the very design itself seems to be the result of
the sensibility of the human creature. The cumulation of
crises rising higher and higher is essentially an emotional
basis of design. The rise and fall and rise again is the
process of uttering an expressive cry, and the relaxation
of tension during which the human creature is gather-
ing itself together for a still more expressive cry. The
Murcian tune is good in this respect, but as a simple

emotional type the following Irish tune is one of the most
perfect in existence :—

The extreme crisis is held in reserve till the last. In the
first half of the tune the voice moves in low ranges of
expression, rising successively to the very moderate crises
A and B. The portion in bracket is merely a repetition
of the phrases A and B, with slight additions of ornament
and a different close, the artistic point of which it is not
necessary to discuss here. At the beginning of the second
half the voice begins to mount to its higher crisis at C,
and intensifies that point by repetition at D, and finally
leaps to its uttermost passion at E, and then falls with a
wide sweep (comprising one more moderate crisis) to the
final cadence. Within the limits of a folk-tune it is
hardly possible to deal with the successive crises more
effectively.

As art-music grows and pervades the world pure folk-
music tends to go out of use among the people. Reflections
of respectable taste invade the homes of the masses more
and more, and familiar fragments which are adopted from
various sources by purveyors of tunes for light popular

operas and such gay entertainments. Civilisation reduces everything to a common level, and "the people" cease to make their own tunes, and accept vulgarised and weakened portions of the music of the leisured classes, and of those who wish to be like them. The rapid extinction of the tunes which successively catch the people's ears as compared with the long life of those that went to their hearts in old days, is an excellent vindication of the fact that what is to be permanent needs a genuine impulse in feeling as well as the design which makes it intelligible. True folk-music is an outcome of the whole man, as is the case with all that is really valuable as art. The features which give it its chief artistic and historical importance (apart from its genuine delightfulness) are those which manifest the working of the perfectly unconscious instinct for design, and those in which the emotional and intellectual basis of the art is illustrated by the qualities of the tunes which correspond with the known characters of the nations and peoples who invent them. Folk-tunes are the first essays made by man in distributing his notes so as to express his feelings in terms of design. Highly sensitive races express themselves with high degrees of emotional force and variety of form; placid races show perfect content in simple design with little meaning; races of moderate intelligence who have considerable skill in manipulation and love of effect introduce much ornamentation; serious and strong races, and those with much reserve of disposition, produce very simple and dignified tunes; and so on in varying degrees. Modes of life and climatic conditions all tell upon the product, and ultimately colour in no little degree the larger artistic developments which are the counterparts of these slender beginnings. Folk-music is an epitome of the principles upon which musical art is founded; and though a long period elapsed from the point where conscious artistic music began, when musicians were busy with other problems than those of design; when the art had progressed far enough for them to concentrate attention on design again, the same principles which appear in folk-music were instinctively adopted in all the forms of mature art.

CHAPTER IV.

INCIPIENT HARMONY.

It can hardly be doubted that music was called into existence by religious feelings as soon as by any of which human creatures are capable. Even the most primitive rites are accompanied by something of the nature of music, and the religious states of awe and wonder and ecstasy and devotion are all familiarly liable to engender musical utterance. The relation of religion to various arts varies with its principles and objects, and with the dispositions of the people who profess it. The religion of the ancient Greeks comprised everything which expressed the emotional inner being of man—such as dances, theatrical performances, orgies, and an infinite variety of curious ceremonies which combined every phase of what a man in modern times would consider essentially secular feelings. Similarly many religions, of all times and types, comprise dancing of a frenzied description, and functions which call forth the most savage instincts of the human creature. In such cases the music is not limited to things which a modern Christian would regard as suitable for church purposes; for the Christian religion is distinguished from all others by its inwardness and quietude, and the absence of any outward energetic signs of excitement; and it is only on rare occasions that eccentric outbursts of ecstatic fervour in any of its professors find utterance

in lively gesticulations or rhythmic dance. From the
very first the spirit of the religion was most perfectly
and completely reproduced in its music, and even its
various phases in many succeeding centuries are exactly
pictured in the art which most closely presents the
spiritual side of man.

In the early middle ages the warlike priest was not
an unfamiliar object; but nevertheless the spirit of the
religion and religious life was essentially devotional and
contemplative; and it followed that all the music employed
in church ceremonies was vocal or choral, and almost
totally devoid of any rhythmic quality or anything which
represented gesticulatory expression. This state of things
was eminently favourable to the development of certain
artistic features which were a necessary preliminary to the
ultimate building up of the modern musical art. Dance
music demands very little in the way of harmony. The
world could go on dancing to the end of time without it;
and whatever harmony is added to pure dance tunes, even
in days of advanced art, is generally of the simplest and
most obvious description. But vague melodic music, and
vocal music which is sung by voices of different pitch,
seem to call imperatively for the help of harmony; and
unless the instinctive craving for choral harmony had led
men to overcome its initial difficulties, the art could never
have developed that particular kind of regularity in time
which is independent of dance rhythm. It was the
necessity of regulating the amount of time which should
be allowed to particular notes when singers sang together,
which brought about the invention of the standards of
relative duration of notes, and the whole system of breves,
semibreves, minims, and crotchets; and also that of the
time signatures; which do not necessarily imply rhythm,
but supply the only means by which various performers
can be kept together, and irregular distribution of long

and short notes made orderly and coherent. It is perfectly easy to keep instruments or voices together when
the music is regulated by a dance rhythm, but in pure
choral music, such as was cultivated from the tenth century till the sixteenth, one of the most beautiful effects,
which composers sought after most keenly, was the
gliding from harmony to harmony by steps which were
so hidden that the mind was willingly deceived into
thinking that they melted into one another. The mystery
was, effected by making some of the voices which sang
the harmony move and make a new harmony, while the
others held the notes that belonged to the previous
harmony; so that the continuity of the sound was maintained though the chords changed. This would have
been impossible without some means of indicating the
duration of the notes, and no style could so soon have
brought men to face the necessity of solving the problem
as the growing elaboration of choral music, of that unrhythmic kind which was the natural outcome of religious
feeling of the Christian devotional type.

It is very remarkable how soon after the first definite
appearance of Christian Church music as a historical
fact men began to move in the direction of harmony.
The harmonic phase of music has been exactly coeval with
the development of that particular kind of intellectual
disposition, which continued to manifest itself more
and more, as modern Europe slowly emerged from the
chaos which followed the collapse of the Roman Empire.
It is as if harmony—the higher intellectual factor in
music — began with the first glimmerings of modern
mental development, and grew more and more elaborate
and comprehensive, and more adapted to high degrees of
expression and design simultaneously with the growth
of men's intellectual powers. As long as the Church
reigned supreme harmony remained more or less in the

background, and made its appearance mainly as the result
of the combination of the separate melodies which various
voices sung at once. But towards the end of the sixteenth century it began to assert itself as the basis of
certain new principles of design, and in the succeeding
century, as secular life grew more and more independent
of ecclesiastical influences, it became more and more the
centre and basis upon which the whole system of artistic
musical design was founded; and it ultimately became
not only the essence of the structure, but a higher and
richer means of expression than was possible by the
subtlest and most perfect treatment of any other kind of
musical device.

But the first steps in this important development were
slowly and painfully achieved under the influence of the
ancient church. There seems no reason to doubt that the
music used in the early Christian ritual was of Greek origin,
and that certain traditional formulas for different parts
of the service had been handed down from generation to
generation by ear. These were certainly quite unrhythmic
and rather indefinite; but the circumstances under which
they were used were favourable to their preservation,
notwithstanding the difficulty which such vagueness puts
in the way of accuracy. For anything which is part of a
ritual has a tendency to be very carefully guarded, and
in course of time to be strictly stereotyped; because
whatever people hear and see when they are in the act
of worship seems to share the sacredness of the function,
and ultimately becomes itself a sacred thing which it is
profanation to meddle with. But nevertheless it was
inevitable that after the lapse of a few centuries the practice of different churches should have ceased to be quite
uniform, and the authorities of the Church endeavoured
in the fourth and sixth centuries to give special sanction
to the traditions which appeared to have the best creden-

tials. It was then that the connection of the music of
the Church with the ancient Greek system was definitely
acknowledged, and though the regulations for systematising the art did not quite agree with the Greek system, owing to lack of opportunity to discover exactly
what that was, the slight discrepancies did not affect the
artistic consequences that followed. The Ambrosian and
Gregorian schemes included a number of vocal formulas,
consisting of traditional melodies, which became the basis
of an extraordinarily prolonged and comprehensive development.   They were the few established facts of
musical art then existing, and upon them the fabric of
modern music soon began to be built.

The immediate source of a most important new departure seems to have been the simple fact that men's
voices were of different calibres; for as some were deep
basses and some high tenors, and some between the two,
it was manifestly inconvenient that they should all sing
their plain song at the same pitch. Some could not sing
it high, and some could not sing it low. In extreme
cases low basses and high tenors could sing an octave
apart, but as a rule that was too wide for convenience,
so men had to find some other relation of pitch at which
it would be convenient to sing the plain song or chants
simultaneously. In such a case it is of first importance
to find a relation of pitch which shall sound agreeable in
itself, and also one which would not cause certain notes
of one part in the reduplicated melody to jar with certain
notes in the other part. It must be clearly understood
that such a process of doubling was not what is called
singing in thirds or sixths in modern times. When people
sing in that manner now they do not each sing the same
melody. The upper voice takes the melody, and the lower
adds major or minor thirds, and sings tones or semitones,
according to the nature of the scale or key in which the

music is written. Thus if two voices sing the following

simple succession of notes together,

it is not a reduplication of melodies, but a process of harmonisation. The upper voice sings a semitone in the first step, A, where the lower sings a whole tone; and in the last step, B, the upper voice sings a whole tone where the lower sings a semitone. If the melodies were justly reduplicated at the third, the result would be as follows,

Such a progression would have the tones and semitones in the same places in both melodies, but the effect would be hideous to modern ears, and impossible to early mediæval musicians, because they had not developed their scale enough to comprise such conflicting accidentals. And the same difficulties present themselves with all the intervals that they could have chosen except two, which are the fifth and the fourth. It also happens that the human mind is so slow to develop any understanding of the effect of harmony, that men only learned to endure some of the simplest combinations by slow degrees. The combination in which there is the least element of discordance after the octave is the fifth,

and after that the fourth, And these two were the first which men learned to endure with equanimity. It took them centuries to settle down to the comfortable acceptance of such familiar combinations as thirds and sixths, and it took fully a thousand years after their sense of harmony had begun to dawn before they could accept the simplest discords without some preliminary devices to save the ear from being too roughly

assailed by the sudden jar. It is a pregnant fact that
the process has gone on till the present day, and the
combinations which human ears accept without preliminary and without protest have been largely added to in
the present century. In later times the progress has
been more and more rapid, but in early times it was
most astonishingly slow. Men allowed some of our most
familiar combinations as notes of passage—purely subordinate details—and by their use in that manner they
became accustomed to the sound of them; but they were
very long in coming to the state of musical intelligence
which recognises even a third as a stable and final combination. The test of complete satisfactoriness for any
interval is the possibility of leaving off upon it without
giving a sense of artistic incompleteness and a desire in
the mind for something further. In modern times no chord
is complete at the end of a composition which does not
contain a third; but the mediæval musicians could not
even put up with it in the final chord till the art had un-
dergone some five centuries of development. Its relative
roughness had much the same effect that a discord has to
modern ears; and so whereas in modern times a man feels
that he wants something more when he is without it, in
mediæval times he would have wanted something more
because he had got it.

These complicated circumstances produced the result
that when men first tried singing anything but pure
melody in one line at a time, they doubled the melody
at the fifth above or the fourth below. This result
seems hideous to modern ears, since fifths have acquired
a new significance in the development of harmonic music.
But to people whose minds are chiefly concerned with
melodic effects it still seems a natural procedure. Not
only is it sometimes adopted in modern Europe by singers
in the streets and by other people of low musical intelli-

gence, but a most trustworthy observer states that the same phase of reduplication is beginning to be adopted in Japan, and is the only thing approaching to harmony which is used in genuine Japanese music. If Japanese music is spared the contamination of European popular music it will probably go through the same phases as early mediæval music, and the Japanese sense of harmony will develop in the same manner as that of Europeans did long ago.

It is well to keep clearly in mind that this new departure did not really amount to harmonisation, nor did it imply a sense for harmony. In the beginning it was merely the doubling of a melody, just like the familiar doubling at the octave in modern times, but at intervals which were less wide apart. Harmonisation implies the understanding of the relations of different chords or combinations to one another. Human creatures had to go through a long probationary period, and to get accustomed to the sounds of chords in themselves, before they could begin instinctively to classify them in the manner in which they ultimately came to serve as the basis of modern harmonic art.

Men began to move in the direction of real effects of harmony when, instead of making their voices go in strict parallels at some definite interval apart, they began to mix up different intervals together. The way in which this was at first effected was chiefly by interchanging fifths, fourths, and octaves or unisons; and by the use of stationary notes (such as are commonly described in modern times as pedals), as an accompaniment to plain-song. The following will illustrate their skill, about the tenth century, in varying the monotony of consecutive fifths or fourths :—

Te hu-mi-les fa-mu-li mo-du-lis ven-er-an-do pi-a.

5 4 4 4 4 1 1

This passage as far as the asterisk is merely the plain chant accompanied by a pedal (the same device as the drone which has been familiar for ages), which does not constitute or imply harmony. From that point there are only three intervals which do not accord with the ancient and crude principle of the "organum"—the one fifth, and the two unisons with which the whole concludes. This, it may be confessed, is not a very great advance in the direction of harmonisation, but it shows how the feeling for variety of harmonies began to develop.

In the course of the eleventh, twelfth, and thirteenth centuries musicians found out how to introduce ornamental notes, and learned to like the sound of the interval of the third, especially at the last step before the final note of all when the movement ended in unison. But their difficulties were enhanced by their attitude towards harmonisation. The basis of operations was always some given melody, such as a passage of an old Church hymn or chant; and to this they endeavoured to add another independent voice part by calculating what interval they would have to move at each step in the part added to obtain satisfactory consonances in relation to each step of the original melody. The theorists of those days, who were surprisingly numerous, endeavoured to give rules by which a musician should be able to fit a new part to any given melody. A treatise of the thirteenth century says:—If the chant (that is, the lower part) ascends the interval of a second, and the organum (the part added)

moves down the interval of a third, they will make a
fifth: If the chant ascends a third, and
the organum descends a tone, they will be at the
fifth: If the chant mounts a fifth, and
the organum descends a fourth, they will be together:
If the chant descends a second, and the
organum beginning at the fifth ascends a third, they will
make an octave: And similar directions
were given for a great variety of contingencies in various
treatises, both earlier and later. The sort of result
obtained may be judged from a fragment of a thirteenth
century hymn:—

This is what was originally meant by counterpoint. It
was point set against point, or note against note; and nearly
all the early work was of this description. Composers
found it quite difficult enough without trying any further
to enhance its effect except by an occasional ornament,
such as the D and C in crotchets just before the end
in the example. They hardly seem to have thought of
varying the monotony of the simultaneous progressions
of the parts until they began to attempt more than
mere two-part counterpoint; and, moreover, composers
or singers who first endeavoured to improve upon such

G

homogeneity of simultaneous motion were hampered by
the fact that they had not the means to indicate it. In
the primitive melodic music of the Church there was neither
rhythm nor any need to regulate the values of the notes
in respect of their length. No doubt they had long notes
and short ones, but it was left to the taste and discretion
of the performer to decide how long and how short they
should be; and the early forms of musical notation (which
were merely marks put over the syllables at varying heights
to help the memory of the singer) gave no indication of
the length of time that the notes were to last. Even
when "organising" in fifths and fourths and the simple
kinds of note against note counterpoint came in, it was still
possible to do without rules of measurement so long as the
singers moved from note to note and from syllable to
syllable simultaneously. But it is inferred that after a
time singers began to extemporise improvements and ornaments to the descant, which made the keeping of the voices
together somewhat difficult; and by degrees the necessity
of infusing order into the proceedings drove musicians to
invent signs which indicated the relative length of time that
the singers should hold the various notes. The rules which
were invented at first were curiously complicated and
puzzling. There were no bars, and even the relative value
of notes varied with certain symbols which were placed
at the beginning of the music, and also with the forms
of certain obscure scrawls and contorted signs called
ligatures, which were allowed to stand for several successive notes at a time. The rules given for some of
these signs are so obscure that even at the present day
they can hardly be considered as decisively understood and
settled, and how the singers managed to read them is a
wonder. It can only be supposed that they did things
very much by ear, as they had done for many previous
centuries. But the result enabled composers to treat

their respective voices with more independence, and to proceed to new kinds of musical achievement.

But every new step they took brought them face to face with new difficulties; the addition of two parts instead of one to the "canto fermo" made the calculations necessary to bring about agreeable consonances much more arduous; and to add three, so as to make an ordinary piece of four-part writing, was considered to be a feat of almost superhuman concentration. The excessive difficulty which such things presented to them is sufficiently indicated by the productions of the most celebrated composers, which present the same sort of aspect to a mind capable of unravelling them, that the artistic efforts of a baby just out of its cradle do, when it tries to represent mankind or its favourite animals. It may have been the severity of these difficulties which caused composers to adopt a less laborious but more hazardous way of arriving at the effect of harmonisation; which was none other than to take two or more tunes and force them to go together by easing off the corners and adapting the points where the cacophony was too intolerable to be endured. It is a proof that their musical sense was developing in respect of the effect of harmony, that they should even endeavour to accommodate the points which to modern ears sound hideous. The actual practice of combining several tunes together is much more common all the world over than is usually supposed. Several savage and semi-civilised races do it, as, for instance, the Bushmen at the lower end of the human scale, and the Javese about the middle. In their case the process usually consists of simultaneously singing or playing short and simple musical figures, such as savages habitually reiterate, with possibly the addition of a long sort of indefinite wailing tune which goes on independently of all the rest. The Javese carry such devices to a very advanced pitch, pro-

ducing a kind of reckless, incoherent instrumental counterpoint, very much like a number of people playing
various tunes at once, with just sufficient feeling for
some definite central principle to accommodate matters.

Of the same type is the combination of dancing and
story singing, which is illustrated in a practice met with
among the Portuguese lower classes, of playing a couple
of simple figures on the mandolin and repeating them
ceaselessly without any change, while a singer wails out
a long poem in extremely long notes which have very
little to do with the accompaniment.

This curious practice is made somewhat easier when
the element of rhythm comes in and makes it possible to
base the combination upon short figures, and present the
result in an instrumental form. With vocal melody, which
is necessarily more wide in its range, it is far more difficult; and whatever the result of the mediæval musicians'
experiments, there was much more of what may be called
artistic intention in them. The practice became very
common quite suddenly, and led very quickly to fresh
developments. And it is worth noting that one of these
developments was precisely the same as that adopted by
the Bushmen and the Javese and other semi-savage experimenters in such things; which was to accompany the main
combination of two melodies by a short musical figure
which could be incessantly reiterated as an accompaniment. In mediæval music this was a sort of nonsense part,
and was sung to nonsense syllables, such as "Balaam,"

or "Portare," or "Verbum," or "Angelus," or any other
single word which could easily be adapted to a sort of
pseudo-rhythmic group of notes, which would fit in while
the other two or three voices got through their respective tunes. When the word "Alleluia" was chosen it
presents a rather more sensible appearance; but this was
clearly an accident, as it happens to be used on one occasion as an accompaniment to two tunes, one of which is
concerning love, and the other about the pleasures of
good fellowship. The practice was so well understood
that the composer merely wrote the word once at the
beginning of the piece, and the singers (generally those
who took the lower part) fitted it in as seemed to them
good. A short fragment of such a motet, combining Latin
and French words with a nonsense part, will be sufficient
to show what a singular art-product resulted :—

Povre se-cors ai en-core re-co-vré,   A ma dame que je avoie servi

Gaude   chorus   om - ni-um fi - del-i - um.

An - ge - lus,   An - ge - lus,   An - ge - lus.

In such pieces as this it was generally rather a matter of
chance what combinations were produced. The composer
was for the most part at the mercy of the tunes he chose
to combine, and he was necessarily absolved from the
rules which theorists laid down for the adding of counterpoint to a canto fermo. Their main object seems to
have been to get the chief points, on which stress could
be laid, to form consonances, and to let passing notes
clash as they would. And it is very remarkable that
their instinct even in adapting tunes together worked

in the direction of successions of fifths and fourths, just as in the early form of the organum. The example quoted above is rather an extreme case of independence, if not of recklessness; but even in this case the old type of the organum is discernible in the relations between the lower and the upper part.

In other compositions it is common to meet with a structure which consists almost entirely of successions of fifths disguised by the ornamental notes which are interspersed. The manner in which this was done may be best judged from an example of the thirteenth century by the Trouvère poet and musician, Adam de la Hale:—

In this the whole basis of procedure is a succession of octaves and fifths, which is almost as regular and unchanged as the old diaphony of the ninth and tenth centuries; but the succession is disguised and made

expressive by ornamental or subsidiary notes introduced
between the main blocks of octaves and fifths. The rest
of the little song (which would take too much room to
quote) is of exactly the same construction, and so are
many pieces of sacred and secular music of these early
centuries. As composers developed their skill in adapting
voice parts to one another, in course of time they even
managed to write in four parts with some facility, and
this necessarily made them more accustomed to the effect
of the less purely harmonious consonances; for though
they tried hard to restrict themselves in the main to what
they called the perfect concords, it was impossible to write
in more than two parts without frequently introducing
a complete triad with third and fifth, and scarcely less
frequently the intervals of the sixth, major and minor. It
is not necessary to follow out the progress of these early
centuries in detail. It pursued its slow course on the
same lines. Composers found out artistic devices which
facilitated their labours, and enabled them to approximate
to more pleasing and artistic results. But the average
quality of their works of every kind is marvellously crude,
harsh, and incoherent.

Almost every elementary rule of art which a modern
musician holds inviolable is broken incessantly, and there
are hardly any pieces of music, by the most learned or
the most intelligent musicians up to the fourteenth century, which are not too rough and uncouth to be listened
to by even the most liberal-minded and intelligent musician
without such bewilderment as often ends in irrepressible
laughter. The little rondeau of Adam de la Hale, part
of which is quoted above, stands almost alone for genuine
expressiveness, and even a certain attractiveness, amongst
a great mass of experiments which are simply chaotically
clumsy and homogeneous.

A still more rare and wonderful exception, which is

important on other grounds besides its musical effectiveness, is the famous English canon, "Sumer is icumen
in," which is probably of little earlier date. This is clearly
a folk-tune (and a very beautiful one) which lent itself
easily to being sung as a round by several voices in
succession, with a sort of drone bass. It is an almost
unique example of its kind for the time when it was
written; and it proves, in a manner which cannot be
ignored, that composers had already at this early date a
very definite idea of the canonic form, which was one
of the earliest and simplest devices of contrapuntal music,
and almost the only one which was cultivated with any
success before the sixteenth century. The significant
point about this canonic form, in relation to the evolution of musical art, is its singular homogeneousness. It
affords hardly any effect of artistic variety or contrast,
and of itself no special means of expression. In fact
it is really no more than a technical device—a sort of
exercise of skill, like any game which men play just for
the amusement of overcoming a difficulty. But in these
early stages of development the distinction between art
and artifice had hardly arisen. Considering the state the
art was in the first appearance of this form becomes a
very important event in the story. It was a very natural
outcome of the improvement of pure choral music that
the different voices should sometimes be made to sing
the same words and phrases after one another instead of
simultaneously; and in later times, when men had developed higher artistic sense, one of the most elastic and
comprehensive of musical forms was developed on this
principle; but in those early days, when musical intelligence was so undeveloped, it was natural that composers
should endeavour to follow out a simple contrivance of
the sort to the bitter end, and should imagine that
they had really achieved an artistic result when they had

manipulated the flow of a voice part in such a way that another voice beginning a little later should be able to sing the same melody always a little way behind the leader. The device undoubtedly took the fancy of early composers very strongly, as was natural when so few devices of any kind were possible; and they expended so much energy upon it that in the fifteenth century they developed quite an abnormal skill in futile note-spinning and puzzle-making. It is not to be denied that canons can be made not only very effective but beautiful; the mistake which most of the early composers and many modern ones have made is to take the means for an end, and assume that the device is worth doing for its own sake. The canonic form is a further illustration of the state of the art from another point of view, as it is purely a combination of voice parts, and not a device of harmony at all. The result is harmony of a sort, but in no sense a phase of harmony which implies any feeling for system or harmonic order. The harmonies are the accident and not the essence of the device; and the result was in the early examples both rhythmically and structurally incoherent, and so far homogeneous.

Another drawback to the form which is characteristic of undeveloped artistic sense is that the voices go on all through without material breaks. There is no relief or change in the amount of sound which the ear receives, and therefore there is a lack of variety. This feature is equally characteristic of a large amount of the early choral music of other kinds. Composers seem to have thought that it was an advantage to keep the parts going; and when they gave any voice a rest of long duration, it was generally less for the sake of artistic effect than because they found it so difficult (in a triplum or quadruplum) to keep all the parts in continual activity. One part indeed was necessarily kept going. For it was

the almost universal practice that each movement was
developed upon some ready-made melody, such as a plain
chant, or even a secular tune put into long notes. This
was generally put in the tenor, and the other parts were
added by calculations such as those quoted on page 97.
And if this canto fermo stopped there was nothing left
to build upon. Here again the product was homogeneous. The principle of adding fresh voice parts to
a given melody on contrapuntal principles suggested of
itself no contrasts except those of pitch, nor any natural
divisions or articulations of the artistic organism, such
as balanced phrases and periods. The music flowed from
end to end indefinitely, and the only indications of completeness were the starting from a definite point in the
scale and the conventional close at the end, sometimes,
but by no means always, on the same tone as the movement started from.

A strong trace of the melodic system to which the old
form of art belonged is recognisable in the cadences.
These were not processes like a modern cadence, in which
two blocks of contrasted harmony succeed one another;
but progressions in which the most important features
were the descent of the modal part—or canto fermo upon
which the contrapuntal structure was built—one step
downwards upon the tonic of the mode; and its accompaniment in another part by a third below or a sixth
above in the penultimate step, passing into the octave or
the unison to finish with.

The whole aspect and texture of this old music is so

different from the modern style, that it seems almost inconceivable to most people when they first come into
contact with it that it could have had any musical effect
at all, much less that it could be the direct source of the
elaborate modern fabric. The most familiar rule that the
tyro in the study of harmony learns to his cost, is to avoid
consecutive fifths and octaves; but the rule of the mediæval
musicians was distinctly and unquestionably to write more
of them than of anything else. As has been pointèd out
before, the basis and substructure of many compositions
was a series of such fifths and octaves disguised by ornamental notes and passing notes. In other particulars also
the difference from modern views is very marked; such as,
for instance, in the use of discords. These early musicians
used many discords, and very harsh ones too, but hardly
ever in any way like modern composers. They were always
purely accidental discords, and were in no sense either used
as means of contrast, nor to propel the music on from
point to point, as is their frequent function in modern
times. The melodic outline of one part jostled against
that of another voice part, and as it were disregarded
what its neighbour was doing for a short while, till it
landed upon some note which brought it again into consonance with its surroundings. The very idea of using
chords of varying degrees of harshness as a means of
effect does not seem to have dawned upon composers
until after some centuries of experience. The early phase
of the progress of harmony from homogeneity to heterogeneity is distinctly traceable in this respect. In the
first stage there is no variety at all; all are fifths or
fourths consecutively. A slight variety appears when
fourths and fifths are mixed up with one another and
with octaves; but it is very slight, as the difference
between one and the other in degrees of consonance is
scarcely marked enough to afford a sense of contrast.

When the force of circumstances drove composers to use
the less perfectly consonant combinations of thirds and
sixths, they enlarged the scope of their resources, and
their materials became more heterogeneous; but it took
them a long time to realise the effects which could be
made with thirds as contrasts to more perfect consonances.
Ultimately the composers with the higher instincts learnt
to use the qualities of the different consonances for relatively similar effects of contrast to such as are produced
by the relations of concord and discord in modern music;
and then going a step still further, composers at last
found out how to use real discords, such as were not the
result of jostling passing notes only, but systematically
introduced and under artistic control. They of course
only used one kind of discord, which was obtained by one
voice holding on a note which had been consonant in one
chord while the other voices went on to other positions
which made the combination into a discord. The appearance of this device immensely enhanced the vitality of the
music; and though the moderation of composers in the
use of it was extreme, it brought a tone into the art which
soon began to dispel the ancient traditions of successions
of fifths and fourths interspersed with discords which
only came by chance and fulfilled no artistic function.
The curious makeshifts of motets made up of several
tunes twisted and hammered into a dubious conformity
ceased to make their appearance. Composers still had to
make their counterpoint upon the basis of a canto fermo,
or a canon, or some equally primitive device, because
without some kind of regulating principle they wandered
and were lost like children without guides. But a more
musical spirit pervaded their attempts, and they found
out how to dispose the progressions of their parts so as
to obtain contrasts of tone, and to make the voices flow
at once with more real independence and interdepen-

dence. The influence of the old organum ceased in time; and a real though limited heterogeneity took its place. And before the end of the fifteenth century composers really understood something of the delicate art of varying the amount and distribution of sound by sometimes having all the voices singing full together, and sometimes letting some of them stop here and there. And they even got so far as to understand how to make the utterances of different voices coherent by making them take up short fragments of melody or musical figures imitatively; and how to make the general texture of a movement uniform by the pervading style and mood of the musical ideas.

But the musical ideas themselves were singularly vague and indefinite. Even the tunes which they borrowed were put into such enormously long notes that whatever individuality there was in them commonly disappeared. It is quite impossible to recognise a tune when single notes are prolonged to an extent equivalent to half a dozen bars in slow time. And this extension was mercilessly practised by the best mediæval musicians in order to lengthen their movements, and give more time for the spinning out of their strange kinds of counterpoint. Spontaneity was of course out of the question. The store of known technical resources was too limited, and every musical work was the product of arduous and laborious concentration, or of peculiar ingenuity. Even expression of any kind was rare, for, strange as it seems, in such immature products the chief pleasure lay in arriving at a new experience through the overcoming of some technical difficulty. Their minds were so fully occupied with the difficulties they had to overcome that they could think of little else. And even up to the end of the fourteenth century the effect produced by getting a

certain number of voices to go together at all seems to
have been so new and attractive that it was hardly necessary to go any further afield to strike men with wonder
at the achievement.

All this development naturally proceeded under the
wing of the Church. The system of the modes pre-
scribed by ecclesiastical authority, and such rules of
counterpoint as ecclesiastical theorists discovered pervaded such secular music as there was quite as much
as the genuine Church music. There were plenty of
attempts made at secular motets, and lively secular tunes
with a sense of rhythm in them made their appearance
therein, but the contrapuntal procedure was the same in
all; and the same phases of progress are noticeable in
one as in the other. Even folk-tunes were influenced
by the modes which were taught by the Church, and the
more highly organised songs of the Troubadours, little as
their authors wished it, had to submit to the universal
influence. The ecclesiastics were the only people who had
devised any system for recording music accurately, and
therefore even if a man wished to strike out an independent line his musical utterances were sure to be recorded
in terms which only the musicians trained in the school
of the Church knew how to use.

The Troubadours indeed stand outside the line of the
direct development of modern music, as their efforts seem
to have been purely melodic; and though there are some
beautiful tunes still remaining which are attributed to
them, they represent a development of lyrical music which
appears to have had no immediate consequences. It was
the fruit of an isolated outburst of refined poetic feeling,
and when its natural home in the South of France was
harried and ruined by the Church the impulse dwindled
and ceased.

But the crude efforts of the early contrapuntists, whether secular or ecclesiastic, served as the immediate foundation of one of the greatest eras in the history of musical art; and through that era as the earliest source of the characteristic system of harmony which forms the distinguishing feature of modern music.

CHAPTER V.

PURE CHORAL MUSIC.

THE early period from the ninth till the end of the fifteenth century was, as it were, the babyhood of modern music, when ideas and modes of musical thought were indefinite, unsystematised, and unpractical. The Church, like a careful mother, watched over and regulated all that was done, and the infantile efforts scarcely emerged at any time into definiteness either of form or expression.

The two centuries which followed, up to the beginning of the seventeenth century, were the period of the youth of modern music—a period most pure, serene, and innocent—when mankind was yet too immature in things musical to express itself in terms of passion or of force, but used forms and moods of art which are like tranquil dreams and communings of man with his inner self, before the sterner experiences of life have quite awakened him to its multiform realities and possibilities. The manner in which the inevitable homogeneity of an early stage of art presents itself is discernible from every point of view. The most comprehensive fact is that almost all the music of the two centuries is purely choral—that is, either written for several voices in combination without independent accompaniment, or devised upon methods which were invented solely for that kind of performance. It followed from this general fact that the methods of art were also homogeneous; for the processes which are fit to be used by voices alone are more limited in range and variety than those which can be employed by instruments,

owing to the greater difficulty of taking awkward intervals and of sustaining the pitch, and to the necessity of
adapting the notes to words; and also to the fact that
the words often lessen the need of absolute principles of
design, by supplying a meaning to the music in general,
when without them it would be incoherent.

The principal reason of this absorption of composers in
the cultivation of choral music is obvious. It is a well
ascertained law of human nature, that men will not go out
and labour in the desert at haphazard when they are fully
occupied in extracting unlimited gold from a rich mine.
Neither will they (in a healthy state of existence) abandon
an occupation which is full of absorbing interest, and constantly presents fresh problems most tempting to solve, for
the mere chance of amusement in some other direction.
At the time when the great era of pure choral composition
was beginning, musical human beings, earnestly disposed,
were just awakening to the singular possibilities of beauty
which the combinations of many singing voices afforded.
They were awakening to the actual beauty of the sound
of chords sung by voices—to the beauty of delicate variety
between one chord and another, and between chords in
different positions (partly owing to the various qualities
of the different registers of the voices)—to the beauty
of the actual human expression of the individual voices;
and to the beauty of the relations of the melodic forms
of the different parts to one another. To win the delight
of realising the various phases of these effects was enough
to keep them fully occupied on even severer labour than
the development of artistic technique; but the incitement
quickened their musical instinct marvellously, and in a
short time developed in them a delicacy of perception of
artistic means and a sense of style which is almost unique
in the history of the art. In later times composers are
distracted by the varieties of style and taste which have

H

been developed, in the necessary course of musical evolution, for different artistic purposes, such as the theatre
and the concert room; and often introduce the formulas
which belong to one kind of an art into another to which
they are quite unsuited; but in the early days there were
no such distractions. Men's minds were occupied by the
conditions of choral performance alone, and the further
they went the more refined and pure their artistic methods
became.

The turning point from the crude experiments of artistic
childhood to the fresh power of intelligent enjoyment of
youth was somewhere about the end of the fifteenth
century. The state of transition is most strongly apparent in the works of the English composer Dunstable,
who in some things still illustrates the helpless crudity
of the early stages of the art, and in others shows a
fair mastery of the disposition of his voice-parts so as to
obtain a really attractive quality of sound, not for the
moment only, but in sufficiently long passages to be fully
appreciable. It marks no little advance in skill, and in
the mastery of technique, that composers were able to look
beyond the mere overcoming of difficulties and to make
use of their devices for a purpose.

It is probably common to all arts that when the early
stages of wrestling with technical difficulties have been
passed the aim of artists seems to be to produce effects
which are more noteworthy for their beauty than for
definiteness of expression and variety of characterisation.
Distinctive definiteness of expression was certainly not the
aim of the composers of the great choral period; and if it
had been they could not have succeeded without launching
out beyond the limits of the art which they understood
into that of experiment without precedent and without
standards of test. Indeed they were quite sufficiently
occupied in applying the skill they had developed to the

simple purpose of making groups of various voices produce effects of smooth and harmonious tone. In the main,
the music was singularly indefinite in almost every respect.
The style had grown up entirely under the influence of
the Church, and composers had learnt how to solve their
earliest artistic problems by using the old Church melodies
as a basis whereon to add voice to voice and make a harmonious combination ; and as the devotional sentiment of
the Christian religion belonged to that inward class of
spiritual emotions which expressed themselves vocally
rather than by animated gestures, it followed that all
this music was unrhythmic ; and consequently it was also
divested of all that kind of regular orderliness of structure which seems so indispensable in the maturer art of
modern times.

It is true the composers had to find methods for
restricting the lengths of the notes, but for a long time
the establishment of their principles of relative duration
tended rather to obscure the rhythmic or metrical order
of the music than to define it. The reason for this lay
in the strong feeling of musicians for the independence
of the voice parts. Their artistic instinct was specially
attracted by the fascinating effect of diverse movement
controlled into the unity of a perfect flow of harmony.
To them it was still essential that each individual voice
part should be pleasurable to sing, and the more subtly
the independence of each was suggested the more fascinating was the artistic effect. The result was that in
one phase of this kind of art composers aimed chiefly
at making the accents and climaxes of the various voice
parts constantly alternate with one another. One voice
part rose when another fell, one held a note when another moved, one came to its highest climax at one
moment and descended, while another moved up in its
turn to another climax, possibly higher than the first.

And as the skill of composers in managing such progressions improved, they found out how to distribute the
climaxes of the various voice parts so as to make them
gain in vital warmth by coming ever closer and closer;
and the hearer could in a moderate degree be excited
by the sound of successive crises in different qualities of
tone, sometimes tenor, sometimes treble, sometimes bass;
each of which seemed successively to rise into prominence
within the smooth texture of the harmonious flow of
sound, and then to be merged into it again, as another
took its place.

The tendency of all such devices was to obscure the
rhythmic element of the music. But the necessity for
orderliness in the relative lengths of notes brought about
a clear understanding of underlying principles upon which
the strong and weak accents were grouped. The mere
fact that some particular long note had to be recognised
as equal to two, three, four, six or more shorter ones,
necessitated the development of a feeling for strong
accents at the points where the longer and the shorter
notes started together; and for a proportionate absence
of accent at the points where the longer notes were
holding though the quicker notes were moving. But
it was rather a point of art with the choral writers to
avoid emphasising these mechanical accents, and to make
the voices have independent cross accents with one another. In respect of pure contrapuntal skill the beauty
of effect of such devices depended upon the manner in
which the composers managed to control them with the
view to keeping the harmonies complete, full in sound,
and ever subtly varying in quality. In early stages
their control of relative qualities of chords and their
power to group them effectively was very limited. Even
their instinct for the actual effect of chords had to be
developed by long experience. As has before been pointed

out, in such devices as the old motets, in which various
tunes were forced to go together, it was a matter of the
purest chance what harmonies, or cacophonies, succeeded
each other. But as composers gained experience they
perceived the effect of contrast and variety which could
be obtained by distributing their chords with regard to
their relative degrees of harshness. And it obviously became a most fascinating study to find out how to control the motions of the various voices so as to obtain
at once constant variety of accent, alternation of crisis,
and the particular effects of harmony of different degrees
of fulness or slightness which were required for the
attainment of satisfactory general effect.

The artistic problem is obviously by no means simple;
and though there was little to distract composers or divert
their energies into other lines of skill, very few arrived
at complete mastery of resource and complete perception
of the various shades of chord effects which are as necessary
to the completely artistic result as the actual management
of the counterpoint. But in one short period at the latter
part of the sixteenth century a small group of composers
achieved a type of art which for subtlety and refinement
in the treatment of delicate shades of contrast has no
parallel in the history of musical art. The very absence
of strong emotional purpose or intention to characterise
gave them a peculiar opportunity. Their whole attention
was concentrated upon a limited field of effort, and the
fruit was a unique phase of a pure, and as it were
ethereal beauty, too delicate to satisfy mankind for long,
and destined to be replaced by a period of reactionary
experiment which produced things almost as crude, ugly,
and barbarous as those of the twelfth and thirteenth
centuries.

But meanwhile, though the central aim of composers
was the development of skill in controlling the diverse

voice parts so as to produce these varying effects of harmonious sound, yet there were many ways in which the tendency to branch out into diversity was shown. Among the most noteworthy of these was the adoption of a method of writing the voice parts which served as a means of variety to the elaborate contrapuntal method above described. In the most characteristic style of choral writing of the old contrapuntal kind a note was but rarely repeated for different syllables. The treatment of the singing voice parts resembled in this the inflections of human speech, in which mechanical reiteration of a note—which implies subordination to some external rule of form or rhythm—is rare. But the constant, ceaseless shifting of every voice is liable to become a strain on the attention when it goes on too long, and the mind begins to feel the need for some kind of repose.

It was probably as a means of relieving this strain that composers adopted a much simpler mode of procedure; in which the effect was not obtained by the relations of the melodic contours of the parts, but by successions of simple harmonies in which the voices often moved in blocks of chords, and also very often repeated the same notes to different syllables. This style is far more like the familiar modern processes of harmonisation; but there remains this marked difference, that whereas in modern harmony the chords always move in subordination to the principles of modern tonality—as illustrating the antitheses of tonic and dominant and other relatively contrasting centres—the old progressions of harmony moved under the regulations of the modes, with much less of definite system in their distribution, and without the melody in the upper part which is commonly the outward and visible sign of the inward principle of design. The importance of the occasional adoption of this procedure was very great, for it not

only called men's attention more directly to the actual
effect of chords as chords, but also led them inevitably to
a more definitely rhythmic treatment of the music. It
became, as it were, the door through which rhythm began
to make its way into choral music of the purest kind;
and though the finer artistic natures never submitted
wholly to its spell except on rare and well chosen occasions, the seduction it exercised was too great to be
resisted, and even before the great period of choral music
had arrived at its zenith its presence made itself subtly
felt here and there in all departments of art.

The most singular result of the adoption of the simpler
method of harmonisation was that it awoke in men's
minds a new feeling for the effect of harmony pure and
simple, which is betrayed by their very helplessness in
sustaining the interest in a long passage which is harmonic rather than contrapuntal in its character. The
increased facility which men gained in the management
of their artistic resources led them to apply their skill
to various forms of both sacred and secular music.
The best secular forms were the madrigals, which were
written under the same artistic conditions as the Church
music, and aimed by similar treatment of independent
voice parts at obtaining beautiful effects of melodic
variety within the bounds of the controlling unity of the
harmony. The moods naturally became a little lighter
and more lively than in Church music, and the expression
even a little more definite and more varied. And it
happened also that the first collections of madrigals which
won very marked success—which were brought out by
Arcadelt in the middle decades of the sixteenth century
—were singularly simple in their treatment of harmony,
and allowed the harmonies to move very much in blocks,
and to present the simple rhythms of the poems set, without the disguise of the familiar cross accents and the

subtleties of choral counterpoint. It was under such circumstances that men began to feel the need of system in the distribution of the harmonies; and as the modes under whose restrictions they still worked hindered their finding any satisfactory system of contrast between one group of harmonies and another, they almost invariably lost themselves in mazes of pointless obscurity in the middle of a composition of any length. For though they could make a good beginning and a good end with simple chords, art required a long period of probation under quite new conditions before men found out how to carry out the development of a long movement on any lines but the contrapuntal ones with which they were familiar. When Arcadelt and his contemporaries tried to sustain the interest without the contrapuntal methods their skill soon failed them. But every effort in this direction told; and as men knew nothing better as yet in the way of harmonic design, it cannot be supposed that they noticed the defects of such early attempts as much as modern musicians do. Undoubtedly the hearing of such effects made them more and more accustomed to effects of harmony of the simpler kind, and undoubtedly in a great many smaller madrigals the composers hit upon very definite and tuneful effects which differ from modern music of a similar kind only in the quaint and attractive peculiarities inevitable to harmonisation in the old ecclesiastical modes. In the madrigals of the best time the finer contrapuntal ways were more generally adopted; but men had so far progressed towards understanding the effect of harmonic design. that in many large examples, especially in those of the English school, tonality becomes sufficiently definite to admit occasionally of clear and effective treatment of modulation of the modern kind; which implies a conception of art quite alien to the purely contrapuntal and modal methods of the great choral composers.

A little consideration will show that the capacity to feel the artistic effect of a change of key implies the adoption of a new method of regarding art which is of the first importance. In melodic systems there is a wide range of possible change of mode, but very little which amounts to change of key. Differences of mode are differences in the relations of various intervals to the most essential notes of the scale, such as the initial or final of a tune, or any other notes on which emphasis is especially laid. But differences of key are much more subtle both in fact and effect. For they do not change the order of the notes, but only the centre round which a uniform series is grouped; and the beauty of the effect is partly derived from the identity of order in relation to a changed centre, and partly from the fact that this identity causes certain notes to appear in one key which do not exist in the other. Now the original conception of the art of the choral epoch was purely melodic: the central thread of orderliness was the modal part, as it was called, which moved according to certain rules within a range of sounds of which either C, D, E, F, G, or A was the most essential note; and whatever parts were added were regulated by their relation to this part, which was most frequently the tenor. Sharps and flats were in no case introduced to give the effect of change of key, but merely to avoid intervals which were considered offensive and inartistic, or to make the close of the movement satisfactory to the ear. The idea of introducing an F♯ into a passage in order to make a modulation from C to G, or a B♭ to pass from C to F, was alien to the very heart of the modal system. When B♭ was introduced it was because the interval of the tritone or augmented fourth between F and B was disagreeable; and when men found that the introduction of a flat to B produced the very interval they wanted

to avoid between B♭ and E, they evaded the obnoxious
interval again by adding a flat also to E, whenever it
was required by the circumstances. But the object was
not to suggest a change of tonality, or to obtain variety
of harmony, but to soften the progress of a melodic
passage. The sharps were. introduced on grounds which
were less purely melodic, as the dissatisfaction in a
cadence consisting of the succession of the chords of
D minor and G, which drove musicians to sharpen the
F, implies quite as much sense of the need for a
penultimate major chord (which is a harmonic consideration) as for the rise of the semitone to the final,
which is the melodic feeling. But at any rate it is quite
clear that when once these additional notes had been
added for one purpose, composers very soon made use of
them for others. They soon saw that it gave them an
additional means of effect, and without thinking of anything so subtle or advanced as a change of key, they
began to use them to obtain the effect of a difference of
quality in harmony in the same position. They delighted
in bringing passages close together which contained chords
with F♯ and F♮, or C♯ and C♮ in them respectively. To
people accustomed mainly to the diatonic series the effect
must have been subtly enchanting; and composers, in
their eagerness to avail themselves of all opportunities,
occasionally overshot the mark, and made experiments
to which modern ears, though as a rule tougher than
ears of the sixteenth century, will not accord any appreciation. But the use of these accidentals gave men
the opportunity to learn not only the important relations
of tonic and dominant chords, but also further to develop
a new conception of the nature of the musical scale.
The truth is, that the frequent use of these accidentals
ultimately assimilated the modes to such an extent that
little more than technical traditions, differences of style,

and forms of cadences distinguished the music written in one mode from that written in another. This might be counted as a loss if it was forgotten that the old modal system was quite unfitted for the artistic purposes of harmony, and that the assimilation of modes into a system of keys was a necessary preliminary to the development of true harmonic music of the modern kind, and of those principles of harmonic design which are vital to its existence.

The masters of the great choral period never arrived at a definite acceptance of the contrast between tonic and dominant as a basis of design; but they understood the principle well enough to use it effectively in cadences of various kinds, and they arrived at a clear enough feeling for tonality in the latest years of the period to use passages which represent such contrasts of key as D minor and B♭ major, E minor and G, D minor and F. But the instinct of the higher class of composers for continuity in the flow of sound militated against any systematic use of such contrasts for purposes of design. Their movements started from some initial point and wandered ceaselessly through unbroken mazes of counterpoint till the return to the starting-point in the close. There was nothing of the systematic modulation to a new key, and definite use of it as the principal element of contrast in the design which is familiar in modern music. But they soon found out the advantage of making subordinate recommencements start from chords which contrasted with one another; and the growth of their feeling for such contrasts grew with their freer use of accidentals, till the relation in which these contrasts stood to one another was sufficiently clear and broad to give to a modern musician the impression of a very effective modulation.

It was in compositions of a lower order that composers

were driven to experiment in rhythmical grouping of
periods more like modern harmonic forms; for as in these
they tried to set their poems directly and simply, they
had no choice but to look for successions of chords
which were effectively alternated and balanced. The
general diffusion of skill in the management of voice
parts brought into being a variety of popular forms which
went by the names of Canzonas, Frottolas, and Villan-
ellas, many of which were simple arrangements of popular
street tunes, which, but for the universal influence of the
modes, would resemble modern part-songs; and besides
these there was a very large amount of dance music
for voices in parts, such as the Balletti, which were
necessarily rhythmic and definite in the distribution of
phrases and periods, and regularly grouped into bars.
Many of these are remarkably bright, sparkling, and
skilfully contrived, with great feeling for vocal effect. The
style reacted upon the higher forms of art, such as the
madrigals; and in the latest phase of that form of art,
which was in England in the latter part of Elizabeth's
reign and in the time of James I., the actual subjects
and figures of melody came to have a far more definite
and distinct character, and the aspect of the works in
general became far more animated, more pointed, and
more harmonic in character. The balance of style was
admirably sustained by the great masters of the English
school, Byrd, Wilbye, Weelkes, Bennet, Morley, Gibbons,
and others, though they clearly aimed at more definite
expression and more close attention to the words than
would have been consistent with the artistic intentions of
the early Netherland and Italian masters. But the expansion of the style in these directions bore with it the seeds
of dissolution; and as soon as composers endeavoured to
enlarge the scope of choral music yet further by imitating the methods of the early operas and cantatas, the

mediæval type of choral art passed into mongrel forms, and very shortly ceased altogether.

But meanwhile the latter part of the century found men laying the foundations of new lines of art in slender but very important experiments. Instruments had hitherto been considerably in the background; they had been very imperfect in construction, and had next to nothing to do with really high class art in any independent form. But the early imperfect types of viols were by degrees improved under the influence of men's growing appreciation of beauty of tone and refinement of feeling for execution, and before the end of the sixteenth century the earliest representatives of the unique and incomparable school of Italian violin-makers were already busy with their inimitable work. In kindred lines of workmanship men arrived at great perfection in the making of those troublesome but very fascinating domestic instruments, the lutes of all kinds; and at the same time the early types of keyed instruments, such as harpsichords or virginals and clavichords and spinets, were rapidly approaching a condition sufficiently practicable to be worthy of the attention of genuine composers; and organs were passing out of the cumbrous and unmanageable state in which there had to be almost as many bellows as notes, and the notes had to be put down with the whole fist, into a practicable condition which admitted of independent music being performed upon them. But the music for instruments was in a very backward state, because composers had no idea what to aim at in writing for them. When they wanted something of a superior artistic order for stringed instruments they simply played madrigals, or wrote music in imitation of any of the varieties of choral music; not realising that without the human tones and the varying degrees of effort and tension in the vocal chords, which gave expression to the rising and falling of the melodic material, the effect was pointless and flat. No doubt the skilful treatment of contrapuntal resources made these movements interesting to the performers to play; but apart from such personal considerations, all the early music of this kind, produced before the rhythmic treatment appropriate to instruments came into force, is altogether shadowy and colourless, and has no independent artistic status.

It was different with dance tunes, for in such rhythmic ranges the instruments were in their proper sphere. There is a very large quantity of such music written for stringed instruments and harpsichords which represents the crude and primitive types of later sonatas and suites. They were written by composers of all countries, and an occasional example is met with which has real vivacity and effectiveness; but for the most part they are singularly clumsy and inartistic, and hardly ever present more than the slightest trace of refined artistic intention. They indicate a dim sense of abstract effect only in the alternations of quick and slow dances, and of dances in rhythm of three or four beats; and in attempts to regulate the structure into equal and balancing groups of bars. The backward condition of the technique of performance on stringed instruments accounts for a good deal of the crudity and absence of expression in the music written for them. Mankind had to develop their skill in performance quite as slowly and with as much effort as it took them to develop the technique of composition; and the progress of both has always been to a great extent interdependent.

The standard of lute music was slightly better. The instrument was very popular in refined sections of society; and the fact that it required less mechanical ingenuity to bring it to perfection, and that it was very portable and well adapted to the conditions of domestic performance and to the social arrangements of wealthy people, caused its technique to be brought to a high pitch before that of any other modern instrument. The sort of music written for it in the early days was much like that written for stringed instruments; and consisted mainly of dance tunes in sets, occasionally of imitations of choral canzonas and madrigals, and occasionally of fanciful movements which would correspond to free preludes or fantasias in modern music. What gives these works a higher importance in relation to later instrumental music than the early viol music, is, that the element of personal skill and expression is much more apparent, and that the style is on the whole much more independent, and more distinctively instrumental. The development of the ornamental department of music had to be achieved in the same fashion as that of all other features of the art; and there can be no doubt that the early stages of the invention of the rich and copious store of decorative materials and of decorative principles, which are so characteristic of modern music, were achieved by the early composers for the lute. Even quite early in the sixteenth century, when the great choral style was by no means matured, lute music was already much cultivated; and though the forms of the movements, such as Ricercare, Passamessos, Preambules, and Pavanas, were at first crude and imperfect, and the ornaments childish and tame, yet they formed the basis of a long and continuous improvement, ultimately finding highly artistic expression in the Ordres of Couperin and the Suites and Partitas of J. S. Bach.

The music for the harpsichord and its close relatives attained very slight independence in the days of the great choral composers. Arrangements were made of choral music, and imitations of the same were attempted; and there was a fair quantity of dance tunes similar to

those written for the violins or viols. Some lute music
was adapted, and a certain number of independent fantasias and preludes were contrived; which were sometimes
written in the choral style, and sometimes consisted of
simple passages of runs and arpeggios. A certain
amount of development of decorative material and of
technique was achieved, but on the whole this branch
of instrumental music was more backward than any other
in those days.

On the other hand, organ music was relatively the most
advanced, and the nearest to complete emancipation and
independence. The requirements of ecclesiastical functions must have made considerable demands on the powers
of organists from comparatively early times; and though
the backward state of the mechanism of the instrument
prevented them from achieving much distinction by
brilliant display, they had ample occasion for experimenting in solo music, and the results they attained to
were as fruitful as they are instructive. As in other
branches of instrumental music, they frequently imitated
the contrapuntal methods of choral music, and with more
appropriate effect. But following the natural instincts of
human kind, they endeavoured to adorn these movements
with flourishes and turns and all the available resources
of ornamental variation. They also developed a kind of
performance which, without disrespect, may be compared
to very bad and unintelligent modern extemporisation.
The systematisation of chord progressions had yet to be
achieved, and they were therefore, through lack of opportunity, in much the same position as any very inefficient
modern organist is through lack of ability. They had
little or no conception of genuine musical ideas of the
kind which is adapted to instruments, and the need
for purely ornamental performance was the more imperative. They therefore devised toccatas and fantasias,

which consisted of strings of scale passages, turns, and shakes, upon successions of chords which are for the most part completely incoherent. Few things could be more instructive, in respect of the fact that our modern music is purely the fruit of cumulative development of artistic devices, than the entire absence of idea, point, and coherence in these early works, which are often the productions of composers who were great musicians and masters of all the resources of refined choral effect. The movements were possibly effective in great churches, from the wild career of the scale-passages in treble, bass, or middle parts, which often rushed (no doubt in moderate tempo) from one end of the instrument to the other. Almost the only structural device which these early organists mastered, was the effect of alternating passages of simple imitation, like those in choral music, as a contrast to the brilliant display of the scales. Further than this in point of design they could not go, except in so far as mere common sense led them to regulate their passages so as to obtain different degrees of fulness in different parts of the movement, and to pile up the effects of brilliant display and gather them all into one sonorous roll of sound at the conclusion. Crude as these works are in design, they were a definite departure in the direction of independent instrumental music on a considerable scale, and were the direct prototypes of the magnificent organ works of J. S. Bach. In fact, the branch of organ music has always continued to be more nearly allied to the great style of the choral epoch than any other instrumental form. The first great representative organist, Frescobaldi, was born in the palmy days of choral music, and made his fame while it was still flourishing; and though the resources of harmonic music were a necessary adjunct to bring this branch to maturity in later days, it did not obliterate the traces of the earlier polyphonic style

I

so completely as was the case in violin and harpsichord music, nor did it entirely obscure the time-honoured dignity of the early contrapuntal traditions. In other branches of instrumental music harmonic conditions necessitated the development of an absolutely new style and new methods of art. In organ music the old methods and something of the ancient style were retained, and were only modified by the new conditions so far as was necessary to make the design of the movements systematic and intelligible in general and in detail.

It remains to consider shortly the essential artistic methods and regulations of this great era of art. The prevailing influence which regulated all things in every department of art was fitness for choral performance. There was practically no solo singing, and, as has been pointed out above, the feeling of musicians for instrumental effect was extremely crude and undeveloped. Harmony was primarily the result of voices singing melodious parts simultaneously; and the highest skill was that which could weave good vocal parts so as to obtain beautiful and interesting successions of chords. In their conception of good vocal parts only the simplest diatonic intervals were admissible, and only the very simplest chords. It was unnatural for voices to assume discordant relations with one another directly, so the only discords allowed were such as were purely transitory, or such as were obtained by the pretty device of holding one or more notes of a harmonious combination while others moved to positions in the scale which made the stationary ones discordant, till they again resolved themselves into the unity of the harmony. All such discords have a double function; they supply contrast, and make that departure from unity, which serves as impulse. They impel the movement onward because it is impossible to rest upon discord, and the mind is not satisfied till the source of disquiet is intelligibly merged in a more reposeful combination. In a perfect work of musical art there is no absolute point of repose between the outset and the close. To make an entirely satisfying and complete close is to make what follows superfluous. The perfect management of such things, even in early stages of art, is much more subtle than it looks. A really great master so adjusts the relative degrees of movement and repose that each step has its perfect relation to the context and to the whole. Every discord must have its resolution, but till the moment of complete repose which brings the work to conclusion, each resolution is only so far complete as to satisfy the mind partially. A problem so complicated is probably more than mere calculation could solve, and its difficulty—combined with hundreds of other artistic problems—accounts for the great length of time that human instinct has taken to arrive at the status of modern music. The difficulty also accounts for the variety of standards which are presented at different periods in musical history which are more or less mature in their way. The great composers of choral music dealt in the very simplest and slenderest materials. They reduced the prominence of their points of repose to a minimum by using extremely few discords, even of the gentle kind above described; and they maintained variety by observing the more delicate shades of difference between the actual qualities of their concords, whose resolutions were not so restricted; and they evaded the feeling of coming to an end in the wrong place by keeping their voice parts constantly on the move, and by avoiding the formulas of their conventional cadences in those parts of the scale which indicated finality.

It was natural that the representatives of typically different races should adopt artistic methods which led to somewhat different results. The Netherlanders, who took the lead so prominently in the fifteenth century, always had a taste for ingenuity and for subtleties of artistic device. It was their composers who carried the homogeneous form of the canon to such lengths of futile ingenuity; but it was also their great composers who achieved all the most arduous part of the early development of their craft, and handed it on to the Italians to complete. In the end the work of the Netherlanders is the most characteristic, but that of the Italians most delicately beautiful; while the English school, which followed both, is far more comprehensive in variety, definiteness, and character, though never attaining to the extraordinary finish and perfection which is met with in Palestrina's work at its best. In the greatest triumphs of Palestrina, Vittoria, and Marenzio, the smooth, easy, masterly flow of separate voice parts seems naturally to result in perfect combinations of sound; in Lasso's work it is easy to see the deliberate ingenuity which contrives some weird unexpected successions, and makes chords melt into one another in ways which have a touch of magic in them; and Josquin and Hobrecht, with all the disadvantages of a less mature state of art, suggest the same attitude. With Byrd and Gibbons there is a touch of English hardness and boldness, and in others of the same school a bright and straightforward freshness which is peculiarly characteristic. The English school came to its best days so late as compared with foreign schools that it is no wonder that it shows many traits of a later development of musical art than do the purest Italian examples. But the same premonitions of a great change were also plentifully shown by the adventurous composers of Venice; especially the great Giovanni Gabrieli, who, besides producing many superb examples of the true old choral style, endeavoured to introduce an element of direct expression both in harmony and figure, and

tried effects of instrumental accompaniment which belong
to a different order of art from that of the pure choral
era, and were among the precursors of the great change
which brought the period of pure choral music to an end.

In a general survey of the aspects of this important
period of art, the condition of homogeneity and indefiniteness appears to be universal. This is especially the
case in respect of the structure of musical movements.
The only form in which a definite principle of procedure
was maintained from beginning to end was the canon
(which the old masters called Fuga), in which different
voices sang the same melody throughout the movement
a little after one another (see p. 104). The device has
occasionally been made interesting by clever treatment in
spite of its drawbacks; but this does not alter the fact
that it is inherently mechanical and inartistic by reason
of its rigidity and monotony. Of definite principles of
design beyond this elementary device these composers had
but few. Their treatment of musical figures and melodic
material is singularly vague. The familiar modern practice of using a definite subject throughout a considerable
portion of a movement, or at certain definite points which
have a structural importance, was hardly employed at all.
The voices which entered one after another naturally
commenced singing the same words to phrases of melody
which resembled each other. But composers' ideas of
identity of subject matter were singularly elastic, and
even if the first half-dozen notes presented similar contours in each voice part successively, the melodic forms
soon melted into something else, and from that point the
movement wandered on its devious way without further
reference to its initial phrases. A few cases occur in
which composers use a well-defined figure throughout
in constant reiteration artistically disposed, but such are
accidents of the composer's mood, and any system in such

things was quite foreign to their aims. The same is the
case with all principles of structure either in general or
in detail. Occasionally composers produced striking effects
by sequences, and by giving parallel passages to different
groups of voices or balancing choirs, but such devices
were not of general application. Occasionally also the
beginning and end of a movement were made to correspond, but that too was extremely rare. The common
modern practice of repeating phrases at long intervals
apart is an abstract musical conception; and its systematic
use in art is the result of the development of instrumental
form in later times.

In no respect is the universal absence of definition
and variety more noticeable than in the actual musical
material or "subjects." Throughout the whole range of
the old sacred choral music these are almost without
decisive significance. It is true that composers adopted
such innocent devices as a long descending scale passage
to express the descent into hell, and a formula which
might be traced into a cross for the "crucifixus," and
a slow passage of simple reiterated chords to express
the awe of the worshipper at the thought of the incar-
nation, and so on in parallel cases; but the position
occupied by subject matter and figure in their scheme
of art is altogether different from that which it occupies in the modern scheme. The subject indeed barely
stands out from its context at all. It is as though the
art was still in too nebulous a state for the essential
elements to have crystallised into separate and definite
entities. This is chiefly the result of the absence of
rhythm, without which every melodic contour is to a
certain extent wanting in complete definiteness and force.
In the matter of expression again the same holds good,
as a consequence of the limited and uniform nature of
the scales. As each complete piece of music was subject

to the rule of some special mode, all the sentiments were restricted by its characteristics. If it was what a modern musician would call minor in character, the musical expression for the "Gloria" had to be got out of it as much as that for the "Miserere." And though the use of accidentals modified modal restrictions to a certain extent, it was not sufficient to obviate the fact that in detail a piece of music had to follow the rule and character of the mode rather than the sentiment of the words. Indeed this is so far the rule that the attempt to introduce direct expression into the scheme at the expense of modal purity was among the immediate causes of the rapid decay and collapse of the whole system of art.

In close connection with the limits of expression were the limitations of the actual chord material or harmonies. No great force of expression could be obtained without more powerful dissonance than the scheme allowed. The scheme was based on consonant harmonies; and the discords, which were mild in character and comparatively rare in use, were no more than artificial modifications of the chain of concords. The incisive striking upon a discord without preliminary was a thing quite alien to the style; and nothing is more decisive as a sign of the approaching end of pure choral music than the appearance of even the slightest and mildest discord without artificial preparation.

In the general aspect of music of the choral time the same homogeneousness prevails. Sacred music, by the end of the period, was subdivided under different names into mass music, motets, hymns, psalms, and many other titles; but as far as style was concerned the distinctions were more nominal than real, for the difference between one and the other was very slight indeed. The main subdivision of the period was into sacred and secular music. But the higher class of secular music was very much like

sacred music in methods, and not very different even in
style; while the branches of lighter secular music, which
differed most from the highest artistic forms in their
more rhythmical character and harmonic structure, were
as yet limited both in range and development.

The chief points which were gained in this period were
a very fine and delicate sense of the qualities of chords
when sung by voices, and the skill in manipulating the
melodic progressions of the separate voice parts so as to
obtain a very delicate variety in the succession of these
chords. While they were achieving this composers unconsciously developed a sense for the classification of such
chords (in accordance with their inherent qualities of
affinity or contrast) in connection with certain tonal
centres. The modification of the modes by accidentals
brought the effect of tonality more and more into prominence, especially in the cadences; and by these processes the basis was formed for the new departures which
followed, and the materials which formed the groundwork
and footing of the structure of the latest modern art were
supplied.

CHAPTER VI.

THE RISE OF SECULAR MUSIC.

WITHOUT taking into consideration the many external causes which influenced and modified the character of various arts about the end of the sixteenth century, it might have been foreseen that a new departure in music was inevitable on internal and artistic grounds alone. The range of the art had been extremely limited so far; and though its limitations had conduced to the development of singularly perfect results, such advantages could not prevent men from wearying of apparent monotony, and becoming restive under restrictions which seemed to be hindrances to the fullest expression of their musical ideals. A reaction, such as in analogous situations in ordinary life drives men accustomed to ease and refinement of surroundings to court hardship, danger, and privation, drove men of the highest taste and refinement, and such as were most thoroughly in touch with the spirit and movement of their age, to cut themselves adrift from the traditions of a perfectly mature art—to cast aside the principles which the accumulated observations and efforts of past generations had brought to an admirable practical issue—and adopt a kind of music which was formless, crude, and chaotic.

The higher type of conservative mind instinctively feels that such well-being as society enjoys, and all the wealth of artistic technique, and the skill by which men achieve all they do well, are the fruits of the experiences and intelligent efforts of previous generations. To a mind so constituted a sweeping rejection of the judgment of ancestry is like cutting away the very ground upon which things are built; and the immediate result of sweeping reforms generally justifies conservative forecasts. To the conservative musician of the early days of the seventeenth century the projects of the enthusiasts who founded modern music must have appeared, as radical reforms generally do, to be based on misconceptions—an outrage to all the best grounded principles of art, and the offspring of brains which were childishly regardless of the most obvious consequences. The reformers, with the hopefulness characteristic of enthusiasts, thought they could dispense with all the results of past experience and develop a new art on the basis of pure theoretic speculation. They gave up the subtleties of polyphonic writing and the devices which were natural to it; the beautiful effects obtainable by skilful combinations of voice parts; the traditions of a noble style, and the restrictions which made it consistent and mature; and they thought to make a new heaven and a new earth where secular expression should be free and eloquent without reference to past artistic experience as a guide to the artistic means.

But they had to adopt unconsciously much that their predecessors had built up for them. It was as often happens in revolutions, when the new constitutions have to be built out of the wisdom of those whose heads have been cut off. Even the earliest experiments were based upon a crude application of chord effects of which they could have had no conception without the development of choral polyphony which their predecessors had laboriously achieved. Their beginnings were essentially steps made in the dark; and the first results that they achieved had the usual aspects of such steps in reform, and look purely infantile and absolutely ineffective by the side of the artistic works which they were meant to supersede. But nevertheless the event proved the reformers to be perfectly right. For unless they had ventured as they did, and had been as blind as reformers sometimes need to be to immediate consequences, the ultimate building up of the marvellously rich and complicated edifice of modern art could never have come about. The conservatives were perfectly right in foreseeing that the methods of the new art would immediately bring the old art to ruin. The reformers were equally right in judging that it was necessary to make that great sacrifice in order that art might obtain a new lease of vitality.

The objects of the earliest reformers, such as Cavaliere, Caccini, Galilei, and Peri, were very innocent. They had no idea of making astonishing effects, or of attracting attention by meretricious effrontery. They aimed, with a sobriety which was artistic at least in its reticence, at devising means to combine music and poetry, so that the two arts should enhance one another. They tried to find some simple musical way of declaiming sonnets, poems, and plays with a single voice, accompanied by such gentle instruments as lutes and harpsichords. The idea was not totally new, for theatrical representations with music and a kind of declamation had been attempted before; solo music of a kind had been practised by troubadours, trouvères, and various independent secularists; while instrumental music —which was such an important element in their scheme —had long been cultivated on a small scale, chiefly in short dance movements, but occasionally also for crude experiments more of the nature of abstract art. But nevertheless they had to begin almost from the beginning and find out the requirements of their art as they went on. At first they seem to have had no idea that any kind of design or even musical figures were required. They thought it sufficient for the solo voice to declaim the poetry in musical sounds whose relations of pitch imitated the inflections of the voice in ordinary declamation; and that it was sufficient to accompany and support the voice by simple chords, such as they had grown accustomed to in the music of the Church and in the simple instrumental music of the early days. Though the composers of some of the early dances had already suggested the principle of design by grouping related and contrasted chords, the intelligence of these speculative enthusiasts was at first scarcely so far advanced as lead them to imagine that a similar practice was advisable in music associated with words. Each individual chord as a lump of harmony served to support the voice for the moment; and the utmost their dormant sense of design seemed to demand in regulating the order of the harmonies, was that in passages which were specially unified by a complete verse of the poetry, the same chord should appear at the beginning and at the end of the phrase. The development of sense for chord relationship had progressed far enough in the days of the great choral music to make men perfectly alive to the effect of the familiar dominant and tonic cadence; and this the composers of the new style used with great frequency, thereby conclusively defining the actual ends of passages; but the general structure of the passages themselves remained incoherent, because, apart from the cadence, composers did not recognise the essential importance of the apposition of the dominant and tonic chords as a means of design. The very necessity of a principle of contrast in the new scheme of art remained to be found out by long experience. In an art so hedged about with limitations as the pure choral art had been, such a principle of contrast was not needed, and the peculiar properties of the old ecclesiastical modes always acted as a hindrance to its discovery; and they continued to do so for some time after the new music

had begun, because the habits and associations of all
kinds of music, both secular and sacred, had been formed
under the influences of the old modal systems; and
these had sunk so deep into men's natures, and had so
coloured their habits of thought, that they could only
shake themselves free and find their true path by slow
degrees. As long as men's minds were so influenced,
they constantly made the harmonies move in directions
which rendered nugatory the one chord which was necessary as a centre of contrast; and definiteness of design
of the harmonic kind was thereby rendered impossible.
The essence of design in harmonic music of the modern
kind is that groups of chords and whole passages shall
have a well-defined connection with certain tonal centres;
and that the centres round which the successive passages
are grouped shall have definite and intelligible relations
of contrast or affinity with one another. The simplest
dance tune or street song is now constructed upon such
principles no less than the greatest masterpieces. But
the early experimenters had no experience of such effects,
and jumbled up their chords together inconsequently.
They thought of little beyond varying their order, and
supplying a support to the declamation of the voice.
The result is that not only each portion of music set
to line and verse, but the whole plan of the works,
is indefinite in structure, and has next to no principle
of necessary cohesion beyond the occurrence of cadences.
The course of the early operas wanders on through pages
of monotonous recitative, varied only here and there by
little fragments of chorus or short dance tunes, which
are almost as innocent of melody or design as the
recitative itself.

This obvious condition of homogeneity appears not only
in the structure of these works, but also in the expression; for whether poignant anguish or exuberant joy is the

theme, there is hardly any variety in the style of the
music, which has therefore hardly any function beyond
formalising the declamation. In Rinuccini's little drama
of Euridice the familiar story is relieved of its poignancy,
and a good deal of its point, by the success of Orpheus
in winning back his lost love from the Shades. Consequently the composers had to set both the expression
of despair at receiving the news of her death, and of
joy at bringing her back to life; and from the manner
in which they addressed themselves to this object much
may be learnt. Two important settings of the little
drama exist, both of which saw the light in 1600. The
best of the two is that by the enthusiastic amateur
Jacopo Peri, which was performed at Florence to grace
the wedding festivities of Henry IV. of France and
Maria Medici. It was not the first work of its kind,
but it is the first of which enough remains in a complete state to afford safe inferences as to the aims and
methods of the new school; and the manner in which he
treated the two highly contrasted situations above alluded
to is very instructive. The following is the passage
which was then held adequate to express the poignancy
of Orpheus' feelings over his loss :—

tol - to   Ohi-me   de - ve segi - - ta

The following is the music in which he expresses his
joy at bringing his lost bride back to the light of day :—

Voice.

Gio - i - te al canto mio

Accomp.

sel - ve fron-do - se   Gio - i - te ama-ti

col - li   e   d'ogni   in - tor - no

Ec - co rim-bom - bi dalle   valle   as-co - se.

The texture of the two passages is obviously very

similar, but it is well not to overlook the points which
show some sense of adaptation to the respective states
of emotion.   Both passages afford fair opportunity to
a competent singer to infuse expression into the ostensibly bald phrases.   And, besides this, they lend themselves very happily to the requirements of the situations,
and show the justness of the composer's instinct in
those respects in which artistic technique is not very
essential.   For the phrases which express bereavement
and sorrow are tortuous, irregular, spasmodic—broken
with catching breath and wailing accent; whereas the
expression of joy is flowing, easy and continuous, and
unusually well defined and regular in form, approaching
as nearly to the types of modern harmonic art as was
possible in those days.   Such general points as these can
be effected by intelligent beings without much training
or experience; but the details are carried out crudely
and baldly, for the day was still far off when men learnt
how to make anything artistically appropriate of the
instrumental accompaniment.

There is very little in the works of the other representatives of this new departure which indicates views or skill
in any special degree superior to Peri's.   Caccini's setting
of the same drama of Euridice is in general character
very like Peri's.   It has the same monotonous expanses
of recitative with accompaniment of figured bass, and
similar short fragments of chorus, consisting of a few
bars at a time, written with quite as obvious a lack of
sense for choral effect.   Perhaps the most noteworthy
point is that, being one of the earliest solo singers of
repute, and the father of a famous *cantatrice*, he introduced roulades and ornamental passages for the singers;
thereby devising some of the first formulas, and prefiguring even in those early days the tasteless and senseless excesses of vain show which disgrace certain schools

of modern opera. The following passage is from Caccini's
Euridice :—

It is noteworthy that these flourishes usually occur close to
the end of verses and phrases, just as simpler ones do in
the old German folk-songs. Caccini wrote a book about
the " Nuove Musiche " which described the objects of the
reformers; and in this work he gave some examples of
the way in which short poems might be set for a solo
voice, which serve as almost the earliest examples of
consciously contrived solo-songs with instrumental accompaniment, as distinguished from folk-songs. These also
serve to emphasise the very slight sense which the composers had of the need for design, or of the possibility
of obtaining such a thing by the distribution of the harmonic successions. What remains of Emilio Cavaliere's
work is similar in character, and shows almost as vague
a sense of design. The introduction to his one Oratorio
is the finest piece of work left by this group of com-

K

posers, and is a very noble and impressive monument of
the man, of whom we know but little beyond the fact
that the invention of recitative is attributed to him by his
fellow composers. To judge from this piece of work he
must have been of larger calibre than they were. Here
and there he even shows some sense of modulation as a
means of effect, and of consistent use of tonality; but in
texture and artistic treatment of detail he is almost as
backward as the rest of his contemporaries.

Though there were a few composers who held by the
old traditions, most of the men of marked powers and
energy were attracted by the new methods, and by the
escape it afforded them from the drudgery of musical
education. They soon became conscious of new requirements in their line of work, and the early homogeneous
experiments were very soon improved upon. The most
noteworthy of all the representatives of the style was
Monteverde, whose adventurous genius found a congenial
field in such a state of art; and who gave the impress of
his personality to a branch of histrionic music which has
maintained certain well-defined characteristics from that
day till this. It may well be doubted if Monteverde would
ever have succeeded in a line of art which required concentration and logical coherence of musical design. He
seems to have belonged to that familiar type of artists
who regard expression as the one and only element of
importance. He had been educated in the learning of
the ancients, but had early shown his want of submission
to the time-honoured restrictions by using chords and
progressions which were out of place in the old choral
style. He had endeavoured to introduce effects of strong
expression into an order of art which could only retain
its aspect of maturity by excluding all such direct forms
of utterance. A decisive harshness breaking upon the
ear without preliminary was shortly to become a necessity

to musical mankind, but to the old order of things it
was the omen of immediate dissolution. The methods of
choral art did not provide for dramatic force or the utterance of passionate feeling; and under such circumstances
it was natural that Monteverde should misapply his special
gifts, which were all in the direction of dramatic expression. The new departure, when it came, was his opportunity. He was not ostensibly a sharer in the first steps
of the movement; but directly he joined it he entirely
eclipsed all other composers in the field, and in a few
years gave it quite a new complexion. For whereas the
first composers had not laid any great stress on expression,
Monteverde's instinct and aim was chiefly in that direction; and he often sought to emphasise his situations at
all costs. His harmonic progressions are for the most
part as incoherent as those of his predecessors, and, as
might be expected with his peculiar aptitudes, he did very
little for design. But he clearly had a very considerable
sense of stage effect, and realised that mere monotonous
recitative was not the final solution nor even the nucleus of
dramatic music. It is true he introduces a great quantity
of recitative, but he varies it with instrumental interludes
which now and then have some real point and relevancy
about them; and with passages of solo music which have
definite figure, and expression, and with choruses which
are more skilfully contrived, and to a certain degree more
effective than those of his predecessors. By this means
he broke up the homogeneous texture of the scenes
into passages of well-defined diversity, and interested his
auditors with contrast, variety, and conspicuously characteristic passages, which heighten the impression of situations as all stage music should.

His ideas of instrumental music were very crude, but
nevertheless immensely in advance of the works of his predecessors. Where they had been satisfied with a single line

and figures to indicate to the lute players and cembalists the chords they were to use, he brought together a large band of violins, viols, lutes, trumpets, flutes, trombones, a harpsichord, and other instruments, and in special parts of his works gave some of them definite parts to play, and distributed them with some sense of effect and relevancy. His experiments sometimes look childish, but in several cases they are the types which only wanted more experienced handling to become permanent features of modern orchestral music. His instinct led him to make his work more definite and alive in detail than the earlier experiments had been; and though it was too early for the articulations of the structure to become distinct, his style of work is a very clear foreshadowing of the state which was bound to ensue. He was especially conspicuous as the first composer who aimed decisively at histrionic effect, and he originated the tradition which passed through Cavalli and Lulli into France and ultimately made that country its home; while Italy fell under the spell of a different theory of art and became the special champion of design and beauty of melody.

The immediate source of this important change in the Italian course of musical development was a reaction from the crude speculativeness of the new style in favour of a revival of the old methods of choral art; and its fruit was an endeavour to adapt what was applicable of those methods to the new theories. The change which came over the new music was so rapid and complete, that it proves that humanity took very little time to realise that something more was wanted than mere moment-to-moment setting of the words of a poem or the scenes of a play. Men who were masters of the technique of the old choral art, such as Giovanni Gabrieli at Venice, tried to apply it in new ways in conformity with the spirit of the new theories; introducing singular experiments of a realistic character, and some remarkable experiments in expression by harmony. This type of art was carried by his interesting pupil, Schütz, into Germany, and by him the first advances were made in the direction of that peculiarly earnest, artistic, and deeply emotional style which is the glory of German music. Each of these and many others contributed their share to the progress of the movement; but circumstances give peculiar prominence to Carissimi, whose experience and genuine feeling for the old artistic methods gave him a good hold upon the artistic possibilities of the new, and helped his judgment to distinguish between what was mere experimental extravagance and what was genuinely artistic expression. He had not the inventiveness or the force and character of Monteverde, but he had more sense of beauty, both of form and sound, and a better artistic balance. This may have been owing to the fact that he did not write for the stage, and was less tempted to trespass in the direction of crude expression. His most important works are in the line of oratorio, and can hardly have been intended (as the earliest oratorios were) to have been represented with scenery and action. In these oratorios he shows a decided revival of the sense for choral effect; but it is noteworthy that the effect produced by his choral writing is very different from the old style. The sense for harmonic design is conspicuously perceptible, and it is obvious that he tries to apply his skill in part writing to the ends of expression. The choruses are often constructed on bold and simple series of chords, and the figures written for the voices strongly resemble passages which are familiar in Handel's choruses—both florid and plain. In his solo music Carissimi is much more refined and artistic than Monteverde; and though he falls behind him in strength of emotional character, he reaches at times a very high degree of pathos and sadness, and has a good hold on many varieties of human feeling. The greater part of the solo music is recitative, but it is of a more regular and definite type than that of his predecessors, and often approaches to clear melodic outlines; while there are plenty of examples of solo music in which the reiteration of a characteristic phrase in contrasting and corresponding portions of the scale gives the effect of completeness of design. Thus the art of choral music sprang into new life through the impulse to express dramatic feeling in terms of harmonic design as well as of counterpoint, while solo music gained definition through the same impulse to make it expressive and intelligible in form.

But instrumental music still hung fire. For that Carissimi seemed to have but little instinct. Possibly he concentrated so much of his artistic impulse on choral music that his mind was distracted from giving attention to the possibilities of purely instrumental effect. By comparison with his skill in vocal effect his instrumental experiments seem too often very crude and tame, and even inferior to Monteverde's in point. But it may be judged that the feeling for instrumental effect was developing among musicians, for Cesti and Stradella (who were younger contemporaries of Carissimi) both show a very considerable skill for that time in writing string accompaniments to their solos and choruses, using the kind of figures which are familiar to the world in Handel's works. Both these composers, moreover, show a very great advance in feeling for design in vocal melody. Cesti's little arias and melodies from cantatas and operas are often as completely modelled and as definite, both in contours and periods, as the best of Handel's. They are not developed to the extent of similar works of the later age; but as far as they go they show a very keen instinct for balancing phrases,

distributing cadences, dovetailing passages, presenting
musical figures in various aspects, and contriving good
stretches of thoroughly vocal melody. Stradella's genius
was of a different cast, and expresses a different group
of types of sentiment. That in itself is a proof of the
widening out of art into heterogeneousness in its larger
aspects. But the tendency to give the effect of definite
design is as clear in Stradella's work as in Cesti's.
Stradella had a very remarkable instinct for choral
effect, and even for piling up progressions into a climax;
and his solo music, though apparently not so happy in
varieties of spontaneous melody as Cesti's, aims equally
at definiteness of structure. His work in the line of
oratorio is specially significant; as he stands comparatively
alone in cultivating all the natural resources of that
form of art—on the lines which Handel adopted later—
at a time when his fellow-composers were falling in
with the inclination of their public for solo singing, and
were giving up the grand opportunities of choral effect
as superfluous. Indeed the branch of oratorio had to
wait for representatives of more strenuous nations for
its ultimate development. But in other respects Italy
continued as much as ever to be the centre of musical
progress. The Thirty Years' War and its attendant miseries
crushed all musical energy out of Germany, and the Civil
War in England delayed the cultivation of the new methods
there, while in France the astute craft of Lulli obtained
so exclusive a monopoly of musical performances, that he
extinguished her own composers in his lifetime, and left
native musical impulse paralysed at his death.

The career of this Italian Lulli illustrates very decisively the manner in which artistic developments follow
the lines of least resistance, by the simple process of submitting to be guided by the predilections of the public
for whom the works of art are devised. Lulli was trans-

planted into France and into the service of the Court in early years; and he had ample time and opportunity for discovering what French tastes were, and for applying his versatility to meet lively demands which afforded excellent prospects of profuse remuneration.   Lulli was undoubtedly made to perceive very early that French taste ran in the direction of the theatre, and more especially in favour of dancing and spectacular effect in connection with it.   He had to provide ballet airs for the King and the Court to dance and masquerade to, and plentiful practice developed in him a very notable skill in knitting these dance tunes into compact and definite forms, and varying their character so as to get the best effect out of groups of them.   The necessity for meeting the artificial requirements of these masquerades (which were like the English Court masques) taught him how to plan scenes with due sense of effect.   It is even possible that he was put in the way of the scheme he adopted by the French themselves; as Cambert, the native composer whom he extinguished, had used the same plan in his operatic works which Lulli afterwards stereotyped on a larger scale.   In the vocal solo part of his work Lulli had opportunity to study the latest and most popular models when Monteverde's famous pupil Cavalli came to Paris to conduct some of his operas for Court festivals.   The Italians had not up to that time given much attention to ballet music, so Cavalli had not been called upon to develop his talents in that direction. But to make his works acceptable to the French public ballet was indispensable; so young Lulli was called upon to fit out Cavalli's work with the necessary tunes, and through being associated with him he gained the opportunity to study the methods of the foremost Italian opera composer in respect of recitative, declamation, and treatment of the vocal part of his work.

Under these circumstances Lulli developed a scheme of
opera which was more mature and complete than any
other of his century. The texture of his work on the
whole is crude and bald, but the definition of the various
items which go to make up his operatic scheme is complete as far as it goes, and he certainly made up his very
astute mind as to the character which each several portion
and feature of his work required.

In the first place, the type of his overture is thoroughly
distinct, and very happily conceived as an introduction
to what follows. It begins almost invariably with a broad
and massive slow movement, which serves as an excellent
foundation, and is followed by a quick energetic movement
in a loosely fugal style, prefiguring the type of Handel's
overtures to operas and oratorios. The play itself commonly
begins with an introductory scene, often mythological,
which comprises choruses, dances, and such other features
as obviously imply spectacular display and much grouping of people on the stage, and lend themselves to a
good deal of musical sound and animation. The drama
proper is interpreted mainly in accompanied recitative,
interspersed with frequent snatches of ballet and a few
definite pieces for solo; and most of the acts end with
choruses and massing of crowds on the stage to give
weight and impressiveness to the final climax.

Lulli shows excellent sense of relief and proportion in
the general planning and laying out of the musical elements in the scenes, and in the relations of the respective
acts and scenes to one another; and he is conspicuously
successful for his time in shaking himself free from the
ecclesiastical associations of the modes, and adopting a
thoroughly secular manner. Where modern methods were
wanting or undeveloped, as in his overtures, he had to
fall back on the methods of the old choral art and write
in fugal or contrapuntal style; but it is clear that he was

not very solidly grounded in the traditional ' science " of music, and was therefore all the more free to work out his scheme in the harmonic style and with more of the spirit of modern tonality. His instinct of the need for orderliness and system in his musical material was in advance of his age; but the realisation of principles of design was still very backward, and he had to use such means of definition as came in his way. He was among the first to make a notable use of what is called the aria form, which consists of three well-defined sections, the first and last corresponding in key and musical material, and the central one supplying contrasts in both these respects. It is essentially the simplest form in music, and might well be called primary form, but in connection with opera it has gained the title of aria-form through its much too frequent and much too obvious use. The conventions of opera were not sufficiently stereotyped for Lulli to use it as his successors did, and he fortunately experimented in other forms which are more interesting and more elastic. One, of which he makes frequent and very ingenious use, is the time-honoured device of the ground bass. This is a principle of unifying a whole movement or passage by repeating the same formula of notes in the bass over and over again. It is attractive to a composer of any real capacity; for the developing of contrast, diversity of sentiment, and variety of harmony and melody upon the same framework requires a good deal of musical aptitude. The reason why Lulli and other composers of his time, such as Stradella and Purcell, made such frequent use of it was that the principles of real harmonic form of the modern order—based upon classification of harmonies—were still unsettled, and they had to adopt principles of design which, like canon and fugue, belonged to homogeneous types, and did not in themselves imply an inherent principle of contrast. But

the fact that Lulli used it, and other principles of like
nature, shows how decisively the human mind was waking
up to the need of clear design and coherence in art, which
the early experimenters in opera and cantata had regarded
as superfluous.

Lulli's type of opera was an immense advance upon the
first experiments in plan, in definiteness of expression and
rhythm, and in variety of subdivision into the component
ballet movements, choruses, instrumental interludes, arias,
recitatives, and so forth; and though the plan of the
drama was very artificial and mechanically subservient
to stage effect, the character of the music followed the
character of the story from moment to moment very successfully, and there is singularly little of superfluous ornament or of passages introduced for the purpose of display.
Indeed the dignity and expressiveness of most of the declamatory portions of these works are creditable alike to Lulli
and to his audiences. The operas are mainly defective in
the very limited sense of instrumental effect which they
imply; in the monotony of the full accompaniments, the
absence of artistic refinement and skill of workmanship
in detail, and in the general stiffness of style. The nucleus
of Lulli's band was a set of strings; probably violins at the
top and a group of viols for lower and inner parts, accompanied by a harpsichord, which was played from figured
bass. These instruments are used in a very mechanical
manner to supply dull harmonies, without attempt at
figuration or any process to lighten or enliven the bass
and filling in. The strings are supplemented occasionally
by trumpets, flutes, hautboys, and other familiar wind
instruments to increase the mass of sound and to supply
variety of colour on special occasions. But the obviousness of these occasions shows how little craving or sense
musicians had as yet for variety of colour. The hautboys
serve to give local colour to rustic scenes, and the trumpets

and drums are called in to illustrate martial ones, and so
forth; but less obvious occasions call for no distinctive
use of such devices.   There is no delicate adjustment of
either mass of sound or special tone for artistic ends.
The whole group of strings plays constantly together in
a monotonous and mechanical manner—extremely homogeneous — in all movements which are "accompanied;"
and recitatives and solo movements have only bass with
figures, for which the accompanyist at the harpsichord
supplied the details.   It is especially this weakness and
ineffectiveness in instrumental matters which would make
even the best of Lulli's operas unendurable to a modern
audience. He was also necessarily backward in feeling
for the actual effects of modulation and for its value as
an element of form, for the principles of modern tonality
were still undeveloped; but in many respects his work is
very noteworthy, and not only indicated principles which
great composers afterwards adopted as the bases of further
developments, but established a form of art which has
served as the groundwork for the later development of
the French grand opera; while his theatrical instinct
strengthened the order of essentially histrionic music
which has survived and sometimes even flashed into
brilliant conspicuousness in modern times.

In Italy, meanwhile, the tastes of the nation soon influenced the course of operatic development, and impelled it
into a different path from that taken by French opera.
The tendency which is most apparent at this time is the
growing feeling for simplicity and clearness of form, and
distinctness and amenity of melody.   The Italians gravi-
tated away from strong direct dramatic expression, and
indeed from immediate expression of any kind, and endeavoured merely to illustrate situations as they presented
themselves by the general sentiment of an entire movement or an entire passage of melody; thus breaking

away altogether from the path which Monteverde had chosen, and leaving it for other nations to follow up to important results. The mission of the Italians at this time was undoubtedly to lay the foundations of modern harmonic art, and to establish those primary relations of harmonies which are the basis of the modern principles of musical design. A certain native easy-going indolence seems to have directed them into the road they chose, while the development of melody of the operatic type (which in itself is equivalent to linear design) sprang from the gift and instinct of the nation for singing. As the century progressed composers became more skilful in the management of their instrumental accompaniments, and more clear about the plan of their operas as wholes, organising the acts into well-defined portions, consisting of instrumental preludes (called either overtures or sinfonias), interludes, recitatives, airs, and even fairly developed choruses. The most important results obtained in these respects are summed up in the work of Alessandro Scarlatti, who became the most prominent composer of his time in opera and church music, and no mean master of instrumental music of the old kind. But the most important part of his contribution to the progress of his art is in the department of opera. The most obvious trait in his career, which typifies the tendencies of his time, was the manner in which he played into the hands of the solo singers. It is singular that a man of such real genius and of such high artistic responsibility of character should have done more than any one to establish that prominence of the solo singer in opera which has in after times been its most fatal impediment. He of course had no idea of the evils to which his practice would lead. The operatic form was still young, and its field was not yet sufficiently explored to make it clear in what directions danger lay; and Scarlatti was led, mainly by his instinct for musical design, to ignore obvious inconsistency in the dramatic development of the plays that he set, in order to obtain a complete musical result which satisfied his own particular instinct and the tastes of his Italian audiences.

The history of opera from first to last has been a sort of struggle between the musical and the dramatic elements; which has resulted in an alternate swaying to and fro, in course of which at one time the musical material was formalised and made artistically complete at the expense of dramatic truth, and at another the music was made subservient to the development of the play. Now that the methods and material of art have developed to such a marvellous degree of richness and variety, it is easy to see that nothing short of the existing profusion admits of both the literary and musical sides being equally respected and being equally satisfactory from the artistic point of view. In the early days it was inevitable that one of the two should give way, and owing to the peculiarities of the Italian disposition, it was not on the musical side that the concessions were made. Scarlatti aimed at making the units of his operatic scheme musically complete, and he succeeded so far that his independent solo movements, called arias, are often beautiful works of art. But the drama, under the conditions which he established, became merely the excuse for stringing a number of solo pieces together, and for distributing them so as to illustrate contrasting moods and types of sentiment. The story of the drama may be dimly felt in the background in such works, but it would be the last thing about which the amateur of Italian opera would concern himself much. Apparently even the spectacular effect was more considered, because it was less likely to interfere with the composer's uncompromising attitude. It soon followed that the interests of the individual singers became the most powerful influence in regulating the scheme, and the type of art became thoroughly vicious and one-sided. The public concentrated so much attention on the soloists that opera became a mere entertainment in which certain vocalists sang, as at an ordinary concert, a series of arias which were carefully adapted to show off their particular gifts. There was a great deal of management required, and the skill of the composer was taxed to devise various types of passages suitable to the several performers. He had to take his soloists with their special gifts as so many settled quantities, and work out a scheme which admitted of their appearing in a certain order, as regulated by their popularity, money worth, or personal vanity; and out of these quantities, whose order was thus mainly prearranged for him, he had to obtain an effective distribution of types of sentiment and style. It was like making patterns with counters of different shapes; and though the process was a mechanical one, it was a field for the expenditure of a good deal of ingenuity, and one not unprofitable to the musical art, because it necessitated the development of so many varieties of melodic figure and vocal phrase.

Scarlatti fell in with the necessities of the situation so completely that he poured out opera after opera in which all the solo pieces were in the same form, and that the simplest conceivable. The principle of statement, contrast, and restatement so completely answered his requirements that he did not even take the trouble to write out the restatement; but after writing out in full his first section, and the section which established the principle of contrast, he directed the first section to be repeated to make the aria complete, by the simple words "da capo." These arias were interspersed with passages of recitative, which, from the musical side of the question, served as breathing space between one aria and another, and prevented their jostling one another;

while on the dramatic side they served to carry on the
plainer parts of the dialogue. It is noteworthy that both
his recitative and his instrumental ritornels are less characteristic than Monteverde's had been. The practical
composer realised that the public did not care much
about them, and he did not care to expend superfluous
effort. All Italian composers soon gave up attempting
to put any expression into their recitatives, and made
them as near as possible mere formalised declamation—
sometimes not even declamation, but formalised talk.
Moreover the progressions of the accompanying chords
became as aimless and empty as the progressions of the
voice, so that the effect depended solely upon the skill
of the singer in delivery; and this retrograde tendency
produced as its natural result one of the most detestable
conventions in all the range of art; which has helped
to kill works which contain many grand and beautiful
features, because the amount of senseless rigmarole with
which they are mated is positively unendurable.

Scarlatti exerted himself occasionally in ensemble movements, but the only department in which he made as
important a mark as in his arias was in his overtures.
The progress made in instrumental performance, and the
attention which music for violins was beginning to attract,
gave him the opportunity to improve the status of certain
instrumental portions of his work. Some of his overtures
are bright, definite, and genuinely instrumental in style.
He commonly wrote them in three or four short movements, distributed in the order familiar in modern symphonies. When he used three movements, the first was
a solid allegro, corresponding to the first movement of
the average modern sonata; the second was a short slow
movement aiming at expression; and the third a lively
allegro; and this scheme came to be universally adopted
even till the time of Mozart, who wrote his early opera

overtures in this form. When four movements were written the scheme was practically the same, as the first was merely a slow introduction. These little symphonies were generally scored with a certain amount of skill and elasticity for a group of stringed instruments, with the occasional addition of a few wind instruments, such as trumpets. As the principles of harmonic form were still undetermined, the style was necessarily rather contrapuntal; but the feeling for tonality is always conspicuously present in the general outline of the movements. There is nothing in them of instrumentation of the modern kind, and the movements are necessarily short and compact; but the nucleus, such as it was, served as the foundation upon which the scheme of modern symphony was based. In course of time these opera overtures (which often went by the name of "symphonies") were played apart from the operas to which they belonged, and then similar works were written without operas to follow them; and as the feeling for instrumentation and the understanding of principles of development and of harmonic design improved, the scheme was widened and enriched and diversified till it appeared in its utmost perfection in the great works of Beethoven.

It is surprising how early national predispositions show themselves in music. They are often more decisively apparent in an early and immature state of art than at later periods; because the special success and prominence of any one nation in things artistic causes other nations which are more slow to develop to imitate their devices and methods in the intermediate state of art, and thus to belie their own true tastes for a time till they have attained sufficient skill to utter things consistent with their own natures, and shake off the alien manner. As early as the seventeenth century both Germany and England showed the tendencies which are evidently

engrained in their musical dispositions, and which have
been carried by the Germans to very extreme lengths.
The real bent of both nations is the same. In sense
of external beauty they are neither of them so keen or
so apt as Italians, and during the period in which beauty
was the principal aim of art they had to follow the
lead of the more precocious nation. But though the
resources of art were not adequate to the ends of characteristic expression, the natural instinct of the northern
nations in that direction is shown in a great number of
instances. It appears mainly in two aspects. One is
the use of curious daring roughnesses and harshnesses in
chords and progressions. Thus Heinrich Schütz in his
choral works frequently contrived strange chords to represent his feeling of the spirit of the words. In his setting
of the first Psalm the words "in the counsel of the
ungodly" are expressed as follows :—

In the late phase of the madrigal period, which was
almost exclusively centred in England, composers aimed
at characteristic expression of the words far oftener than
the great Italian masters had done ; and they often showed
that tendency towards realistic expression which Purcell
carried to such an excess. Purcell was indeed the greatest
musical genius of his age, but his lines were cast in most
unfortunate places. His circumstances put him completely
out of touch with the choral methods of the great period ;
and the standards and models for the new style, and
the examples of what could and what could not be done,
were so deficient that his judgment went constantly
astray ; and in trying to carry out his ideals according

to the principles of the "new music" he occasionally
achieves a marvellous stroke of real genius, and not un-
frequently falls into the depths of bathos and childishness.
The experiments which he made in expression, under the
same impulse as Schütz in church choral music, are quite
astounding in crudeness, and almost impossible to sing;
while in secular solo music (where he is more often highly
successful) he frequently adopts realistic devices of a
quaintly innocent kind, for lack of resources to utter
otherwise his expressive intentions :—

that pants . . . . for breath

do glide . . . .

Precisely in the same spirit Schütz describes the angel
descending from heaven at the resurrection as follows :—

Der En - gel des Her-ren steig vom Him - mel her - ab

And when he rolls away the stone from the sepulchre
he does it in this wise—

Und wäl - - - - - - - - zet den Stein

In the instrumental line the works of the early Italian
violinists form a very important historical landmark. The
development of the art of violin-making to the unsur-
passable pitch attained by the great Italian violin-makers,
such as the Amatis, Guarnerius, Stradivari, and Bergonzi,
naturally coincided with a remarkable development of
the technique of violin-playing. The crude experiments

of earlier generations in dance movements, fantasias, variations, ·and movements copied from types of choral music, were superseded by a much more mature and artistic class of work, in which the capabilities of the violin for expression and effect were happily brought into play. The art gained immensely for a time through composers being also performers, for they understood better than any one what forms of figure and melody were most easily made effective. They made a good many experiments in diverse forms, and ultimately settled down to the acceptance of certain definite groups of movements whose order and arrangement approved themselves to their instincts. The scheme is in the main always the same, consisting of dignified animation to begin with, expressive slow cantabile for the centre, and light gaiety to end with. And it may be noted in passing that ·this too is in conformity with that universal principle of design which it seems to be the aim of all music to achieve; and almost all modern works in which several movements are grouped together are mainly variations of it, or outcomes of the essential artistic necessity of contrast and restatement. The names the violin composers gave to their works were various. A Sonata da Camera was mainly a group of dance movements, essentially secular in style; a Sonata da Chiesa was a group of abstract movements in more serious style, generally comprising a fugue or some other contrapuntal movement, derived ultimately from the old choral music. Concertos were variable in their constituents, and were written for more instruments. The modern sonata was an outcome of all three, and of the general development of instrumental expression and technique, which also went on under the names of Suites, Lessons, Ordres, Partitas, and many other titles. Corelli's works stand at the head of all these types, and indeed of all modern instrumenta. music, for hardly anything written before his time appeals to the modern hearer as being sufficiently mature to be tolerable; and though in point of technique his range was rather limited, he managed to produce something which in its way is complete, well-balanced, and perfectly adapted to the requirements of instrumental performance. The appearance of crude helplessness and uncertainty which characterises the works of earlier composers is no longer perceptible, and his compositions rest securely upon their own basis. This was indeed an extremely important step to have achieved, and can hardly be overrated as an epoch in art. All music whatever which was of any dimensions, except rambling fantasias, organ toccatas, and contrapuntal fugues, had hitherto been dependent on words for its full intelligibility. Real artistic development, independent of such connection, had not been possible till men changed their point of view and developed their feeling for tonality and for the classification of harmony.

Corelli's methods are ostensibly contrapuntal, but it is noteworthy that his is not the old kind of counterpoint, but rather an artistic treatment of part-writing, which assimilates into chords whose progressions are adapted to the principles of modern tonality. He uses sequences for the purposes of form, and modulations for purposes of contrast and balance, and cadences to define periods and sections, and other characteristic devices of modern art; and though the traces of the old church modes are occasionally apparent, they are felt to be getting more and more slight. There is more of art than of human feeling in his work, as is inevitable at such a stage of development; but his art as far as it goes is very good, and the style of expression refined and pleasant.

There is no need to overrate the absolute value of Corelli's works as music to establish their historic importance. The fact that they are the earliest examples of pure instrumental music which have maintained any hold upon lovers of the art implies that men's instincts do not justify the methods upon which earlier works were constructed. And they therefore mark the point where imperfect attempts are at last replaced by achievement.

Corelli's contemporary, Vivaldi, who was a more brilliant executant than Corelli himself, had even keener sense for harmonic principles; and though his work has not the substance nor the uniform interest nor the smoothness of part-writing, nor, finally, the permanent popularity of Corelli's work, it was extremely valuable at the moment for supplying various types of instrumental passages and for helping to establish the feeling for harmonic design. In his concertos and sonatas the harmonic plan is clear even to obviousness, and there is much less of contrapuntal and free inner development than in Corelli's works; but they are more characteristically fitted out with the typical figures of harmonic accompaniment, brilliant *fiorituri*, and passages which show a high instinct for instrumental effect. From Corelli and Vivaldi sprang that wonderful school of Italian violinists and composers who did more than any others to give the modern harmonic system of design a solid foundation, and to establish those principles of development which have been refined and elaborated by many generations of instrumental composers up to the present time.

Among other lines of progress later events made the development of organ music of peculiar importance. As has before been pointed out, organ music obtained an independent status sooner than any other branch of instrumental music, probably because organists were afforded such frequent opportunities of experiment in solo-playing in the services of the church. Many of the kinds of work in which they experimented led to nothing particular, but their imitation of choral works led to the development of fugue, which is one of the most important and elastic of all forms of art. The immediate source of the method of its construction was the manner in which the voices in choral movements entered one after another singing the same initial phrase at the different pitches which best suited their calibre—the tenor taking it a fourth or fifth above the bass, and the alto a fourth or fifth above the tenor, and the treble at the same distance above the alto, or *vice versâ*. In the old choral music the initial phrases were usually rather indefinite, and but rarely reappeared in the course of the movement. But when the same process was adopted for instrumental music without words, composers soon felt the advantage of making the initial phrase characteristically definite, and common sense taught them the advantage of unifying the movement throughout by making the initial phrase, as it were, the text of the whole discourse. Then again common sense equally taught them that mere repetition of the initial phrases in the same order and at the same pitch was wearisome; and they soon found the further advantage of associating the principal phrase or subject with contrasting subordinate phrases, and of making the order and pitch of subsequent reiterations of the initial phrase afford contrast by varying from the first order of statement. Then as their sense of tonality grew clearer, the practice naturally followed of making the course of the movement modulate into new keys, and of presenting the initial phrases or subjects, and the subordinate figures or counter-subjects, in relation to new tonics. Thus the general aspect of the fugue came to resemble some of the simpler forms of harmonic music, by beginning in one key, passing to extraneous keys by way of contrast, and ending by bringing the course of the progressions round to the original key, and by recapitulating the initial phrases prominently to round the whole movement into completeness.

However, the fugal form had an advantage over pure
harmonic forms through its allowing composers to dispense with the cadences which defined the various sections,
but broke up the continuity of the whole. But it was so
inviting to musicians of an ingenious turn of mind that
it became vitiated by sheer excess of artifice, in manipulating subjects and counter-subjects, and interweaving
the strands into all manner of curious combinations;
and the possibilities of pure contrapuntal device were
discussed up and down to such an extent that most composers who used the form forgot that all this artifice was
superfluous except as a means to express something over
and beyond their own ingenuity. In the end the elastic
capabilities which it possessed for variety of expression,
and for effective general development based upon the use
of well-marked subjects, attracted many of the greatest
composers; and not only served for toccatas, movements
of sonatas, and even dance suites, but was readapted for
choral purposes, and became one of the most effective
forms for choruses possible, and far better adapted for
genuine choral effect than the so-called sonata forms.
It was not indeed till the resources of music were
developed all round to the very highest pitch that any
better form for choral use was found; and then finally
the old pure type of fugue gave way to forms of art
which are more elastic still. The early organists, from
the two Gabrielis, Sweelinck, and Frescobaldi onwards,
served the art nobly in the fugal and kindred forms;
devising types of figure and traits of style which were
well suited to the instrument, and contriving many
schemes of design which were worked out in course of
time till they became noble types of complete and
expressive art.

Music for the harpsichord and clavichord rather lagged
behind for a time, as, for domestic purposes, neither was

so attractive as the violin; and in the early part of the
century they still had a formidable rival in the lute.
Works for these instruments began to be produced very
early in the century, but of these all except rare and exceptional specimens by Orlando Gibbons and Bird are chiefly
interesting on account of their containing the crude fore-
shadowings of later developments of technique. The first
nation to make successful mark in this line were the
French, especially the famous Couperin, who had a very
lively sense of the style which was best suited to the instrument, and developed a happy knack of writing tuneful
and compact little movements which he grouped, with
great feeling for contrast and consistency, into sets called
Ordres, which are much the same as the groups more
familiarly known as Suites. His prototypes were probably
the sets of little movements for lutes, such as those of
Denis Gaultier. He was evidently a man of considerable
musical gifts of a high order, but he sacrificed more
dignified lines of art in concession to the French popular
taste for ballet tunes. He was one of the first to write
tuneful little movements of the kind which became so
popular in later days; and it is noteworthy that he, as
well as the earlier lutenists, and his later compatriot,
Rameau, foreshadowed the taste of the French for illustrating definite ideas by music, and for making what may
be called picture-tunes, in preference to developing the
less obvious implications of pure self-dependent music,
in lines of concentrated and comprehensive art.

The progress of this somewhat immature period shows
the inevitable tendency of all things from homogeneity
towards diversity and definiteness. In its widest aspects
art is seen to branch out into a variety of different
forms. The difference in style and matter between
choral movements and instrumental works begins to be
more definite and decisive. The types of opera, oratorio,

cantata, and of the various kinds of church music become more distinct, and are even subdivided into different
subordinate types, as was the case with Italian and French
opera.　Instrumental music, from being mainly either
imitations of choral music, or vague toccatas and fantasias
or short dance tunes, established a complete independent
existence, and began to branch out into the various forms
which have since become representative as sonatas and
symphonies.　The treatment of instruments began to be
characteristic, and the style of expression and of figure
appropriate to different kinds began to be discerned.　In
the works themselves the articulation of the component
parts attains more and more definiteness and clearness
of modelling, and methods were found out for making
each movement more logical and coherent.　Among the
most important achievements of the time is the final
breaking away from the influences of the old modes,
which made the design and texture of the older works so
indefinite.　The earliest phases of the developing feeling
for tonality of the modern kind, which implies a classification of harmonies and an adoption of systematic harmonic
progressions, already gave the new works an appearance
of orderliness and stability which marks the inauguration
of a new era in art; while the use of definite rhythmical
grouping enabled musicians to make their ideas infinitely
more characteristic and vivid, and caused the periods and
sections of the movements to gain a sense of completeness
and clearness which was impossible under the old order
of things.

CHAPTER VII.

COMBINATION OF OLD METHODS AND NEW PRINCIPLES.

THE development of principles of design in music must inevitably wait upon the development of technique. Very little can be done with limited means of performance; and adequacy of such means is dependent on the previous perfecting of various instruments, and on the discovery of the particular types of expression and figure which are adapted to them. One of the reasons why instrumental music lagged behind was that men were slow in finding out the arts of execution ; and even when the stock of figures and phrases which were adapted to various instruments had become plentiful, it took composers some time to assimilate them sufficiently, so as to have them always ready at hand to apply to the purposes of art when composing. It was this which gave performers so great an advantage in the early days, and accounts for the fact that all the great composers of organ music in early days were famous organists, and all the successful composers of violin music were brilliant public performers. In modern times it is necessarily rather the reverse, and the greatest composers are famous for anything rather than for their powers as executants.

But though form is so dependent upon technique of every kind, the development of both went on in early days more or less simultaneously. The management and disposition of the materials and subjects used by the composer is all part of the business of designing, and while the violinists and organists were devising their types of figure they learnt to fit them together in schemes which had the necessary general good effect as well as the special effect in detail; and all branches of art contributed something of their share towards the sum total of advance in art generally. But the various methods and resources of art were developed in the different departments in which they were most immediately required. Composers found out what voices could do and what they could not do in writing their church music, oratorios, cantatas, and so forth. They studied the forms of expression and melody best suited for solo voices in operas and cantatas, and they studied the effects and forms of figure which were best adapted to various instruments, and found out by slow degrees the effects which could be produced by various instruments in combination when they were trying to write sonatas, suites, concertos, and overtures. Each genuine composer then as now added his mite to the resources of growing art when he managed to do something new. And in those days when the field had not been so over-cultivated it was easier to turn up new ground, and to add something both effectual and wholesome to the sum of artistic products.

It must not be overlooked that all branches of art became more and more interdependent as musical development went on. Opera and oratorio required instrumental music as well as solo and choral music, and instrumental music had to borrow types of melody and expression as well as types of design from choral and solo music. Hence it followed that each department of music could only go ahead of others in those respects which were absolutely within its own range; and there were several occasions in the history of art in which a special branch came to a standstill for a time because the development of other branches upon which it had to draw for further advance was in a backward state. This was mainly the reason why opera, which was cultivated with such special prominence in the seventeenth century, came practically to a standstill for some time at the point illustrated by Scarlatti and Lulli. The actual internal organisation of the component parts, such as the arias, improved immensely in style and richness and dimensions as men gained better hold of principles of melodic development; and Handel and Hasse and Buononcini, and many others, improved in that respect on the types of their predecessors. But the general scheme of opera stood much where it was, and the best operas produced in the next fifty years (even those by Handel) are not in the least degree more capable of being endured as wholes by a modern audience than those of Lulli and Scarlatti.

As has before been pointed out, the early representatives of the new style of music had been extremely inefficient in choral writing, because they thought the methods and learning of the old school superfluous for their purposes. But in the course of about fifty years musicians found the need of again studying the fruits of the experience of earlier generations, and something of the old choral style was revived. However, by that time men's minds were thoroughly well set in the direction of modern tonality and harmonic form as distinct from melodic modes and essentially contrapuntal texture, and the result was that the old contrapuntal methods were adapted to new conditions when they came into use again ; and this made them capable of serving for new kinds of expression and effect. The old methods were resumed under the influence of the new feeling for tonality. Composers began anew to write free and characteristic parts for the several voices in choral combinations, but they made the harmonies, which were the sum of the combined counterpoints, move so as to illustrate the principles of harmonic form, and thus gave to the hearer the sense of orderliness and design as well as the sense of contrapuntal complexity. And it is not too much to say that their attitude soon changed the principle of their work. Where formerly they had simply adapted melody to melody, they now often thought first of the progression of harmony, and made separate voice-parts run so as to gain points of vantage in the successive chords. In the old state of things counterpoint sometimes appeared, chiefly by accident, in the guise of harmony; in the new style simple harmonic successions were made deliberately to look like good counterpoint.

This was partly the result of the peculiar disposition of the Italians. They attained to very considerable skill in manipulating voice-parts smoothly and vocally, but they were not particularly ardent after technical artistic interest or characteristic expression. Their sense of beauty shows itself in the orderliness and ease of their harmonic progressions, and in the excellent art with which general variety is obtained. But as usual a certain native indolence and dislike of strenuous concentration made them incline too much towards methods which lessened the demands upon their attention. They preferred that the design of an enormous number of movements should be exactly the same, and commonplace and obvious as well, rather than that they should have any difficulty in following and understanding what they listened to. The result was favourable to the establishment of formal principles in choral music, but it put a premium on carelessness in the carrying out of detail and in the choice of musical material; and the result was that composers got their effects as cheaply as they could, and too often fell into the habit of writing mere successions of chords without either melody or independent part-writing, trusting to the massive sound of many voices in chorus for their effect. But, granting these drawbacks, it may well be conceded that the Italians were pioneers in this new style of choral writing, as they were in most other things; and both in the direction of harmonic form in choral works and in the new style of counterpoint they did invaluable service to art.

Another new feature of this phase of choral music was its combination with instrumental music. In the old order of things the instruments had sometimes doubled the voices, but very little attempt had been made to use the instrumental forces as separate means of effect. The new mode of combining voices and instruments made a very great difference to the freedom with which the voices could be treated, and to the effect of form and expression which could be obtained. But at the same time it is important to note that the instrumental element was still very much in the background, and did not in any sense divide the honours with the choral effects. The instrumental forces were accessories or vassals, not equals. Even the most responsible masters were forced by the backwardness of instrumental art to adopt a contrapuntal style for their orchestral work, and to write for their several instruments as if they were so many voice-parts; and when they attempted variety of colour they used it in broad homogeneous expanses, such as long solos for special wind instruments. The sense for variety of colour was undoubtedly dawning, but as yet composers had to produce their impression with very moderate use of it.

The result was a paradoxical vindication of the inevitable continuity of artistic as of all other kinds of human progress. For although the first beginnings of the new movement were prominently secular, and diverged from the traditions of church music, the first really great and permanent achievements in the new style were on the lines of sacred and serious art, because it was in that line alone that composers could gain full advantage from the old traditions. And whereas the early representatives of the new style had cast away the study of choral methods, it was in their choral aspects that these oratorios were specially complete and mature. But it did not fall to the Italians to bring these new experiments to full fruit.

It was indeed the first time that the Teutonic temper found full expression in the art which now seems most congenial to the race. Through various causes German progress in music had so far been hindered. While the Netherlands, England, Italy, and even France, had each had important groups of composers, Germany had as yet had but few and more or less isolated men. But now that social conditions had quieted down, and the spirit of the nation had better opportunity to expand, her composers rose with extraordinary rapidity to the foremost place, and in their hands comparatively neglected forms of art, such as the oratorio and church cantata, reached the highest standard of which they have proved capable. All the German composers undoubtedly learned much of their business from Italian examples; and it is noteworthy that on this occasion, as on many others, the composers who were the most popularly successful adopted altogether Italian principles, merely infusing into their work the firmer grit and greater power of characterisation which comes of the stronger and more deliberate race. But by far the greatest and most important results were obtained where the Teutonic impulse for characteristic treatment was given fullest play; and where the resources made available by the combination of old contrapuntal principles and the principles of the new kind of art were applied to the end of lofty and noble expression.

The difference of result following upon the difference of method is illustrated to the fullest degree in the familiar oratorios of Handel on the one hand, and in

Bach's Passions and the best of his church cantatas on the other. The Italian development of oratorio had been stunted and perverted, but there were sufficient types and models for Handel to follow. It is a noteworthy instance of the influence of circumstances that for his first oratorios, which were written in Italy for Italian audiences, he hardly wrote any choruses at all, and only such as are of the slightest description. But when, some years later, after plentiful experience of English tastes, he began writing for London audiences, he at once adopted the familiar scheme, in which the most prominent and the most artistically important features are the numerous grand choral movements. But it so happened that the English of that time had lost touch with their own native traditions, and had become thoroughly Italianised; it therefore naturally followed that Handel adopted an Italian manner in his choral writing, as he had done previously in his operatic works. This was entirely consistent with all the previous part of his career, for ever since he had left Hamburg and his native country in his youth, every new line he took up showed invariably the influence of Italian methods and Italian musical phraseology. He was so saturated with musical Italianism of all kinds that actual phrases of Corelli, Alessandro Scarlatti, Stradella, Carissimi, and others constantly make their appearance in his works; while his instrumental movements —such as slow introductions and fugues—are in texture most like similar movements by Corelli and Scarlatti, and his choral style was modelled upon the facile, smooth, and eminently vocal style of the Italian masters, as exemplified in various kinds of church music of the new kind. Where he improved upon them so immensely was in the use of the resources of artistic technique for the purposes of expression. As has been frequently pointed out, the Italians cared very little for expression in the music itself, though they liked to have it put in by the performers.

M

Intrinsically it was sufficient for them if the music was melodious and vocal in solos, and if the counterpoint in the choruses had a pleasant sense of orderly form in the progressions of the harmonies. Now both English and Teutons have always had a great feeling for direct expression in the music itself; and when in immature times they could not get it in any other way, their composers tried to get it by obvious realistic means. Italians had tried realistic expression now and again, but always in a half-hearted and ineffectual manner; and they always ended by dropping it. But to genuine Teutons and English such intrinsic expression is a necessity, and it is the force of their instinct for it which has enabled the former to carry to their highest perfection all the forms of the art which the Italians initiated, but had not sufficiently high artistic ideals or sufficient persistence of character to bring to maturity.

This is what makes so great a difference between Handel's choral work and Italian choral work; and the same is the case with his arias and other solo music. The fact is so familiar that it hardly needs emphasising. He not only gives in his choruses the direct expression of the feelings of human creatures, whose places the singers might be said to take, in exultation, mourning, rage, devotion, or any other phases of human feeling; but he makes most successful use of them for descriptive purposes, and for conveying the impression of tremendous situations and events. This may have been somewhat owing to his English surroundings, as the German bent is to use music more for the expression of the inward emotion and sentiment than for direct concrete illustration. But this was a part of the development of the artistic material of music which had to be achieved, and as it might not have been done so thoroughly under the influence of any other nation, it

is fortunate that Handel did his part of the work under
English influences, for the thoroughly Teutonic part of the
work was assuredly as perfectly done as is conceivable by
J. S. Bach.

Bach also was a close student of Italian art, as he
was of the methods of all skilful composers of whatever
nation; but nevertheless his circumstances and constant
Teutonic surroundings made him take, in his most
genuinely characteristic works, a thoroughly Teutonic
line. The circumstances of his career were peculiar,
as his life was divided definitely into periods in
which he specially studied different departments of art.
In his earliest days, at the period in man's life when
impressions most easily become permanent, he was most
particularly occupied with organ music, with organ
style, the technique and methods of all the greatest
organists that he could hear, and the compositions for the
organ which he had opportunity to study. Fortunately
the organists of that day were exceptionally worthy of
their instrument. They did not try to make it gambol
or mince trivial sentimentalities, but to utter things that
had dignity and noble simplicity; and to produce those
majestic effects of rolling sound which were peculiarly
suitable to the great vaulted buildings which were the
natural homes of their art. Bach's musical organisation
became well steeped in organ effects, and the phraseology
which was most appropriate to the instrument became
the natural language for the expression of his musical
ideas, and remained so for the rest of his life, though tem-
pered and enlarged by the wide range of his sympathetic
studies in every branch of composition. Together with
organ music he heard and absorbed the church music
of his country; and the peculiar mystic sentiment, full of
tender poetical imagery and personal devotion, which was
then characteristic of Teutonic Christianity, took firm

hold of his disposition. Unlike Handel, he remained all his life in one small part of Germany, always amid thoroughly Teutonic influences; and the result was that when in the latter part of his life he addressed himself most particularly to the composition of great choral works, the Italian influences are but rarely apparent; and all the details, the manner, the methods, and the type of expression are essentially Teutonic. Great as was his contrapuntal skill, it was in no sense the contrapuntalism of the Italians; for it may be confessed that his voice-parts are by no means smooth, facile, or even vocal. The origin of the style of his vocal part-writing was the kind of counterpoint that he had learnt from studying and hearing organ works when young. He had a marvellous instinct for choral effect of many kinds, in no way inferior to Handel's though so extraordinarily different. But where Handel aimed at the beauty of melodic form, Bach strove for characteristic expression. Where Handel used orderly progressions of simple harmony, Bach aimed at contriving elaborate interweavings of subtly disposed parts to give the effect of the subtlest shades of human feeling. Where Handel used the most realistic means to convey the hopping of frogs, or the rattling of hailstones, or the rolling of the sea, or the buzzing of flies, Bach attempted to express the inner feelings of human creatures under the impress of any exciting causes. It must not be supposed that either composer was restricted to these particular lines, for Handel at times succeeded better than most composers in uttering the inner spirit of man's emotions, and Bach at times adopted realistic methods; but the larger portion of Handel's choral work tends in the one direction, and of Bach's in the other. Nowhere is the difference of their attitude better illustrated than in their use of recitative. Handel, accepting the conventions of Italian art without hesitation, ruined

an enormous number of his works by the emptiest,
baldest, and most mechanical formulas; while Bach, dissatisfied with anything which had not significance, endeavoured by the contours and intervals of his voice-part,
by the progressions and harmonies of his accompaniment,
and by every means that was available, to intensify from
moment to moment the expression of the words. Bach's
recitative was consequently extremely difficult to sing,
but the intrinsic expression of the music is as strong
as it can be made in such a form. Handel's may be
easy to sing, but it means nothing, and the formulas
often suit one set of words as well as another.

Bach's feeling for melody was not so happy as Handel's.
His Teutonic attitude is shown again in the fact that he
sought for richer, deeper, and more copious expression
than can be achieved by conventional treatment of
melody with simple secondary accompaniment. Solo
music indeed was not the most congenial form for the expression of his ideas, and faithfully as he tried to achieve
a perfect scheme and principle of procedure, he never made
sure of a satisfactory result. He aimed at something which
is a little beyond the capacity of a formal solo movement to express, and the soloist is often sacrificed to the
exigencies of artistic development. He could not rest
satisfied with the apparent superficiality of Italian treatment of melody, and but rarely even attempted to produce
a suave or ear-catching tune. When the mood he wished
to illustrate lent itself to melodic expression, he produced exquisitely touching or innocently joyous fragments
of tune, which lay hold of the mind all the more firmly
because of their characteristic sincerity and the absence
of any pretence of making the thing suave and agreeable
at the expense of the truth of the sentiment. The only
respect in which he falls under the spell of convention
was in following without sufficient consideration the

principle of repetition familiar through the direction "da capo." It is as though, when he had carried out his artistic scheme with all the technical, richness and care in detail he could master up to a certain point, he felt he had done what art required of him, and wrote "da capo al fine," without consideration of the length to which it would carry his movement; and thereby impaired some of his happiest inspirations by want of the practical observation that even a good audience is human. And it may be confessed that though his artistic insight, power of self-criticism, and variety of inventiveness were almost the highest ever possessed by man, his fervently idealistic nature was just a little deficient in practical common sense. He worked so much by himself, and had so little opportunity of testing his greatest works by the light of experience in performance, that he sometimes overlooked their relation to other human beings, and wrote for the sheer pleasure of mastering a problem or developing to its full circuit a scheme which he had in his mind.

In instrumentation both of these giants among composers were equally backward, though their aims, methods, and results were very different. They were necessarily restricted to the standard of their time at starting, and Handel did as little as it is possible for a great master to do in adding to the resources of the instrumental side of music. He tried interesting experiments, occasionally, even in his earliest works, but his mind was not set on making much use of new resources or on using colour as an enhancement of expression. His mastery of choral effect and gift of melody, and power of portrayal by vocal means, were sufficient for his purposes, and the instruments served chiefly to strengthen and support the voices, and to play introductory passages to the arias and choruses, and simple marches and dance tunes, which were written mainly for stringed instruments in the contrapuntal manner. He looked to the present, and finished up much as he began. Bach, on the other hand, looking always forward, showed much more purpose in his use of instrumental resources. He used a great variety of instruments of all kinds, both wind and strings, not to increase the volume of tone in the mass, but to give special quality and unity of colour to various movements. The days when composite colouring and constantly altering shades of various qualities of tone are an ordinary feature of the art were yet very far off; and he never seems to have thought of adopting anything like such modern methods. But as far as his unique principles go, they are at times singularly effective. He realised the various expressive qualities of the tone and style of hautboys, flutes, solo violins, horns, trumpets, viole da gamba, and many others; and with the view of intensifying the pathos, or the poignancy, or the joyousness, or the sublimity of his words, he found suitable figures for them, and wove them with the happiest effect throughout the whole accompaniment of a movement. The device was not new, for it was the first method that composers adopted in trying to make use of variety of orchestral colour; but Bach's use of it for the purposes of expression was new, and was an important step in the direction of effectual use of instrumental resources. To the object of obtaining great sonority from his instrumental forces Bach does not seem to have given much of his mind. Both he and Handel relied so much upon the organ to fill in accompaniments and supply fulness of sound, that it does not seem to have struck either of them as worth while to look for any degree of richness or volume from combinations of orchestral instruments. In loud passages neither of them attempt to dispose the various instruments in such a way as to get the best tone out of them; and when played in modern times, under modern conditions, the wood wind

instruments are often totally drowned by the strings.
The proportions were very different in those times, but
even if the old proportions of wind and strings were
restored, many contrapuntal effects in which flutes or
hautboys have to take essential parts would be quite
ineffective.

Their scheme of oratorio and church music being what
it was, the backwardness of instrumental effect was but of
small consequence. The means they used for their effects
were essentially choral forces and solo voices, and these were
amply sufficient for the purposes in hand. Instrumental
music and the arts of instrumentation have been developed
almost entirely under secular conditions. In such works
as Handel's and Bach's, which illustrated mainly religious
aspects of human feeling and character, the absence of
subtle sensuous excitements of colour was possibly rather
an advantage than otherwise. Whatever lack of maturity
is observable in both is felt not so much in the lack of
instrumental effect as in the crude recitative of Handel,
and in the overdoing of contrapuntal complexity in places
where it is not essential in Bach. Their works are mature
without instrumentation, and even the exquisite skill of
Mozart's additional accompaniments to Handel's work
cannot disguise the fact that the phraseology of modern
instrumentation is out of touch with the style of the
older masterpieces.

In considering the aspects of their great sacred choral
works it is of importance to note the circumstances which
called them into existence. Both composers came to the
writing of such works quite at the end of their careers,
when their mastery of their art was most complete; and
they brought the fruits of their experience in all branches
of art to bear upon them. Moreover, the circumstances
of their respective careers had great influence upon the
quality of the products. Handel had all through been a

practical public man, constantly in touch with the public,
and constantly watching their likes and dislikes, and
catering for his supporters in accordance with them. He
began as a subordinate violin-player in Keiser's Hamburg
Opera-House, where his abilities soon caused him to be
promoted to the position of accompanyist on the harpsichord; which was excellent training for an opera composer,
and taught him the ins and outs of that branch of public
entertainment. This short preliminary was soon succeeded by brilliant successes as a composer in Italy, and
these in turn led to his long and brilliant career as an opera
composer in England, which lasted some twenty-six years.
Then, finally, the accident of having an opera-house on his
hands in Lent on days when opera performances were
not allowed led to his trying the experiment of setting
sacred dramas for performance on the stage of his theatre.
These differed from the operas in their more serious
and solid character, the absence of action, and the introduction of grand choral movements. But he began this
experiment purely as a business manager, and did not
attempt to write complete new works, but merely patched
together choruses and other numbers out of earlier works,
giving them new words and adding some new movements to
make the whole pass muster, and calling the patchwork by
a scriptural name. The success of the experiment encouraged him to proceed to compose or patch together more
works of the same kind. It is a strange fact that the
grandest and most impressive of all his works is actually
a piece of patchwork; for Israel in Egypt contains a
most surprising number of old movements which may
have been early compositions of his own, and also a very
large quantity of musical material which was unquestionably by other composers. He transformed some of
the borrowed materials into extremely effective choruses,
and wrote other new choruses which are among his finest

achievements; and the greatness of his own work has
carried the second-rate work along with it. But his procedure shows that he did not treat the form of oratorio at
first as a responsible conscientious composer might be
expected to do, but as a man who had to supply the public
with a fine entertainment. It cannot indeed be doubted
that though he was capable of rising to very great achievements, and was capable of noble and sincere expression,
he thought a great deal of the tastes of a big public, and
not very intently of refinements of art, or originality of
matter or of plan. His disposition was not so much. to
work up to any exalted ideals of his own, as to feel sympa-
thetically what was the highest standard of taste of the
public for which he was constantly working, and to supply
what that demanded. This must not be taken to mean that
he habitually wrote down to a low standard of public taste.
Composers who persuade themselves to do that generally
take a very low view of their public, and write even worse
than they need. Handel had on the whole very good
reason to think well of his public, notwithstanding their
unwillingness to listen to Israel in Egypt without some
sugar-plums in the shape of opera airs to relieve its
austere grandeur. They thoroughly appreciated others
of his works, and the reception accorded to the Messiah
was sufficient to encourage him to put all his heart into
his later works of the oratorio order. Thinking so much
of the big public may therefore have been no great
drawback to him; and some of the thanks are due to
the good taste and sense of the people for whom he
catered. His position made him practical, and helped
him to that definite and wholesomely direct style which
was congenial to his English audiences; and though they
may be answerable for a certain amount of commonplace and complacency in his work, they deserve credit
for encouraging him in the line of choral work, which

resulted in the achievement of those effects of genuine grandeur, simple dignity, and cosmic power which mark his culmination as one of the great eras of art.

The circumstances which led to Bach's great choral works were absolutely different, and account for a great deal of the marked difference in the product. The contrast in the circumstances of the two composers is noticeable from their earliest years. When Handel was absorbing the influences of an opera-house, Bach was listening to the great organists of his time. When Handel was practising Italianisms in every branch of art, Bach was studying mainly the ways and tastes of his own people. But the relation of a composer to his public is of supreme importance in respect of the line he takes, and in that respect Bach's position was most peculiar. By comparison with the public nature of Handel's career Bach's life seems like that of a reflective recluse. So far from catering for a public, all through his life he rather lacked audiences and opportunities to feel the public pulse. He could hardly in any case have brought himself to see his art through other people's eyes; for it was his nature to judge solely for himself, and he laboured throughout his life with simplicity and singleness of heart to come up to his own highest ideals in all branches of art, and to satisfy his own critical judgment without a thought of the effect his work would have upon any but an ideal auditor. His principle of study is most happily illustrative of the manner in which all musical progress is made. For he early adopted the practice of studying and copying out the works of composers who excelled in all the different branches of art, and endeavouring to improve upon their achievements. Sometimes he actually rewrote the works of other composers, and oftentimes he deliberately imitated them both for style and design; and wherever he recognised an artistic principle of undoubted value and vitality, he as it were absorbed

and amalgamated it as part of his own artistic procedure.
He ranged far and wide, and studied the methods of
Italians, Frenchmen, Netherlanders, and Germans—writers
of choral music and of organ music, of violin music and
of harpsichord music. And not only that, but he always
sedulously criticised himself, and recast, remodelled, and rewrote everything which new experiences or a happier mood
made him feel capable of improving. This would have
been impossible in the busy public life of Handel, and
was not in that composer's line. Bach's was a far more
individual and personal position. He wanted to express
what he himself personally felt and approved. Handel
adapted himself to feel and approve what the public
approved.

It naturally followed that Bach's style is far more
individual and strongly marked, and, as a consequence,
that he went far beyond the standard of the musical
intelligence of his time; and his most ideally great
and genuine passages of human expression were merely
regarded by his contemporaries as ingenious feats of
pedantic ingenuity. A man could not well be more
utterly alone or without sympathy than he was. Even
his sons and pupils but half understood him. But we
do not know that he suffered from it. We can only
see plainly that it drove him inwards upon himself, and
made him adopt that attitude which alone is capable
of producing the very highest results in men who have
grit enough to save them from extravagance and in-
coherence. He wrote because it interested him to write,
and with the natural impulse of the perfectly sincere
composer to bring out what was in him in the best form
that he could give to it; and his musical constitution
being the purest and noblest and most full of human
feeling and emotion ever possessed by a composer, the
art of music is more indebted to him than to any other

composer who ever lived, especially for the extension of the arts of expression.

The peculiar services he did in the branch of pure instrumental art must be discussed elsewhere. The services he did to choral art, especially in his Passions, the B minor mass and smaller masses, the great unaccompanied motets and the various cantatas, are equal to Handel's, though on such different lines. The effect of the isolation in which his work was produced was no doubt to make it in some respects experimental, but it ensured the highest development of the art of expression and of the technique which serves to the ends of expression. To the same end also served the Teutonic aspect of his labours. The oratorios of other nations were not part of religious exercises nor the direct expression of devotional feeling. They had merely been versions of lives of famous scriptural heroes or events set to music partly in narrative and partly in dramatic form. But the Germans had fastened with peculiar intensity of feeling on the story of the Passion, and set it again and again in a musical form as though determined to give it the utmost significance. The plan was to break up the story into its most vivid situations and intersperse these with reflective choruses and solos which helped the mind to dwell intently and lovingly upon each step in the tragedy. It was essentially a devotional function in which every one present took a personal share. Even the audience, apart from the performers, took part in the noble chorales—so characteristic of Teutonic nature — which were interspersed throughout. Many poets and many composers tried their hands at this curious form of art, Bach himself several times. And the crown was put on the form of art finally by the famous Passion according to St. Matthew which Bach wrote and rewrote towards the end of his career, for performance at Leipzig.

It is not necessary to emphasise further the difference between Bach's treatment of a great choral form of art and Handel's. The oratorios of the latter were nearly all dramatic or epic, and the subjects were treated as nearly as possible histrionically. There are portions of Bach's Passions which treat the situations with great dramatic force, but in the main they are the direct. outcome of personal devotion, and in them the mystic emotionalism of the Teutonic nature found its purest expression. Thus in the works of the two great composers the types of musical utterance which represent epic and narrative treatment on the one hand, and inward immediate feeling on the other, were completely realised on the largest scale that the art of that day allowed. Handel's direct and practical way of enforcing the events and making his story vivid by great musical means has given great pleasure to an immense public, and as it were summed up the labours of his predecessors into a grand and impressive result. Bach, with higher ideals, produced work which was often experimental, and even at times unpractical; but he used the sum of his predecessors' work as his stepping-stone, and did much greater service to his art. He appeals to a much smaller public than Handel, and is totally unacceptable to shallow, worldly or unpoetical temperaments; but he has given much higher pleasure to those whose mental and emotional organisation is sufficiently high to be in touch with him, and there are but few of the greatest composers of later times who have not felt him to be their most inspiring example.

CHAPTER VIII.

ALTHOUGH the principles of design upon which modern self-dependent instrumental music are based had hardly dawned upon the minds of men till the eighteenth century was nearly half spent, the instrumental music of the earlier period, written almost entirely upon the same general principles as choral music, is not only historically important, but of more genuine vitality than a very large proportion of the music which has been written since the cultivation of pure harmonic music has enlarged the resources of composers. The situation is parallel in many respects to the earlier crisis of Palestrina and Marenzio. There is less of the sense of immaturity in their work than in the work of Lulli and Scarlatti of nearly a century later; and there is far less of immaturity in the instrumental works of Bach and Handel and their fellows than in the works of Galuppi or Paradisi, or even in the early works of Haydn. Maturity is a relative term altogether. If a man's ideas are worth expressing, and are capable of being expressed completely within the limits of his resources, his productions may be completely mature at almost any epoch in the progress of artistic development. If Palestrina had introduced discords more freely and treated them with less reserve, and had aimed generally at a stronger type of expression, the balance of his work would have been destroyed; he would have gone beyond the limits which were then inevitable for completely artistic work. Part of his greatness consisted in

feeling exactly where the limitations were, and achieving
his aims within the field of which he was complete master.
The position of the composers in Bach's time was much
the same; and part of his own particular greatness consisted in seeing within what particular range the technical
resources of art, which preceding development had placed
in his hands, were most fully available.

It is very necessary to keep in mind the fact that different types of artistic procedure representing different
epochs frequently overlap.   Just as in the arrangements of society a monarchy may be thriving successfully in one country, while its neighbour is trying
experiments in democratic institutions.   So in art it constantly happens that a new style has broken into vigorous
activity before the old style has produced its greatest
results.   And there is a further parallel in the fact that
as the theories and practices of the republican country
may filter into the country where the more antiquated
form of government still prevails; so the new ideas
which are beginning to be realised in other departments
of artistic energy often creep into the heart of an old
but still active system, even before it has come to full
maturity.   Even the strictest representatives of an ancient
and well-developed style try occasional experiments on
revolutionary lines.   The bounds of the old order were
transgressed before Palestrina's time, and many men
began to have clear ideas of harmonic form of the sonata
order long before John Sebastian Bach put the crown on
the old style of instrumental music.   Bach himself tried
experiments in this line, and did his utmost to master and
gauge the value of the new style, by copying, rearranging,
rewriting, and imitating the works of prominent representatives of the new school.   But it is clear that he was
not satisfied with the results, and that the style was not
congenial to him.   His peculiar gifts would not have

found sufficient means for employment on the simple lines of harmonic form as then understood, and the necessity of submitting to uniform distribution of the various parts of his design would have hampered him in the experiments in modulation and harmonisation which are among his greatest glories.

So it came about finally that he attempted but little of a sonata order, but concentrated his powers on works of the old style—the toccatas, canzonas, fantasias, fugues, suites, partitas, and other varieties; and his work in those lines sums up the fruitful labours of all his predecessors, and provides the most perfect examples of all the older forms. The essence of the being of the old instrumental forms was the polyphonic texture in which every part or voice is on equal terms with every other one. There is no despotic tune with subservient accompaniment, nor strict conventions as to the distribution of chords according to their tonalities. The use of chords as chords had undoubtedly become quite familiar, but it was not on any principle of their systematic distribution that works were designed. They were of secondary importance to polyphonic elaboration of musical figures; by the interweaving of which, like the strands of a rope, the works were made coherent and interesting.

Of all the forms of instrumental music which were characteristic of this phase of art, the fugue is the most familiar and the most perfectly organised. It was the form in which Bach most delighted, and the one which gave him fullest variety of scope and opportunity for expression. Its beginnings have already been sketched. The earliest forms were clearly imitations of choral music adapted for the organ or for sets of viols. The type of choral work which was imitated was extremely indefinite as far as the musical ideas were concerned, and the musical "subjects" were not necessarily reiterated in the course of the movements. But when the form came to be used independently of words, the barrenness of mere meandering counterpoint soon became apparent, and characteristic musical figures became more definitely noticeable, and were frequently reiterated in the course of the work to give unity to the whole. The early composers who speculated in these lines called their works by all sorts of names—canzonas, ricercari, fantasias, and so forth; and they were very unsystematic in their ways of introducing their "subjects." But experience led them by degrees to regulate things with more attention to symmetry and better distribution of their materials. By degrees the aspect of the form became sufficiently distinctive for theorists to take note of it, and the simplicity of the conditions of procedure led them to imagine that an artistic scheme might be very successfully devised by mere speculation, without regard to the existing facts of art; and they contrived such a multiplicity of directions to show composers how to expend their superfluous inartistic ingenuity according to the letter of their law, that men in general came to think that the fugue form was invented for nothing else but to enable pedants to show how clever they are. As a matter of fact, the rules were devised without consideration of the necessities of the case, and it naturally follows that hardly any of the finest fugues in the whole range of the musical art are strictly in accordance with the directions of the teachers on the subject; and if it had not been for Bach and Handel this most elastic and invaluable form would have become a mere dead formality.

The essence of the form in its mature state is simply that the successive parts shall enter like several voices, one after another, with a "subject"—which is a musical phrase of sufficiently definite melody and rhythm to stand out from its context and be identifiable—and that this

subject shall give the cue to the mood of the movement at
the outset and reappear frequently throughout. Artistic
interest and variety of effect are maintained by the way
the voices or parts sometimes sound all at once, and sometimes are reduced to a minimum of one or two. Climaxes
are obtained by making them busier and busier with
the subject; making it appear at one time in one part,
and at another time in another, the voices or parts catching one another up like people who are so eager in the
discussion of their subject that they do not wait for
each other to finish their sentences. Subordinate subjects are made to circle round the principal one, and
the various ideas are made to appear in different relations to one another, sometimes high and sometimes
low, sometimes quick and at other times slow, but
always maintaining a relevancy in mood and style. And
the course of the movement simultaneously makes a complete circuit by passing to subordinate keys, which allow
of constant change in the presentation of the subject,
and ultimately comes round to the first key again and
closes firmly therein. All sorts of devices had been found
out for giving additional effect and interest to the scheme,
and in Bach's time fugue became the highest representative form of the period of art.

It had been first used for the organ—the association of
the instrument with choral music in church services ensured that—and many of Bach's predecessors obtained
more effective results in this form than any other that they
attempted. Many attempts had been made before Bach's
time to adapt it also for harpsichord and for stringed
instruments, so that Bach had plenty of models to improve
upon, according to his wont, in each department of art.

It ought not to be overlooked, moreover, that his predecessors in the line of organ music were an exceptionally
high-spirited group of composers. It is difficult to find

a finer or more true-hearted set of men in the whole range of the art than such as Frescobaldi, Froberger, Swelinck, Kerl, Reinken, Buxtehude, Pachelbel, Kuhnau, John Michael Bach, and many others of the same calling and similar musical powers. Each one of them had contributed a considerable number of items of their own both to the materials of art and to the solution of the problems of their manipulation. Bach's own work has thrown theirs into the shade, but the world which has forgotten them is under great obligations to them all. For though their work never reaches the pitch of equal mastery which satisfies the fastidious judgment of those who have enjoyed maturer things, it is only through their devoted pioneering that the musical revelation of the personality of Bach in instrumental music became possible.

In the passionate eagerness to express his thoughts as well as was conceivably possible, Bach studied the works of every man who had distinguished himself in any branch of art. And with the true instinct which is so like concentrated common sense, he took each department of art in turn, and always at times when he had opportunities to test his own experiments in similar lines. At one time he devoted himself to organ music, at another to secular instrumental music, at another to choral music. As has been pointed out elsewhere the organ period came first, and coloured his style for the rest of his life.

The organ is obviously not an instrument which is capable of much expression in detail, but it is undoubtedly capable of exercising great emotional effect upon human beings, partly through its long association with feelings which are most deeply rooted in human nature, and partly through the magnificent volume of continuous sound that it is capable of producing. The latter quality supplies in a great measure the guiding principle for its successful treatment by a composer; and the effect of the most

successful works written for it, depends in great measure
on the manner in which the crises of voluminous sound
are managed. The fugue form happens to be the most
perfect contrivance for the attainment of these ends.
For it completely isolates the text of the discourse, which
is the principal subject; and the successive entries of
the parts necessarily make a gradual increase of general
sonority. Looking at fugue from the sensational side,
the human creature is made to go through successive
states of tension and relaxation; and the perfection of a
great master's management lies in his power to adjust
the distribution of his successive climaxes of sonority
and complexity proportionately to the receptive capacities of human creatures, beginning from different points,
and rising successively to different degrees of richness
and fulness. The difficulty of the operation lies in the
necessity for building up the successive effects of massive
complexity out of the musical ideas. A great master
like Bach is instinctively aware that appeals to sensation
must be accompanied by proportionate appeals to higher
faculties. It is only in the crudest phases of modern
theatrical music that mere appeals to sensation are dignified by the name of art. In modern opera climaxes of
sound are often piled up one after another without doing
anything but excite the animal side of man's nature.
The glory of Bach's management of such things is that
the intrinsic interest of the music itself is always in
proportion to the power and volume of the actual sound.
Indeed the volume of the sound is sometimes made to
seem tenfold greater than the mere notes sounding would
warrant, by reason of the extraordinary complexity and
vitality of the details out of which it is compounded.
Moreover, Bach has such a hold upon the resources of
his art, that when he has to reduce the number of notes
sounding to a minimum, the relation of the passage to

its context prevents the interest from flagging. It was in such circumstances that his predecessors often failed. They could often write several pages of fine, rich, and noble music, but never held the balance so perfectly but that at some time or other the movement seems to fall to pieces. Bach at his best manipulates all his resources so well that even his quietest moments have some principle of interest which keeps the mind engaged, and his final climax of sound and complicated polyphony comes like the utmost possible exultation, taking complete possession of the beings who hear with the understanding as well as the senses, and raising them out of themselves into a genuine rapture.

Of course Bach did not restrict himself to such types of procedure. There are plenty of works which are mainly intellectual from end to end, relying on the beauty of some melodic phrase or the energy of some rhythmic figure to supply what is necessary on the side of feeling. In such works a characteristic subject is taken as a *thesis*, and presented in every possible light with byplay of subordinate *theses*, like little commentaries, which are often beautifully expressive melodic figures, and are all welded together into a complete whole by the endless resource and acute instinct of the composer.

The style of the organ works is always eminently serious, as befits the character of the instrument. But Bach uses subjects with regular dance rhythms, as well as those of the choral type; and those which are most popular are generally the rhythmic fugues. In the toccatas, fantasias, and preludes he is but rarely rhythmic to any pronounced extent. He finds figures which have a natural animation without too much lilt, and welds them into great sequences, which have a coherence of their own from the point of view of tonal design, without having anything of the sonata character about them.

The sonata mood and type of form is conspicuously absent, and most happily so. That grew up under secular conditions, and the style represents totally different habits of mind and manner from those which were natural to the men who cultivated the old polyphonic forms. Bach succeeded in finding forms for himself which in relation to his polyphonic methods are completely satisfying to the mind, and admitted of wide range of modulation and variety in the presentation of subjects without distracting the attention from the polyphonic treatment which is the essence of his style. He had complete mastery of all genuine organ devices which tell in the hearing. The effects of long sustained notes accompanied by wonderful ramifications of rapid passages; the effects of sequences of linked suspensions of great powerful chords; the contrast of whirling rapid notes with slow and stately march of pedals and harmonies. He knew how the pearly clearness of certain stops lent itself to passages of intricate rhythmic counterpoint, and what charm lay in the perfect management of several simultaneous melodies—especially when the accents came at different moments in the different parts; and he designed his movements so well as to make all such and many other genuine organ effects exert their fullest impression on the hearers. He rarely allows himself to break into a dramatic vein, though he sometimes appeals to the mind in phases which are closely akin to the dramatic—as in the great fantasia in G minor, the toccata in D minor, the prelude in B minor. He occasionally touches on tender and pathetic strains, but for the most part rightly adopts an attitude of grand dignity which is at once generous in its warmth and vigour, and reserved in the matter of sentiment.

His work in this line seems to comprise all the possibilities of pure organ music. Everything that has been written since is but the pale shadow of his splendid conceptions;

and though the modern attempts to turn the organ
into a sort of second-rate orchestra by means of infinite variety of stops are often very surprising (and
very heterogeneous), they certainly cannot compare with
his work for intrinsic quality or genuine direct impressiveness. The organ is naturally associated with types
of thought and emotion which are traditionally referred
to a religious basis; and the later development of purely
secular music has hardly touched its true field.

In the line of orchestral music, such as orchestral
suites and concerti grossi, Bach's achievements are often
supremely delightful—vigorous, vivacious, and characteristic. But they are not of any great historical importance.
The backward state of the arts of instrumentation tells
against them, as does Bach's natural inclination to treat
all the members of his orchestra on equal terms as so
many counterpoints. On the other hand, his work for
harpsichord and clavichord is of supreme importance; for
in this line again he put the crown on a special type of
development, and made the final and most perfect exposition of the varieties of the suite form, and of the old
instrumental fugue, as well as of all those varieties of
forms of toccata and fantasia which were especially
characteristic of the polyphonic period.

In connection with these lesser keyed instruments his
objects were necessarily different from those which he had
in view in organ composition. No volume of sound nor
sustainment of tone for any length of time was possible.
While the organ had ancient associations and great echoing buildings to lend enchantment to the performance,
the lesser keyed instruments were chiefly confined to the
intimate familiarities of domestic life. Bach's favourite
instrument, the clavichord, admitted of some tender expression and delicate phrasing; but the harpsichord, with
a certain noble roughness of tone, admitted of hardly

any expression or variety of volume. Here indeed was a great temptation to subside into purely intellectual subtleties. But there was an amount of human nature about Bach which prevented his wasting his time in ingenious futilities. Considering how infinitely capable he was of every kind of ingenuity, it is surprising how few examples there are of misuse of artistic resources. He was incessantly trying experiments, and it was natural that he should test the effect of pure technical feats now and then, but the proportion of things which are purely mechanical to those which have a genuine musical basis is very small. He exercised his supreme mastery of such resources very often, as in the canons in the Goldberg Variations, but in most cases the mere ingenuity is subordinate to higher and more generous principles of effect. Exceptions like the Kunst der Fuge and Musikalisches Opfer were definitely contrived for definitely technical purposes, and hardly come into the range of real practical music.

Among the most important of his clavier works are the several groups of suites and partitas. These are sets of dance tunes grouped together in such a way as to make a composite cycle out of well contrasted units, all knit together in the circuit of one key. The idea of grouping dance tunes together was of very old standing; and composers had tried endless varieties, from galliards and pavans to rigadoons and trumpet tunes. But by degrees they settled down to a scheme which was in principle exactly the same as that of the distribution of sonata movements in later times—having the serious and more highly organised movements at the beginning, the slow dances in the middle, and the gay rhythmic dances at the end. Many composers had succeeded admirably in this form, especially Couperin, who generally fell in with the taste of his French audiences by adding to the nucleus

a long series of lively picture-tunes which savoured of
the theatrical ballet. Bach took Couperin for one of his
models, and paid attention chiefly to the most artistic
part of his work, and set himself to improve upon it.
The form in which he cast his movements is always on
the same lines. They are divided into two nearly equal
halves, the first passing out from the principal key to a
point of contrast, and closing there to emphasise it; and
the second starting from that point and returning to the
point with which the movement began. This is all that
the movements have of actual harmonic form, though
they frequently illustrate an early stage of typical sonata
movements, by the correspondence of the opening bars of
each half, and of the closing bars of each half. The
texture of all the movements—even of the lightest—is
polyphonic. The two first movements of the suite are
generally an allemande and a courante, which are often
very elaborate in intricacy of independent counterpoint.
The courante was also made additionally intricate by
curious cross rhythms. In these movements Bach is
more often purely technical than in any other branch
of his work; and though very dignified and noble, they
are occasionally rather dry. On the other hand, the
central movement (the sarabande) almost always represents his highest pitch of expressiveness and interest; and
it is, moreover, the movement in which he is least contrapuntal. There are sarabandes of all kinds. Some are
purely melodic, some superbly rich in harmonisation,
some gravely rhythmic, and some treated with beautifully expressive counterpoint. In almost all Bach strikes
some vein of very concentrated expression, and maintains
it with perfect consistency from beginning to end. After
the central expressive point of the sarabande the light and
gay movements naturally follow. A suite was held to be
complete which had but one of such merry movements

(a gigue) at the end. But as a sort of concession to human weakness very light and rhythmic movements were commonly admitted directly after the sarabande, such as the bourrées, gavottes, minuets, and passepieds. In such movements Bach was wonderfully at home. In perfect neatness and finish of such rapid, sparkling little movements, no one has ever surpassed him; and he contrived them throughout in the terms of perfect art. For they are not of the modern type of dance tune with dummy accompaniment, but works in which everything sounding has vitality, most frequently in the form of busiest and merriest two-part counterpoint. The final gigues also are nearly always contrapuntal, and often almost fugal. But they are by no means severe. Such examples as the gigue of the G major French suite and the F major English suite are sufficient to prove that uncompromisingly artistic methods are by no means inconsistent with most vivacious gaiety.

Of all the works with which Bach enriched the world, the one which is most cherished by musicians is the Collection of Preludes and Fugues which is known in England as the "Forty-eight," and in Germany as "Das wohltemperirte Clavier"—which means "The clavichord tuned in equal temperament." The very name of this work brings forward a point which is of great moment in the story of the art, namely, the final settling of the particular scale which serves for all our later music.

In choral music wide diatonic intervals are so much preferable to semitones that in the early days, when all music was choral, composers found a very limited number of flats and sharps sufficient for all their requirements. Modulations from one key to another were not thought of in the way in which they are now, for men were very slow in arriving at a clear understanding of the principle of tonality or definition of key. But when instrumental

music began to be cultivated, and men developed a sense
for various keys, and began to use modulations as a basis
of design as well as a means of effect, they were brought
face to face with a perplexing problem.   It is a familiar
paradox of acoustics that if a series of fifths are tuned
one on the top of another, the notes at which they arrive
soon begin to be different from notes at the same position in the scale which are arrived at by other methods
of tuning.   Thus, if starting from C, the notes G, D, and
E, are successively tuned as perfect fifths, the E is not
the same E that would be produced by tuning a true
third and transposing it by the necessary octaves.   And
the same happens if the fifths are tuned one on the
top of another till they appear to arrive at the same
note from which they started.   B♯, according to modern
ideas, is the same as C, but if theoretically in tune it would
be practically out of tune, and many of the other sharps
and flats which coincide on the keyboard are in the same
category.   This was of course no great obstacle as long as
composers only wanted to use B♭, E♭, C♯, F♯, and G♯.
The old methods of tuning made these possible without
modifying the essential intervals, such as the fifths and
thirds.   No provision was made for the other accidentals,
because they were not required until music had gone a long
way beyond the limits of the ecclesiastical modes.   But
by Bach's time the feeling for the modern system of keys
and of major and minor scales was quite mature.   All composers perfectly understood the status of the various notes
in the scales, at least instinctively, and modulation from
one key to another had become a vital essential of art.
No music was possible without it.   But it still took some
time for music to expand so as to make modulation to
extraneous keys seem a matter worth contending for.
Cautious conservatives would not be persuaded that any
modification of the old system of tuning was wanted; but

the more adventurous spirits would not be gainsaid. They found that they required to assume A♭ to be the same as G♯, and D♭ as C♯, and the fact that the chords which resulted were hideously out of tune in the old method of tuning would not stop them. It became more and more obvious that modulation must be possible, for the purposes of the new kind of art, into every key represented by a note in the system. Otherwise there would be blanks in particular directions which would inevitably make the system unequal and imperfect. In other words, it was necessary that all the notes in the system should stand on an equal footing in relation to one another. Bach foresaw it with such clearness that he tuned his own instrument on the system of "equal temperament," and gave his opinion to the world in a most practical form, which was this series of preludes and fugues, major and minor, in every key represented by a note in the system. Till his time certain extreme keys had hardly ever been used, and his action emphasises the final crystallisation of the modern scale system, which makes it as different from the system used by the musicians of the middle ages as the heptatonic system of the Persians is from the pentatonic system of the Chinese. In all cases the scale is an artificial product contrived for particular artistic ends. The old scale, with a limited number of available notes, was sufficient for the purposes of the old church music, because the aims of the art were different. The growth of modern instrumental music brought new aims into men's minds, and they had to contrive a new scale system to satisfy them. The division of the octave into twelve equal intervals, to which Bach in this objective way gave his full sanction, is now a commonplace of every musical person's experience. Some people imagine that it was always so. But in reality the existing system is only a hundred and fifty years old, and was resisted by some musicians even till the present century.

The two books of preludes and fugues represent an extraordinary variety of artistic speculation on Bach's part. They have much the same standing in his artistic scheme as the concentrated lyrical pieces of Chopin and Schumann have in modern times. The system of design upon which the modern pieces are devised had yet to be developed, and the only well established and trustworthy form for concentrated expression of abstract ideas was the fugue. As the fugues in this collection belong to various periods in Bach's life, they naturally illustrate purely technical as well as expressive aims; but there are very few that have only technical interest. Most of them obviously illustrate such states of feeling and of mind as music is especially fitted to express, and they do so in terms of the most perfect and finished art. There are fugues which express many shades of merriment and banter (C minor, C♯ major, B♭ in first book; F minor in second book). Strong confident fugues (D major, first book; A minor, second book); intensely sad fugues (B♭ minor and B minor, first book); serenely reposeful fugues (E major and B major, second book); tenderly pathetic fugues (G♯ minor in both books). In every case his subject gives him his cue, and the treatment of harmonisation, modulation, counterpoint, design, and general tone, follows consistently the mood which the subject indicated. Bach's objects were absolutely different from those of the theoretical writers on fugue. He aimed at designs which are more akin to the devices of harmonic form; making different parts of the work balance with one another in style, by special characteristic runs, or special sequences—anything which gives an additional value and interest to the mere technicalities of the treatment of the subject. He never makes the mistake of writing a fugue in sonata form, which is little better than a forcing together of incompatible types of style. From the point of view of polyphonic writing the fugues are as pure as they can be made, but his frequent use of sequences and similar devices gives an additional sense of stability to the design without distracting the mind from the true objects of the form. The fugues have the reputation of being the most important part of the work, but in reality the preludes are fully as interesting, and even more unique. They are very varied in character, and many are evidently experiments in compact little forms, the schemes of which Bach worked out for himself. Several of them exist in more than one version; which seems to imply that he gave them much consideration, and revised them several times before he was satisfied. No collection of equal interest and variety exists in the whole range of music. Some of them are of the nature of very carefully considered extemporisations. The art of preluding was very much practised in those days, and consisted mainly of stringing together successions of chords in the guise of arpeggios, or characteristic figures devised on the frame of an arpeggio. Successions of harmonies had not as yet got stale by conventional usage, so Bach employed his gift for contriving beautiful and neat little arpeggio figures to make complete movements out of chord successions, which range through dreamy modulations without ever losing coherence, or falling out of the natural order required to make a complete and compact unity. A happy extension of this typical prelude-device is to break off the arpeggios and add a coda which serves as a peculiarly apt contrast. Both the preludes in C♯ major are happy in this respect, especially the one in the second book. Another development of the same type, but in a much more impulsive and expressive style, is that in D minor in the first book, in which the characteristic progressions of harmony are so directed as to arrive at

quite a passionate climax just before the end. Following the same line again, the figures corresponding to the
arpeggio forms of the chords are sometimes made much
more definite as musical figures, and a whole movement is
developed out of various phases of the same compact
musical idea (D major in first book). And so device
was built upon device to make new types of movements.
Of quite a different order is the wonderful prelude in
E♭ minor in the first book, which is a highly emotional
kind of song, with a most remarkable succession of inter-
rupted cadences at the end, which exactly illustrate the
longing mood of the principal idea. Of similar type is the
highly ornamental solo rhapsody in G minor in the first
book, which might be a beautiful violin piece with a
compactly consistent polyphonic accompaniment. A few
are dance movements in disguise (A♭ in first book). One
is either an imitation or an arrangement of a typical
orchestral movement of the period with violin and trumpet
passages interchanging (D major in second book). A very
few are on the lines of a modern sonata movement, though
the style is so different that the relationship is barely recognisable (F minor in second book). A few are studies
based on short but beautifully expressive figures which
make the movement coherent by their constant interchange
(B minor in second book). The variety is so extraordinary
that it is impossible to give a full account of them; and
every individual movement is a finished piece of workmanship, perfect in design and full of refined expression;
and few things in the range of art are so full of sugges-
tions for fresh possibilities on quite unconventional lines
in the treatment of harmonic expression, melody, and
rhythm. The preludes and fugues as a whole have been
subjected to the closest scrutiny by numberless musicians
of the highest intelligence for the greater part of a
century, and they bear the test so well that the better

men know them the more they resort to them; and the collection is likely to remain the sacred book of musicians who have any real musical sense as long as the present system of music continues.

In their particular phase of art they appear to touch the highest point imaginable. Bach was fortunate in occupying a unique position at the end of the purely polyphonic period, before the influence of the Italian opera had gained force enough to spoil the fresh sincerity of such polyphonic works. The moment the balance swung over to the harmonic side, and men thought more of the easy progressions of the harmony than of the details of the polyphonic texture, work on his lines became almost impossible. The change is curiously illustrated by the difference between the ring of such a work as his Chromatische Fantasie, and of the experiments in the same line by so true a composer as his son, Philip Emmanuel. The first is one of the greatest movements ever written for a keyed instrument; the latter soon reveals a mechanical emptiness, when the formulas and types of phrase of an Italian pattern are given in ecstatic fragments, which are utterly inconsistent with the formal Italian style. It is perhaps possible to write something new on the lines of the toccata as well as on the lines of the suite; but in his particular polyphonic line Bach's work is so high and noble that it entirely forbids all hope of advance beyond his standard. People have very rarely attempted toccatas of his type again. The modern type is a totally different thing, for some curious convention seems to have grown up that a toccata is a movement in which rapid notes must go on from beginning to end. Bach's works were founded on the types of the old organists, and it was a very congenial style to him—as he revelled in the grand successions of powerful harmonies, and the contrasts of brilliant

o

passages, and the varieties of all possible imitative passages, and expressive counterpoint.　Indeed he had a
gift for rapid ornamental passages almost unequalled
by any other composer; for they never suggest mere
emptiness and show, but have some function in relation
to the design, or some essential basis of effect, or some
ingenious principle of accent, or some inherent principle
of actual melodic beauty which puts them entirely out of
the category of things purely ornamental.　Thus even into
the merest trifles he infused reality.　The same genuineness and sincerity look out from all his work; and—art
having been at the right stage for his purposes—give the
world assurance of a man.

CHAPTER IX.

THE BEGINNINGS OF MODERN INSTRUMENTAL MUSIC.

It would have been an eminently pardonable mistake for any intelligent musician to have fallen into in the third quarter of the eighteenth century, if he concluded that J. S. Bach's career was a failure, and that his influence upon the progress of his art amounted to the minimum conceivable. Indeed the whole course of musical history in every branch went straight out of the sphere of his activity for a long while; his work ceased to have any significance to the generation which succeeded him, and his eloquence fell upon deaf ears. A few of his pupils went on writing the same kind of music in a half-hearted way, and his own most distinguished son, Philip Emmanuel, adopted at least the artistic manner of working up his details and making the internal organisation of his works alive with figure and rhythm. But even he, the sincerest composer of the following generation, was infected by the complacent, polite superficiality of his time; and was forced, through accepting the harmonic principle of working, to take with it some of the empty formulas and conventional tricks of speech which seem to belie the genuineness of his utterances, and put him out of touch with his whole-hearted father.

The fact of J. S. Bach's isolation is so obvious that it is often referred to and accounted for on the ground that he was so far before his time. It is true that his gift for divining new possibilities of combination, new progressions of harmony, and new effects and procedures of modulation, was so great that his contemporaries' wits were fatigued before they got to the point of following his drift; and succeeding generations plodded on for a long time before they came up with him, and grasped that he aimed not at pure intellectualities, but at expression. This, however, is not a complete explanation of the facts, but only a superficial illustration of more widely acting causes which governed the progress of art. The very loftiness of Bach's character and artistic aims prevented his condescending to do some of the work which had to be done before modern music could be completely matured; and the supremacy of Italian music, both operatic and otherwise, in the next generation, and the simultaneous lowering of standard and style, was as inevitable as a reaction as it was necessary as a preliminary to further progress.

Handel and Bach had carried the art of expressive counterpoint to the utmost extremes possible under the artistic conditions of their time, in the combination of polyphonic writing with the simplest kind of harmonic form. The harmonic quality is still in the background in their work because so much energy is expended upon the complexity of the choral and contrapuntal expression. As long as composers aimed chiefly at choral effect, they were impelled to individualise the parts out of which the harmony was composed, to make them worthy of the human voices ; aiming rather at melodic than rhythmic treatment. And though they submitted to certain general principles of harmonic sequence, the actual principle of harmonic design was more or less a secondary consideration. But after Handel and Bach there did not seem much to be done in this line. Genuine secular influences began to gain strength, and with them the feeling for instrumental music; and men began to feel their way towards a line of art which

could be altogether complete without the ingenuities of
counterpoint or the words which formed a necessary part of
vocal utterance.   As has been pointed out, an instinctive
desire for harmonic design and for clear definite distribution of harmonies had been in the air for a long time.   It is
as though there had been a wrestle for supremacy between
the two principles of treatment.   Composers who belonged
to the same class as Handel and Bach looked upon the
independent and equal freedom of motion of all parts
(which is called counterpoint) as the essence of good
style; and the massing and distribution of the harmonies
as secondary.   The two great masters carried their feeling for contrapuntal effect into every department of art.
Even in their arias the principle is generally discernible.
For though they generally only wrote out the voice part
and special instrumental parts, and left the harmonies to
be supplied from figures by the accompanist, yet in a large
proportion of cases even the bass part moves about quite
as vivaciously as the melody, as for instance :—

It is true that the use of harmony in the lump was early
attempted in solo arias and recitatives, and examples, such
as " Comfort ye," may be quoted to show that Handel could
use harmonic methods of accompaniment with effect; but
by far the larger proportion of the solo movements in his
operas and oratorios have accompaniments which are contrapuntally conceived ; and Bach's impulse was even more

strongly to make all parts of his scheme equally alive and individual.

But as soon as their work was done the index swung over, and the balance went down on the harmonic side. Counterpoint, and interest in the subordinate parts of the music, became of secondary importance (or even less), and clearness and intelligibility of harmonic and melodic progressions, became the primary consideration. Composers made a show of counterpoint now and then, but it was not the real thing. The parts are not in the least interesting. They are mechanically contrived to have the appearance of being busy, and serve for nothing more; and it was no great loss when such pinchbeck was undisguisedly replaced by the conventional figures of accompaniment which became so characteristic of the harmonic period even in the palmy days of Mozart and Haydn. But such traits and contrivances had to be found out like everything else, and in the time at present under consideration they were not in common use. Indeed as far as the Italian share of the work of developing harmonic form goes, the early period contemporaneous with Handel and Bach is the purest and most honourable. That most remarkable school of Italian violinists and composers who began with Corelli and Vivaldi forms as noble and sincere a group as any in music; and to them, more than to any others, the credit of establishing the principles of harmonic form on a firm basis is due.

The great Italian violin-makers had, in the course of the seventeenth century, brought their skill up to the highest perfection, and put into the hands of performers the most ideally perfect instrument for expression that human ingenuity seems capable of devising. Their achievement came just at the right moment for artistic purposes, and Italian musicians of the highest gifts took to the instrument with passionate ardour. In the violin

there is so little intervening mechanism between the
player and his means of utterance that it becomes almost
part of himself; and is as near as possible to being an
additional voice with greater compass and elasticity than
his natural organ of song. To the Italian nature such
an instrument was even specially suitable, and as the
inartistic sophisms, to which Italians have proved so
lamentably prone to succumb, had not yet darkened
the musical horizon, their instinct for beauty of form
and melody led them under its influence to very notable
achievements. Corelli's style was noble and healthy, but
the range of his technique was limited. In that respect
his great successors—many of them his pupils or their
pupils in turn—progressed by leaps and bounds. Men
like Veracini, Tartini, Geminiani, and Locatelli, possessed
with the passion to attain some ideal joy that their instrument seemed to promise in possibility, soon brought their
department of art to almost the highest pitch of perfection. The congenial nature of their instrument seems
to have inspired them to find out with extraordinary
rapidity the forms of melody and figure and the kinds
of phrasing and expression that suited it; and adding
contrivance to contrivance, they soon learnt the best way
to overcome the mechanical difficulties of stopping and
bowing in such a way as to obtain the finest tone, the
purest intonation, and the greatest facility and fluency of
motion.

But what was still more notable and important was
their successful development of a scheme which could
be completely intelligible on its own account, without
either systematic dance rhythm or contrapuntal devices
or words to explain it. The speed with which they advanced towards an intelligent grasp of the necessary
principles for such a purpose of design is very surprising. It was probably due to the fact that they were all

performers, and performers on a solo instrument. The central idea in the violin soloist's mind was to make his effect by melody, with subordinate accompaniment; that is, melody supported by simple harmonies, and not melody as only the upper part of a set of equal independent parts. The violin has been forced—and forced with success—to play contrapuntal movements; but it may be confessed, without disrespect to J. S. Bach, that counterpoint is not its natural mode of expressing itself, and that its resources of expression could not have led to the development of the typical Italian solo sonata if the accompaniment had been on equal terms with the solo instrument. It is naturally a single-part instrument—a singing instrument with great capacity for enlivening and adorning its *cantabile* with brilliant passages. It was therefore imperative for the player-composers to find a form which should not depend for its interest upon contrapuntal ingenuities and devices — a form which should mainly depend upon distribution of melodious passages, supported by systematic and simple harmonic accompaniment. The opportunities for testing their experiments being plentiful, they soon found and established a solution of the problem; and their solution forms the groundwork of the development of those principles of design which ultimately served Haydn, Mozart, and Beethoven in all their greatest and most perfect works.

The types which served these composers for models were the Sonate da Chiesa and the Sonate da Camera of the Corellian time. Their instinct impelled them to develop movements which were not purely dance tunes, but of wider and freer range; which should admit of warm melodic expression without degenerating into incoherent rambling ecstasy. They had the sense to see from the first that mere formal continuous melody is not the most suitable type for instrumental music. For, as

was pointed out in the first chapter, there is deep-rooted
in the nature of all instrumental music the need of some
rhythmic vitality, in consonance with the primal source
of instrumental expression. And for instrumental music,
pure, continuous, vocal melody, undefined by rhythm, is
only temporarily or relatively endurable; even with such
an ideal melodic instrument as the violin. These player-
composers, then, set themselves to devise a scheme in which
to begin with the contours of connected melodic phrases
(supported and defined by simple harmonic accompaniment) gave the impression of definite tonality—that is, of
being decisively in some particular key, and giving an
unmistakable indication of it. They found out how to proceed by giving the impression of leaving that key and passing to another, without departing from the characteristic
spirit and mood of the music, as shown in the "subjects"
and figures; and how to give the impression of relative completeness by closing in a key which is in strong contrast
to the first; and so round off one-half of the design. But
this point being in apposition to the starting-point, leaves
the mind dissatisfied and in expectation of fresh dis-
closures. So they made the balance complete by resuming
the subjects and melodic figures of the first half in the
extraneous key and working back to the starting-point;
and then closing in that key with the same figures as
were used to conclude the first half, but in the principal
key instead of the key of contrast. This was practically
the scheme adopted in dance movements of suites; but
the great violinists improved upon the suite type by much
clearer definition of the subjects; and by giving them a
much wider range, and making them represent the key
more decisively. As time went on they extended the
range of each division of the movement, and made them
balance one another more completely. They also lengthened the second half of the movement by introducing

more extensive modulations in the middle of it, and thus introduced a new and important element of contrast. How this simple type of form was extended and developed into the scheme uniformly adopted in their best movements by the three great masters of pure instrumental music must be considered in its place.

This was the highest type of harmonic design used by the early composers of sonatas. They also used simpler ones like the primitive rondo, which is the least organised and coherent of forms; and the aria type, which is the same thing in principle of structure as the familiar primitive minuet and trio. As instrumental art was still in a very experimental stage the character and order of the movements which they combined to make a complete group or sonata varied considerably; but the general tendency was towards the familiar arrangement of three movements:—1. A solid allegro; 2. an expressive slow movement; 3. a lively finale—to which was often most suitably appended a slow and dignified "introduction." The reasons which made men gravitate towards this grouping of movements appear to be obvious. The slow introduction was particularly suitable to the noble qualities of the violin, and was the more needful in violin sonatas, as it not infrequently happened that the first allegro was in a loose fugal form, following the model of the canzonas in Sonate da Chiesa; and as that would necessitate beginning with only a single part sounding at a time, it was not sufficient to lay hold of the audience's attention at once. Whereas a massive full-sounding introduction insists upon being heard. Moreover, the instinct of the composers was right in adopting a serious style to put the audience in proper mood for what was to follow. It is a familiar experience that when people are appealed to on trivial and light grounds they can with difficulty be brought to attend to anything serious afterwards. The principal allegro movement which follows the introduction always tends to be the most elaborately organised of all the movements; and to appeal to the intellectual side of the audience. In this the composer puts forth all his resources of development and richness of design. The intellectual tendency was illustrated in the early days by the fugal form in which the movement was usually cast, as in the Sonate da Chiesa; and when in harmonic form it was the one in which the design above described was adopted. Sometimes it was an allemande, as in the Sonate da Camera, and the suites and partitas and ordres. The allemande was nominally a dance form, and was distributed in regular groups of bars in accordance with the requirements of the dance; but it was always the most solid and elaborate of all the movements in the group in which it occurred (except sometimes the French courante), and it often contained imitations and elaborate counterpoint. The position of a movement of this character fits with the requirements of an audience, for people are more capable of entering into and enjoying serious matters and subtleties of intellectual skill when their attention is fresh and unwearied.

After the intellectual came the emotional. The slow movement which follows, not only serves as a marked contrast, but appeals to the opposite side of men's natures. The intellectual faculties are, comparatively speaking, allowed to rest, and all the appeal is made to sensibilities by expression. Strange as it may seem, it was in this movement that the Italian violin-composers most frequently failed; and the same is the case with Haydn and Mozart and the whole school of harpsichord-composers; and the full perfection of the slow emotional movement was not attained till Beethoven's time. The reason is that music had to wait for the development of the technique of expression much longer than for the technique of mere design. And it may be noted in passing that nothing marks the difference between extreme modern music and the earlier phases than the different degree and quality of passionate emotion it expresses. But at least these performer-composers aimed at expression in this movement; and when they were at fault and found nothing sympathetic to say, they took refuge—like opera singers and people in ordinary circumstances in life—in ornamental flourishes and such superfluities as disguise the barrenness of invention and feeling under the show of dexterity.

The function of the lively last movement is equally intelligible. It is usually in dance rhythm of some kind, and was always more direct and free from intellectual subtleties than the other movements. It was gay—spontaneous—headlong. At once an antidote and a tonic. Restoring the balance after the excitement of too much sensibility, and calling into play the healthy human faculties which are associated with muscular activity. As though the composer, after putting his auditors under a spell of enchantment, called them back to the realities of life by setting their limbs going.

In short, the sum of the scheme is—

1. The preliminary summons to attention, attuning the mind to what is to follow.

2. The appeal to intelligence; and to appreciation of artistic subtleties and refinements of design.

3. The appeal to emotional sensibilities.

4. The re-establishment of healthy brightness of tone— a recall to the realities of life.

This is the natural outline of the scheme, which in the main has persisted from the beginnings of genuine instrumental music till the present day. It has of course been varied by the ingenuity and insight of really capable composers, as well as by the fatuity of musical malaprops.

Nearly all the violin sonatas of the Italian type were written by violin players, with the exception of a few by John Sebastian Bach, Handel and Hasse, and such comprehensive composers. The quality of these works is on the whole far higher than that of the examples of other forms of instrumental music of the early time, but very important results were also obtained by composers of harpsichord sonatas.

Keyed instruments did not find so much favour at this time with Italians. The superior capacities of the violin for cantabile purposes attracted the best of their efforts, and met with most sympathy from the public. It remained for Germans, with their great sense of the higher resources of harmony and polyphony, to cultivate the instruments which offered excellent opportunities in those directions, but were decidedly defective for the utterance of melody. Nevertheless Italians contributed an extremely important share to the early establishment of this department of art; and even before the violin sonata had been cultivated with so much success, the singular genius of Domenico Scarlatti had not only laid the foundations of modern music for keyed instruments, but contributed some very permanent items to the edifice. His instinct for the requirements of his instrument was so marvellous, and his development of technique so wide and rich, that he seems to spring full armed into the view of history. That he had models and types to work upon is certain, but his style is so unlike the familiar old suites and fugues and fantasias and ricercare, and other harpsichord music of the early times, that it seems likely that the work of his prototypes has been lost. His musical character makes it probable that he studied players rather than composers; for the quality that is most conspicuous in his work is his thorough command of the situation as a performer. His work, at its best, gives the impression

that he played upon his audience as much as he did on
his harpsichord. He knows well the things that will tell,
and how to awake interest in a new mood when the effects
of any particular line are exhausted. Considering how
little attention had been given to technique before his
time, his feats of agility are really marvellous. The
variety and incisiveness of his rhythms, the peculiarities
of his harmony, his wild whirling rapid passages, his rattling shakes, his leaps from end to end of the keyboard,
all indicate a preternaturally vivacious temperament; and
unlike many later virtuosos, he is thoroughly alive to the
meaning of music as an art, and does not make his feats
of dexterity his principal object. They serve as the means
to convey his singularly characteristic ideas in forms
as abstract as modern sonatas. The definiteness of his
musical ideas is one of the most surprising things about
him. For when the development of any branch of art
is in its infancy, it generally taxes all a man's powers
to master the mere mechanical problems of technique and
style. But Scarlatti steps out with a sort of diabolic
masterfulness, and gives utterance with perfect ease to
things which are unmistakable images of his characteristic personality. In spirit and intention his works
prefigure one of the latest of modern musical developments, the scherzo. For vivacity, wit, irony, mischief,
mockery, and all the category of human traits which
Beethoven's scherzo served so brilliantly to express, the
world had to wait for a full century to see Scarlatti's
equal again. He left behind him a most copious legacy
to mankind, but his successors were very slow to avail
themselves of it. The majority of harpsichord composers
immediately after his time were more inclined to follow
a path that was redolent of the saponaceous influences
of opera, and made their works but slightly distinct as
forms of instrumental art. His influence is traceable

here and there, but it did not bear full fruit till the development of genuine pianoforte playing began.

His sense of design was not so strong as his ideas or his feeling for effect. His works consist of single movements, which are almost invariably in the same form as the earlier movements of suites, such as the allemandes and courantes; only considerably extended after the manner of the violin sonatas, and singularly free from systematic dance rhythm. He rarely wrote fugues, and when he did they were not particularly good, either technically or intrinsically. He was too much of a performer to care much about the conventional ingenuities of fugue form, and too much of a free lance to put his thoughts in so elaborate a form; though he often makes a beginning as if he was going to write a serious fugue, and then goes on in a different manner. The harmonic principle of design came to him most naturally, and, as far as they go in that respect, his movements are singularly lucid and definite. But they are not operatic. They are genuine representatives of a distinct branch of art; and the expression of ideas in terms exactly adapted to the instrument by means of which they are to be made perceptible to the human mind.

Of the other Italians who did service in the line of harpsichord music the most deserving of mention is Paradisi. His technique is nothing like so extended as Scarlatti's, and the style is much less incisive; but he shows a very excellent instinct for his instrument, and a singularly just and intelligent feeling for harmonic design. The best of his sonatas (which are commonly in two movements without a slow movement) show considerable skill in modelling ideas into the forms necessary for defining the key. The design of his best movements is the same as that of the great violin composers; but even more structurally definite. He deserves credit also for devising true sonata subjects, and escaping the temptation of writing fragments of operatic tunes with dummy accompaniments —a rock upon which the Italians and even some very wise Germans later were very liable to split.

The true centre of progress in the line of the harpsichord sonata soon proved to be in Germany. As has been before remarked, many of Germany's most distinguished composers, such as Graun, Hasse, and John Christian Bach, adopted Italian manners to suit the tastes of the fashionable classes; but there were a few here and there who did not bow the knee to Baal; and noteworthiest of these was Philip Emmanuel Bach. Though gifted with little of the poetical qualities or the noble loftiness of idea and expression of his father, he was in a position to do considerable service to his art. He adopted without reserve the Italian harmonic principle of design which had become universal by his time, and adapted to it a method of treating details, and harmonisation, and rhythmic and figurative interest, which was essentially Teutonic. The high intellectual qualities come out both in his scope of harmony, and in the richness and ingenious subtlety with which he manipulates his sentences and phrases. He did so much to give the harpsichord sonata a definite status of its own that he is sometimes spoken of as its inventor. This he obviously was not, but he was for some time its most prominent representative. He owed a good deal to his father's training and example, though more in respect of detail and texture than in style or design. His father had made some experiments in the harmonic style, but on the whole he was rather shy of it, and rarely achieved anything first rate in it. But his son, taking to it at a time when it had become more familiar and more malleable, was the first to treat it with Teutonic thoroughness. Italian influence is sometimes apparent, but happily it is not often the influence of the opera. Instrumental music had developed far enough for him to express his ideas in a genuinely instrumental style—frequently in figures as compact and incisive as Beethoven's—to make his modulations as deliberately and clearly as Mozart, and to define his contrasting key with perfect clearness, and to dispose all the various ingredients of his structure with unmistakable skill and certitude. His sonatas are usually in three movements—the central one slow and expressive, and the first and last quick. It is characteristic of his Teutonic disposition that he is a little shy of adopting the traditional lightness and gaiety as the mood of his last movement. But he finds an excellent alternative in forcible vigour and brilliancy.

There is yet another branch of instrumental music which was very slow in developing, but has come in later days to form one of the most conspicuous features of the art.

As has before been pointed out, all the composers of the early part of the eighteenth century, even the giants, had been specially backward in feeling for orchestral effect. They used instruments of most diverse tone-quality in a purely contrapuntal manner, just as they would have used voices, or the independent parts of an organ composition. Those methods of using colour which enhance the telling power of ideas, and exert such moving glamour upon the sensibilities of modern human creatures, were quite out of their range. The adoption of harmonic principles of treatment were as essential to the development of modern orchestration as to the development of forms of the sonata order. As long as composers were writing accompaniments to contrapuntal choral works they disposed their instruments also contrapuntally; and it was not till they had to write independent instrumental movements that the requirements of instrumentation began to dawn upon them.

P

The first occasions which induced composers to attempt
independent orchestral movements of the harmonic kind,
were for the symphonies or overtures of operas. These
had been written at first, as by Scarlatti and Lulli, for
stringed instruments only, and occasionally with the
addition of trumpet solos. Composers insensibly got into
the habit of enhancing the effect of their strings by a
few other wind instruments; and before long the group
of instruments was stereotyped (as every other department of opera was) into a set of strings and two pairs of
wind instruments, such as two hautboys, or two flutes and
two horns. The conventional opera writers had no very
great inducement to make their overtures either finished
works of art, or subtly expressive, or in any way interesting, for they felt that very little attention was paid to
them. They appear to have produced them in a most
perfunctory manner, to make a sort of introductory clatter
while the fashionable operatic audiences were settling into
their places, and exchanging the customary greetings and
small talk which are inevitable in such gatherings of light-
minded folk. The musical clatter was distributed into
three movements, in the same order as the movements of
violin sonatas, and in thoroughly harmonic style of the
very cheapest description. There inevitably were some
composers who could not help putting tolerably artistic
touches and lively points into their work, and in course
of time the symphonies came to be considerably in request
independent of their connection with the operas; and
enormous numbers were written both for people to listen
to, and also for them to talk and eat to. Composers
usually saved themselves all the trouble they could. They
put musical material of such slight definiteness into them
that it is often hardly to be dignified by the name of
ideas; and they also spared themselves the labour of
writing in the parts for the various instruments whenever

possible. They made the second violins play with the first
violins, and directed the violas to play with the basses—
which must have caused the viola players to spend a good
deal of their time in not playing at all, or otherwise in
producing extremely disagreeable effects, when the bass
part went below their compass. Moreover, the wind
instruments that were sufficiently agile were generally
directed to double the violins, or to hold notes and
chords while the violins ran about in scales or figures.
There was little or no idea of differentiating the various
parts to suit the respective instruments, and equally little
attempt to use their various qualities of tone as means of
effect. The horn parts had the most individuality through
the mere accident that they were not agile enough to play
violin or viola parts; and composers being driven to give
long notes to these instruments, by degrees found out
their great value as a means of holding things together
and supplying a sort of background of soft steady tone
while the other instruments were moving about.

When these "symphonies" or "overtures" were played
more often independent of the operas, both composers
and performers began to realise that they were wasting
opportunities by slovenliness. The process of coming
round to more sensible and refined ways is very interesting to watch in the successive publications of these
very numerous symphonies. It is like the gradual return
of a human being to intelligence and serviceableness after
being temporarily submerged in levity. At first the style
of the passages was empty and conventional, and it is quite
clear that the players hacked through the performance
in a careless style, which perhaps was quite as much as
the music and the audience deserved. There were hardly
any indications given for the most ordinary refinements of
performance—such as phrasing, bowing, or *pianos* or *fortes;*
and gradations of more delicate nature are implied to

have been entirely ignored. But as time went on the directions for expression and refinements of performance became more numerous; and composers even began to use mutes to vary the effect, and to see that hautboys are capable of better uses than mere pointless doubling of string parts, or playing irrelevant holding notes. Little by little things crept into a better state of artistic finish and nicety; the varieties of instruments in the group were more carefully considered, and their qualities of tone were used to better purpose; and the style of the passages was better suited to the qualities of the instruments. Composers began to grow more aware of the sensuous effect of colour, and to realise that two colours which are beautiful when pure may be coarse and disagreeable when mixed. And so, by degrees, a totally new and extremely subtle branch of art is seen to be emerging from the chaotic products of indifference and careless-ness. The refinements of modern orchestration, and those subtleties of sensuous colour-effect which are among the most marvellous and almost unanalysable developments of human instinct, took a very considerable period to mature, and many generations of men had a share in developing them. But the inherent difference of nature between the old and new is perceptible even in the course of one generation. For even in a symphony of John Christian Bach's there is a roundness and smoothness in the sound of the harmony, as conveyed by the different instrumental *timbres*, which is quite different from the unassimilated counterpoint of his great father's instru-mental style. In the instrumentation of the great masters of the earlier generation the tone-qualities seem to be divided from one another by innate repulsion; but in the harmonic style they seem to melt into one another insensibly, and to become part of a composite mass of harmony whose shades are constantly shifting and varying.

Amongst the men who had an important share in the early development of orchestral music, a Bohemian violinist named Stamitz seems to have been most noteworthy. He was leader and conductor of the band at the little German court of Mannheim, and seems to have been fortunate in his opportunities of carrying out reforms. He set his face to organise his band thoroughly. to make his violins play with refinement and careful attention to phrasing, and to obtain various shades of *piano* and *forte,* and all the advantages which can be secured by good balance of tone. He succeeded in developing the best orchestra in Europe, and established a tradition which lasted long after he had passed away; even till Mozart came through Mannheim on his way to Paris, and had an opportunity of hearing what refined orchestral playing was like—probably for the first time in his life—with important results to the world in general.

A similar line was pursued by the Belgian Gossec in Paris, who tried to stir up the Parisians to realise the possibilities of instrumental effect. He in his smaller way followed something of the same line as Berlioz, laying very great, even superfluous, stress on the importance of elaborate directions to the performers.

The position of Philip Emmanuel Bach in this line of art was important, though peculiar. In his best symphonies he adopted a line of his own; similar in principle to the ways of his father in his orchestral suites and concerti grossi. They are harmonic in style, but not so decisively as his sonatas. Indeed they are quite different in design and style from the symphonies of the Italians above discussed; and though remarkably vigorous, animated and original in conception, they have not led to any further developments in the same line. His management of instruments shows considerable skill and clear perception of the effective uses to which they can be

put; and he treats them with thorough independence
and variety of effect. His feeling for orchestration is
even more strikingly illustrated in his oratorios "The
Israelites in the Wilderness" and "The Resurrection."
In these he makes experiments in orchestral effects
which sound curiously like late modern products, and
he tries to enforce the sentiment of his situations with a
daring and insight which is very far ahead of his time.
But in this, as in many other noteworthy attempts, he
was considerably isolated, and out of touch with the easy-
going spirit of his day. His works, apart from the
sonatas, seem to have taken no hold upon his contemporaries, and serve chiefly to illustrate the rapidity with
which change of view, and the new conditions of art,
helped men to discover the possibilities of orchestral
effect. The application of instrumental effect to the
oratorio was destined ultimately to give that form a new
lease of life, and to lead to new ulterior developments,
but Philip Emmanuel's attempt was at that time, as far
as public taste was concerned, premature.

The enormous number of symphonies which were produced and published in those days, by composers whose
very names are forgotten, proves that public taste was
gravitating strongly towards orchestral music; and it is
pleasant to reflect that the more composers improved the
quality of their art, the more prominently they came into
the light of day. When they escaped out of the Slough
of Indifference they made progress very fast; and considering how complete is the change of attitude between
Bach and Mozart, it is very creditable to the energy and
sincerity of musical humanity that this new phase of
orchestral art was so well organised in the space of about
half a century. But it must be remembered that it was
the outcome of a separate movement which began before
the time of Handel and Bach, and was going on, though

on different lines from those they followed, during their lifetime. Their work, as it were, branched out from the direct line of harmonic music into a special province of its own. The purely harmonic style was not sufficiently matured to allow of their expressing themselves fully in it; otherwise a development like Beethoven's would have come nearly a hundred years sooner. It was the possibility of combining the polyphonic principles of the old choral art—painfully worked out in the ages before harmonic music began—with the simpler principles of the new harmonic music, which afforded them the opportunity they used so magnificently. And while they were busy with their great achievements, it was left to smaller men to get through the preliminaries of such forms as the sonata and the symphony—for even such insignificant business as the devising of an "Alberti bass," and of similar forms of conventional accompaniment, had to be done by somebody. But by the multitude of workers the requirements of art were brought up to the penultimate stage ready for the use of the three great representatives of instrumental music.

The main points so far achieved may be summed up.

The Italians initiated an enthusiastic culture of the violin, and in a very short time developed the resources of its technique and the style of music adapted to it. The same was done simultaneously for the harpsichord by other groups of composers in Italy, Germany, France, and England. To supply these typical solo instruments with intelligible music, composers laboured with excellent success to devise schemes of design and methods of development, which without the help of words became sufficient reason of existence and principle of coherence. At the same time, the growth of feeling for the effect of massed harmonies placed composers in a position to develop the possibilities of effect of orchestral instruments

in combination; and before long the sense of the adap-
tability of various kinds of technique and the relations
of different qualities of tone to one another, and the
possible functions of the different instruments in the
scheme of orchestral composition, put things in the right
direction to move on towards the development of the
latest episodes in the story of music—the employment
of the complicated resources of an immense aggregate
of different instruments for the purposes of vivid and
infinitely variable expression.

CHAPTER X.

THE MIDDLE STAGE OF MODERN OPERA.

EVERY form of art has a variety of sides and aspects which appeal to different men in different degrees. A work may entrance one man through the beauty of its colour, while another finds it insupportable for its weakness of design. One may care only for melody, when another is satisfied with grand harmony; one wants artistic skill when another cares only for expression. This is true even of symphonies and sonatas, and such pure examples of human artistic contrivance; but in opera the complication and variety of constituents intensify the situation tenfold, for the elements that have to be combined seem to be almost incompatible. Scenic effect has to be considered as well as the development of the dramatic situations, and the dialogue, and the music. The action and the scenery distract the attention from the music, and the dialogue naturally goes too fast for it. Music, being mainly the expression of states of mind and feeling, takes time to convey its meaning; and in all but the most advanced stages of art the types of design which seem indispensable to make it intelligible require the repetition of definite passages of melody, and submission to rules of procedure which seem to be completely at variance with dramatic effect. If the action halts or hangs fire, the dramatic effect is paralysed; but if a phase of human passion which has once been passed has to be re-enacted to meet the supposed requirements of music, the situation becomes little less than ridiculous. So, in early days it seemed as if people had to take their choice, and either accept the music as the essential, and let the dramatic effect cease to have any significance; or to fasten their attention on the action and dialogue, and allow the music to be merely an indefinite rambling background of tone, which was hardly fit to be called music at all. The Italians, who enjoyed the distinction of developing the first stages of the operatic form, were much more impressionable on the musical than on the dramatic side, and as soon as the new secular type of music began to take shape, they gave their verdict absolutely in favour of the former; and the drama rapidly receded farther and farther into the background. The scheme was well devised up to a certain point; but as soon as the aria type had been fairly established, the ingenious artifices which seemed to settle the plan of operations degenerated into mere conventions, and even musical progress itself came to a dead standstill. It was impossible for the music to grow or develop, for there was nothing in the occasion to call for any human expression or human interest. The sole purpose of existence of the opera was to show off a few celebrated Italian singers, who required to be accommodated according to fixed rules of precedence, which precluded any kind of freedom of dramatic action. The only glimpse of life which was apparent for some time was in the little humorous operas which began to come into notice about the beginning of the eighteenth century. The regular singer's opera was a most solemn and sedate function, and hardly admitted of anything so incongruous as humour. Humorous scenes had been attempted, even by Alessandro Scarlatti; but apparently they were considered out of place, and humour in general was relegated to the little separate musical comedies called intermezzos, or "opera buffa," which were performed in between the acts of the opera seria. From one point of view this made the situation even more absurd. It was like performing King Lear and the School for Scandal in alternate acts. But the ultimate result was eminently beneficial to opera in general. The composers who took the opera buffa in hand developed a special style for the purpose—merry, bright, vivacious, and pointed, and in its way very characteristic. In the music of the *opera seria* no attempt was made to follow the action in the music, because action in such situations could have amounted to nothing more than stilted gesticulation. But the composers of the intermezzi tried to keep the scene in their minds, and to accentuate gestures by sforzandos and queer surprising progressions, in accordance with the meaning of the actions. And this is a point of more importance than might appear without paying a little attention to it. As has before been pointed out, music mainly implies vocal expression in melody, and expressive gesture in rhythm and accent; and in the condition into which Italian opera had degenerated, the rhythmic element had for the most part retired into the background. Under the circumstances, the rhythmic animation and gaiety which was adapted to humorous purposes was the very thing that was wanted to reinfuse a little humanity into the formal torpor of opera seria.

The importance of the new departure may be judged by its fruits. A direct result of considerable importance was the French light comic opera, which started into existence after a visit of an Italian opera troupe to Paris in 1752, who performed Italian intermezzi, and aroused much controversy mainly on the ground that Italians were not Frenchmen. But the style took root and was cultivated by French composers, who developed on its basis a type of light opera of the neatest and most artistic kind. But of still more importance was its actual influence on opera in general. The style inaugurated by the Italians in intermezzi is the source of the sparkling gaiety of

Mozart's light and merry scenes in Seraglio, Nozze di Figaro, and Don Giovanni. Osmin's famous song in the Seraglio is a direct descendant of the style which Pergolese so admirably illustrated in La Serva Padrona ; and so is all Leporello's and Figaro's music. The style indeed was so congenial to Mozart's disposition that it coloured his work throughout; and traces of it peep out in symphonies, quartetts, and sonatas, as well as in his operas. And even Beethoven sometimes gives clear indications that he knew such ways of expressing lighter moods.[1]

The powerful influence which such a slight and rather trivial style exerted upon music in general at that time is clearly owing to the fact that it was the only line of operatic art which had any real life in it. When serious art becomes a formality, and shows that composers or artists are only conforming to barren formalities, light music, and even vulgar and trivial music, which gives people a strong impression of being genuinely human, is bound to succeed. The audiences of the opera were at least allowed to take some genuine interest, and to get a genuine laugh out of the human perplexities and comic situations, and to feel that there was a reality about them which the heroic complacencies of the opera seria did not possess. But as far as solid reforms of the opera seria itself are concerned, the public might have allowed things to go on in the same perfunctory way till the present day. The courtly fashionable people neither wanted nor deserved anything better ; and the general reforms had to be forced on the notice of an indifferent world by the irrepressible energy of a personal conviction.

Gluck deserves great homage as a man of the rarest genius. But he deserves fully as much again for the splendid sincerity with which he refused to put up with

---

[1] Quartett in B♭, Op. 18, No. 6, at beginning. Opening scene of Fidelio. Violin sonata in C minor, last movement.

the shams which the rest of the world found quite good
enough to amuse them, and made men wake up to realise
that opera was worth reforming. He brought about the
first crisis in the history of this form of art, by calling
attention to the fact that a work of art is always worth
making as good as possible, and that opera itself would
be more enjoyable and more worthy of intelligent beings
if the dramatic side of the matter received more consideration. He was premature, as it happened, for the resources
of his art were not yet fully equal to such undertakings
as he proposed; but at least he succeeded in dispelling
a good deal of apathy, and in persuading people that real
dramatic music was a possibility.

He himself received his operatic education in the school
of Italian opera, and wrote a good many operas on the
usual lines, which had good and characteristic music in
them, but did not make any great impression on the world
in general. The conviction that reforms were necessary
was forced upon him by degrees; and he was encouraged
by the similar views held by prominent people who were
connected with operatic matters, such as the famous lib-
rettist, Metastasio, himself. He made several isolated
attempts at re-establishing the lost element of dramatic
effect in opera from 1762 onwards. In 1767 Alceste was
brought out in Vienna; and to the published edition he
appended a preface, which so well expressed his view of
the situation that a few of its sentences must necessarily
be quoted. He proclaimed his object to be "to avoid all
those abuses which had crept into Italian opera through
the mistaken vanity of singers and the unwise compliance
of composers," and proceeded :—

"I endeavoured to restrict the music to its proper function, that of seconding the poetry by enforcing the expression of the sentiment and the interest of the situations,
without interrupting the action or weakening it by

superfluous ornament. . . . I have been very careful never
to interrupt a singer in the heat of the dialogue in order
to introduce a tedious ritornelle, nor to stop him in the
middle of a word for the purpose of displaying the flexi-
bility of his voice on some favourable vowel. . . . I have
not thought it right to hurry through the second part of a
song if the words happened to be the most important of
the whole in order to repeat the first part four times over;
or to finish the air where the sense does not end in order
to allow the singer to exhibit his power of varying the
passage at pleasure.

"My idea was that the Sinfonia ought to indicate the
subject, and prepare the spectators for the character of
the piece they are about to see; that the instruments
ought to be introduced in proportion to the degree of
interest and passion in the words; and that it was necessary above all to avoid making too great a disparity
between the recitative and the air in the dialogue, so as
not to break the sense of a period or awkwardly interrupt
the movement and animation of a scene," &c.

The Viennese were not so much moved by these considerations, or by his practical exposition in the shape of
opera, as he had naturally hoped; and ultimately he had
to transfer the scene of action to Paris, where conditions
were on the whole likely to be more favourable. The
French in their national opera had always managed to
keep the dramatic side of things more steadily in view
than the Italians. Lulli had established the type before
described, and his operas held the stage, to the exclusion
of nearly all others, for some time after he had departed
out of the world. Ultimately Rameau, one of the greatest
of all French composers, improved very materially upon
Lulli's work by a better handling of his instrumental resources, more lightness and variety and geniality in the
music, and a better artistic standard of work all round. He

was a man of musically sincere character, with more grasp
of harmonic expression than is usual with Frenchmen,
and with far more genuinely dramatic perception of the
theatrical kind than any other man of his time—for it is
noteworthy that he was born two years before Handel. It
is highly probable that he had considerable influence upon
Gluck; for that composer passed through Paris in 1746,
and heard and was impressed by Rameau's work, which
was so conspicuously different from the average Italian
product to which he was accustomed. And though Gluck's
own work went ultimately far beyond Rameau's in every
respect, whether artistic or expressive, there is a touch
of the spirit of Rameau even in his mature and most
characteristic works.

Paris then was the most hopeful place for him to get
his views on dramatic matters attended to; and though
it is obvious that the real evils which he attacked were
in the Italian form of opera, and that the natural form of
French opera was not so amenable to his criticisms, yet
it was better to promulgate them in a place where people
might pay a little attention than to address the worse
than deafness of indifference.

The summary of his Parisian campaign is that he
began by enlisting able literary men on his side, and
rousing public curiosity by getting his theories discussed.
He then brought out the first practical illustration of his
theories in a version of Racine's "Iphigénie en Aulide" in
1774; and followed it up with a revised version of his
earlier Orfeo under the name of "Orphée et Eurydice,"
and a revised version of Alceste in 1776, and Armide
in 1777. After this a very estimable Italian composer,
Piccini, was brought over from Italy by Gluck's opponents
in the hopes of defeating him in a practical contest;
and for a while the fervours of the rival partisans divided
Paris. Gluck brought out his final manifesto, "Iphigénie

en Tauride," in 1781, with great success. Piccini's
setting of the same subject was acknowledged to be
inferior, and the Gluckists remained masters of the field.

The point which is of highest importance in Gluck's
victory, as far as the development of the art is concerned,
is the restoration of the element of genuine expression
to its place in the scheme of art. Gluck, like every one
else, was forced to accept the work of his predecessors
as the basis of his own, and even to retain some of the
most conspicuous features of the scheme which he aimed
at destroying. He had to write arias on the old lines,
for they were the only definite types of design then
understood; and Gluck was far too wise to think he
could dispense with definite design. He had also to
accept the ballet, for it was too vital a part of the
French operatic scheme to be discarded without almost
certainty of failure. But, in the case of the arias, he did
his best to make them as characteristic of the situations
as the backward state of the art allowed; and he often
replaced them by short movements of very complete
and simple form—more like the type of folk-songs—into
which he concentrated a great deal of genuine expression.
For the ballets he had the justification of the ancients;
and he undoubtedly applied them in many cases extremely
well. Wherever it was possible they were made part
of the action, and became a very effective part of it.
As, for instance, the dance and chorus of furies at the
threshold of the infernal regions in Orfeo, and the chorus
and ballets of Scythians in "Iphigénie en Tauride." For
his treatment of recitative he had the earlier examples
of Lulli and Rameau, who both adopted a free style of
expressive declamation with definite accompaniment; often
with very successful results. Since their time music had
very much enlarged its resources of expression and had
become more elastic; and Gluck, while working on the same

lines, arrived at far more refined and finished results.
Moreover, the expressive qualities of his admirable recitatives are very much enhanced by his way of dealing with
the accompaniment. He neglected no opportunity to make
use of the qualities of his orchestral instruments—as far
as in him lay—to enforce and accentuate the situations,
and even to intensify the passing moment of feeling implied by the dialogue. Composers were beginning to
develop a little sense of the effects of instrumentation.
Even Gluck's rival, Piccini, made some very appropriate
effects by using his instruments consistently with the
spirit of the situations. But Gluck applied himself to
the matter with far more intensity, and far more genuine
perception of the characters of the instruments. Indeed
it would hardly be an exaggeration to say that he was
the first composer in the world who had any genuine
understanding of this very modern phase of the art.
Mozart was the first to show real natural gift and genuine
feeling for beautiful disposition of tone, but Gluck anti-
cipated modern procedure in adapting his colours exactly to
the mood of the situation. A good deal had been attempted
already in a sort of half-hearted and formal manner, but
he was the first to seize firmly on the right principles and
to carry out his objects with any mastery of resources.

The texture of his work is such as might be expected from his training. He has very little feeling
for polyphony, or for the effects which are produced
by those kinds of chords which become possible only
through the independent treatment of parts. In this
respect he was the very opposite of Bach. His early
experience of choral writing was in a bad school; and
his choruses, except when animated by some powerful
dramatic impulse, are flat and badly managed, both for
vocal tone and general effect. But his orchestration is
as much more mature than Bach's and Handel's as his

Q

choral writing is inferior. There is no attempt to treat
his instruments like voices or counterpoints, nor to use
them solely because artistic effect, apart from dramatic
effect, makes it advisable. The treatment is in every
respect harmonic, not contrapuntal; and his harmonies
are extremely simple and limited in range. But he
uses them with such an excellent sense of proportion
that the general result is, even harmonically, more impressive than the work of modern composers who have
a more copious supply to draw from, but less discretion
and discrimination. It may be confessed that in his
efforts to infuse expression into every possible moment
he very much overdoes the use of appogiaturas, till the
device becomes a sort of pointless mannerism; but the
greatness of his genius is emphasised by the fact that
he contrived to attain a very high pitch of genuine expression, and to sustain the general musical character of
whole works in conformity with the nature of the subjects
at a time when the resources of expression, especially in
the dramatic line, were very limited. It must be remembered that the development of modern instrumental forms
of art had only just begun. It so happened that the first
of Mozart's symphonies which is really notable from the
point of view of style and design was first performed in
Paris in the middle of the war of the Gluckists and
Piccinists. But no great symphony had been written
before, and when Gluck was formulating his theories and
speculating on the possibilities of musical expression, the
art of modern instrumentation was still in its infancy.
Naturally Gluck's management of general effect is not
like Mozart's. His powers as a composer were developed
mainly under the influence of his strong feeling for things
dramatic and poetical, and it was the intensity with which
he felt the situations which gave him musical utterance.
His orchestration has none of the roundness or balance or

maturity of Mozart's. It is unequal and uncertain, and requires humouring in performance to make it produce the effect which is intended. But, like the rest of his work, it is essentially sincere, and its very crudity is sometimes apt to the situations that he required it to illustrate.

His influence upon the history of art in certain directions was great, but not such as might be expected. Upon Italian opera seria he had scarcely any influence at all. It went on its absurdly illogical and undramatic way unmoved. The kind of people who patronised it did not want anything good; they only wanted to be amused. Italian composers were not troubled with convictions as Gluck was, and they have too often liked bad music quite as much as their audiences. Upon French opera the influence of Gluck was more permanent; and his schemes were developed by later composers to grandiose proportions, sometimes with excellent results, sometimes with an unfortunate tendency to emphasise histrionic display, which certainly does not chime with Gluck's refined intentions.

His system was too ideal for the world of his time, and the niche which he occupies is singularly isolated, through the inadequacy of musical means to meet his requirements. His singular energy and clearness of dramatic insight forced a special path for himself out of the direct course of musical progress. It was as though he pushed for himself a special short cut up a very arduous ascent where other men could not follow him. And it was not until music in general had gone by a more circuitous route, which avoided the rocks and precipices, that it finally arrived at a position which made his ideals attainable. No one in his time could pursue the path he had marked out, for no one but himself had sufficient mastery of dramatic expression even to equal his work in that respect, much less to improve upon it.

Though the genuine opera seria of the Italians was not destined to be lifted out of the ruts into which it had fallen for a long while, the scheme which their composers had inaugurated served as the basis upon which composers of the more enduring Teutonic race gradually developed the resources necessary for the achievement of the operatic ideal. Germans had been for some time dominated by Italian influences in every department of art as badly as the Italians themselves; and when Mozart came upon the scene, it is probable that he heard next to nothing in his earlier years which was Teutonic either in style or in name. Italian music reigned supreme in Vienna and Salzburg; and throughout his most impressionable years he constantly imbibed the phraseology, the principles of design, and the artistic methods of Italian composers and their German imitators. He was no reformer by nature, and the immense services he did to art were in no sense either speculative or theoretic, but merely a sort of natural growth; amounting to a general improvement of the texture of things rather than to a marked change either in principles or details. He was gifted with an extraordinarily keen sense of beauty, and with the most astounding natural facility in all things artistic which ever was the lot of man. The inevitable consequence was that he began to see how to improve upon the work of his predecessors in every direction very early; and he was afforded ample opportunities.

Before he was ten years old he had made a triumphal progress through the most important cities in Europe, and had tried his hand at most of the branches of composition; and by the age of twelve he was writing operas for the Italians themselves, and had surpassed most living composers in all departments of artistic workmanship. All his earlier operas were on the usual Italian lines; and

though they show his unusual powers in finished modelling of melody, and skilful management of accompaniment, they do not need any special consideration. The
first really important mark he made was an indirect
result of his visit to Mannheim on the way to Paris in
1777. The town was, and had been for some time, the
centre of the best musical activity in Germany; and it was
here that Mozart first heard refined and careful orchestral
playing, and came into contact with patriotic schemes
for developing national art and national opera. The
experiences he enjoyed during a rather prolonged stay
thoroughly roused him to give his full attention to the
possibilities of orchestral effect; and the enthusiasm for
thoroughness in all departments of art, which possessed
the people of Mannheim, undoubtedly led him to treat
the operatic form of art with more consideration for fitness
and dramatic effect, than it would have occurred to him to
do if he had remained entirely under Italian or Viennese
influence. The first important fruit in the line of opera
was Idomeneo, which he produced three years later (1781)
for the Carnival in Munich, where he had every inducement to distinguish himself; as the taste of the public
was better there than in Vienna, and the resources of the
orchestra and chorus were very large. His libretto was
modelled on an old Italian one which had been used nearly
seventy years before; but this did not affect the quality of
his work, which is so very much richer and better than any
earlier opera of its class that it marks a point in the story
of the art. To begin with, he used an unusually large
orchestra, and he used it in a way which was quite new to
the world. He did not aim at characterisation so much as
Gluck had done, for in that respect Gluck was speculatively
too much ahead of his time. But his method shows far
more spontaneous skill, through his keen feeling for beauty
and variety of tone, and his perfect use of each several in-

strument in the way best suited to its special idiosyncrasies.
Nothing is wasted. No player of a wind instrument merely
blows into his pipe to make a sound to fill up a gap, nor
do the violin players now and then merely draw out an
isolated sound to make a chord complete. Everything is
articulate, finished, full of life; and that without adopting a
contrapuntal manner, or obtrusively putting in figures that
are not wanted and merely distract the attention. Mozart
at this early stage shows himself a completely mature
master of all the practical resources of orchestration; and
in almost every department and every aspect of the work
a like fine artistic sense is shown. The early composers
had to concentrate their attention and almost all their skill
on the solo singer's voice part, and the care which they
bestowed on the rest of their work was mainly to keep
it in the background. Mozart's spontaneous instinct for
artistic fitness brought things to their proper level, and
simultaneously raised the standard of interest in every
respect. Even in the matter of singing and acting the
soloist has to share the honours with the chorus; which is
now brought forward not only to give the requisite mass
of tone and scenic animation to the ends of acts, but
to take an important part in the action throughout.
The chorus becomes a living portion of the scheme, and
is wielded by the composer in a way which shows that he
tried to feel what real people would do in the situations in
which he had to put them, and not what mere theatrical
chorus singers would be doing among the wings and
stage properties. The same story repeats itself again and
again. When any scheme like the presentation of a
stage play has been contrived, and there arises a large
demand for new works, men who supply them get into
the habit of thinking of nothing but the artifices of the
stage. They put the machinery in motion, and all they
succeed in presenting is a property shipwreck, or a stage

murder, or the passion of a prima donna in full sight of
an audience. Mozart showed a superiority to that weakness of the imagination, most notably in his comic scenes
in the later operas. But it is easy to see that in Idomeneo
too he tried to keep in mind the reality of the human
circumstances of which the stage machinery is but the
symbol. Mozart never trespassed through laying too much
stress on expression. It was necessarily quite the reverse,
for he belonged to a formal period, when the machinery
of art claimed a great deal of attention. But within the
limits of formality he often succeeded in infusing true and
sincere human expression, and he used his resources of
colour, rhythm, and melody with perfect relevancy to the
situations. In those respects the distance between his
work and that of the Italians is really enormous. But
there are still a great deal too many of those formalities
which are inevitably brought in to hide the gaps made by
unsolved problems. The arias are too rigid in form, and
the various complete pieces are crudely introduced. The
divisions do not assimilate into a well-moulded whole,
but are separate items, like the old singers' arias, though
so immensely superior to them in intrinsic qualities, and
so much more varied in general character. And, moreover,
a great deal of the dialogue is set in the insupportable
makeshift manner of the middle-period Italian recitative;
which makes an almost insuperable blot in any serious
work in which it occurs. It passes muster in comic works,
because it can be accepted together with other confessions
of human weakness as conceivably humorous. But in a
work of serious interest it breaks the continuity of things
worse than even ordinary speech does; for its chaotic
inanity is such a perversion of the purpose of music that
it becomes far more noticeable than dialogue, which pretends to be nothing more than it is.

Apart from these recitatives, Mozart probably carried

expression as far as was then possible within the limits
by which he was bound. His instinct for design was too
true to allow him to venture upon untried methods which
fitted more closely to the dialogue and to the progress
of the action. He had to repeat his passages, and to take
his "tonic and dominant" quite regularly according to
the laws of form as then understood, and to write set
melodies on familiar lines. He had hardly any experience
of methods of immediate concentrated expression, such as
Bach's mastery of harmony and counterpoint enabled him
to use. And even if he had known how to achieve such
things the types of procedure would not have fitted into
his scheme of art; for they would have betrayed their
incongruity, and thrown the balance of style out of gear.
Art had to go a long way before such amalgamation was
possible. Even Mozart himself was as yet far from the
standard of his greatest symphonies; and, far as Idomeneo
is beyond the standard of any previous Italian operas, and
interesting and rich in artistic power and resource, its
formality and inadequacy as a solution of the operatic
problem is indicated by the fact that it is almost totally
unknown to the musical public.

The national desire for genuine Teutonic opera was
spreading and growing more eager in Mozart's time; and
the Emperor of Austria took up the cause, and invited
him to write a regular German opera. The principal
obstacle was that a national opera, like anything else
in art, had to be built up by slow degrees; and there
was a conspicuous lack of models for style and plan,
and treatment of things dramatic in a German manner.
Keiser's attempts lay too far away in the past, and were
too crude to have much bearing in Mozart's time; and
the only form which had succeeded at all in later times
was the Singspiel, which was little more than a play
with incidental music and songs, very similar to the type

in vogue in England about Purcell's time. These plays
had generally been very slight, and sometimes farcical, so
there was very little in them to serve as a basis for work
of a solid kind.   But such as it was, Mozart accepted
the form as the type to follow in his "Entführung aus
dem Serail."   In the event very little came of it that was
characteristically Teutonic.   The music itself is admirable, and every artistic accessory and detail is managed
.as only Mozart could manage such things at that time.
But the light scenes were in the Italian buffo style, and
the harmonisation and instrumentation and everything else
are in the style Mozart usually employed in Italian opera.
Every one who understands anything about art will
know that this was inevitable; for a man can only work
on the lines and in the terms he is master of.   The most
that Mozart could do was to impart a more genuinely
warm and expressive feeling to a few of the airs, and
in no other respect is any Teutonic flavour discernible.
Mozart for the moment elevated the form of the Singspiel into the regions of loftiest art; but that was not
what a Singspiel audience wanted, and his work was
not characteristically Teutonic enough, either in subject
or style, to enlist the national sympathies; and though
on the whole it succeeded very well, its success was on
the old grounds, and not on the grounds of its being
a satisfactory or complete solution of the problem of
national opera.   Further action in the same direction
was postponed, and Mozart resumed the composition of
Italian operas.   His next effort was the brilliant Nozze
di Figaro, founded on Beaumarchais' play.   It came out
in 1786, and Don Giovanni followed in 1787.   These are
not on such a grand scale as Idomeneo, but they have
the superior attraction of a great deal of real fun, which
is essentially a human element.   The stories of both
Figaro and Don Giovanni are rather trivial and quite

unfit to be taken seriously, but it is easy to follow and
to be amused by all the escapades and scrapes of the Don
and Leporello, and by Figaro and Cherubino and the
rest of the merry throng. They are just as much realities as Mozart's merry tunes; and the necessary stage
conventions do not jar so noticeably as they would do if
the works had often touched upon deeper chords, and
portrayed stronger and more vital emotions. It is just
in those situations where, owing to the nature of his story,
he has to touch on the tragic vein, that the formality
necessarily becomes prominent. Real tragic intensity of
feeling would be quite out of place in such surroundings;
and such sorrows as Elvira's are not in any case capable
of being adequately expressed in the old-fashioned form
of the aria, with its complacent orderly melody, and
mechanical repetition of the same words of sorrow. It
is in such cases that the utter inadequacy of the old
operatic scheme becomes too conspicuously glaring.

The process of development in the right direction is
shown by the way in which Mozart often knits together
a number of movements into a continuous series, especially at the end of an act. This was the way in which
complete assimilation of the musical factors into a composite whole was gradually approached. In some cases,
as in the finales in Figaro, he contrives to make the interchange of dialogue between the characters very rapid for
a long time at a stretch, producing an extremely animated effect. But it illustrates the immaturity of the
operatic form that he still felt it necessary to repeat
his musical phrases again and again to make them lay
hold of the minds of the audience. The lightness of
the subjects he dealt with necessitated his carrying out
every feature of his scheme very simply and spontaneously;
and this device of phrase repetition he used without the
least disguise. He probably borrowed it from the Italian

composers of opera buffa, and it became so much a part
of his system that he employs it in every class of work,
in symphonies and sonatas as well as in operas. The
result is that the works become very easy to follow;
but the practice cannot be said to be a characteristic of
an advanced state of art. Mozart undoubtedly brought
his music into very close connection with the action,
especially in comic scenes. It sometimes fits so perfectly
that it seems as though he had the whole scene before
him, and followed all the by-play and gestures in his
mind while writing. This also was probably a development of the methods of the composers of opera buffa.

Of Mozart's two last Italian operas little need be said.
"Cosi fan tutte" is a comic opera which was written
by order of the Emperor of Austria to an unsatisfactory
libretto, which made the success, which the real brightness of the music might have otherwise obtained, completely impossible. La Clemenza di Tito was an opera
seria of the old kind written for a coronation at Prague
to an old libretto by Metastasio, which had been set by
most of the earlier stock composers before it came to
Mozart's turn, and did not contain any elements which
could inspire him to fresh achievements.

His last operatic work was far more important, for
once again it made him the representative of the German
aspiration to have a national opera. On the previous occasion the experiment had been made under the auspices of
the Austrian Emperor and his court; the new one was
made for an essentially popular audience. The invitation
came from the actor-manager Schikaneder, who had been
catering for the Viennese public for some time with fair
success. He conceived the idea that the German public
would be attracted by a magic opera; and to judge
from the surprising number of magic operas which have
since appeared in Germany, he gauged the Teutonic

disposition in that respect very acutely. The play, which Schikaneder himself prepared and called "Die Zauber-flöte," is almost unintelligible; but it contained some good opportunities for musical effect, and as the interest of the play was supposed to centre round some mystic secrets of Freemasonry, which at that time were especially interesting to the German mind, it was not altogether inappropriate that it should be unintelligible to the general and the feminine public. Mozart's setting was again mainly Italian in style, but he infused a degree of dignified and noble sentiment into certain parts of the work which was quite unlike what was to be met with in Italian operas; and in the end, between his music and the mystery of the play, the work became a spontaneous success of a pronounced description, and was taken up very eagerly all over Germany.

It can hardly be said, however, that it quite satisfied the aspirations after a national opera, but it was decidedly a step of some importance in that direction. The actual solution of the problem depended on conditions which at that time were unattainable, for the national style for operatic purposes had yet to be found. What little there was of distinctly Teutonic style had not been applied in such a manner; neither had the accessories, such as the appropriate type of harmonisation and of accompaniment, been cultivated sufficiently to be available on such a large scale as opera. German melodic ideas would not fit to the conventional types of harmonic accompaniment used for Italian melody, any more than a Gothic roof and steeple would fit on to an Ionic building. The racial musical instincts of Teutons and Italians were different. The instinct of Italians was all in favour of beauty and simplicity. They cared little for intensely vivid expression of any kind, and their most natural method of utterance was melody, and the forms of accompaniment which supported melody in the very simplest manner. They were perfectly content to hear the same formulas again and again. For instance, the same formulas of harmony, and even of melody, were used for the last few bars before the cadence in endless different arias and scenas; and the same successions of chords served for the song of the lady bewailing her murdered father and for that of the gentleman rejoicing over the success of a love suit. The bent of Germans, on the other hand, was not so much towards beauty as towards expression and character. Their very type of beauty was different from that of the Italians. The Italians looked for beauty of externals, and the Germans for beauty of thought. The instinct for beauty of thought comes out analogously in their artists' work. To the eye there is not much beauty of externals in Albert Durer and Holbein, but of expression and thought there is ample to engage the mind and the sensibilities again and again. So it was in music from the earliest time, in Schütz's work as in Bach's and in Brahms'. And though melody was a factor in the German scheme, characteristic harmony became one also very early. And as harmony has more power of immediate expression than melody, the Teutonic nature was drawn towards it more and more. And as polyphonic treatment enhances the capacity of harmony for expression, and gives vitality to its inner details, the Teutonic mind was also drawn in that direction. Polyphony is melody multiplied, and represents the composite nature of man's character and man's moods and motives of action in a way that mere single melody can never do. The Germans having the feeling and instinct for these higher things, it was clearly impossible for their ideals of operatic art to be satisfied with such immature conditions as are represented in Mozart's operas, admirable though the works themselves are as representing the Italian conception of art. But though Mozart, owing to his circumstances, and the state of art at that time, could not satisfy the full aspirations of the Germans in their own field, he raised Italian opera to its highest point. His more earnest German surroundings, and his experiences at Mannheim, led his impressionable disposition to the full development of his marvellous aptitude for orchestration; to a higher, richer, and more characteristic standard of melody; to a wider range of harmony, and more perfect modelling and management of design, than had ever been attained by Italians. In all these things he enriched the art to an enormous extent, and left it more highly organised in nearly all its various departments than when he took it up.

CHAPTER XI.

THE MIDDLE STAGE OF "SONATA" FORM.

THE principles upon which self-dependent instrumental music was being developed in the greater part of the eighteenth century were quite new to mankind. Before men developed the capacity for understanding the classification of harmony in connection with certain tonal centres, such principles were altogether inconceivable. But when once the idea of harmonic centralisation was well established, progress in readiness to grasp the artistic purpose of the composer in disposing his groups of harmony so as to convey the impression of design, was extraordinarily rapid; as may be judged by the difference in obviousness between a concerto of Vivaldi's and a symphony of Mozart's.

It may be admitted, parenthetically, that there was a considerable falling off of style in instrumental music when it came more decisively under operatic influences. The standard of Tartini and his fellow-violinists is much higher than that of most of their successors; who infused the fashionable style of opera music into their instrumental works, to gratify the feeble taste of their fashionable pupils. But the development of the great branch of instrumental music did not follow in a straight line from Corelli and Tartini and such masters, but was the result of a process of filtration through the minds of all sorts and conditions of composers. Haydn and Mozart, and Beethoven in his turn, were in their younger days influenced by the flood of all sorts of music which came

under their notice. And though their higher sense of
style and expression rejected the more trivial and superficial things that they heard, their own work became a
sort of instinctive generalisation, which was based on
the general average of all that attracted their attention.
Everything has its degree and proportion in such matters,
but great work is always the sum of an immense range
of influences, and not the product of the impressions
produced by a few isolated pieces of perfection. Thus
in painting, if a man study only the manner in which
some single master overcomes some special difficulty, his
own treatment will probably be only a reflection of that
master's work. But if he studies the methods of several,
and finds the particular excellencies of each, and grasps
their principles of application, he has enlarged his own
resources; and then he will not merely reproduce the
external aspects of the works of one man, but will find
out how to express his own individuality in terms which
are the fruit of wider understanding of technique.

The special department in which the sum of all sorts
of experiments was leading to a satisfactory establishment of principles, in the early part of the eighteenth
century, was the extremely important one of harmonic
design. Musical instinct was leading men to give the
best of their powers to the development of the types of
design now familiar in sonatas, and out of a multiplicity
of experiments Mozart and Haydn, and their lesser contemporaries, gave their verdict very decisively in favour
of a type of movement which looks at first most peculiar
and enigmatical; but which not only proved to be most
elastic and satisfying in practice, but becomes amply intelligible when the course of its history is taken into
consideration.

The aim of composers was first to establish a point of
departure; and then setting out from it to find an orderly

series of contrasts of as many and various kinds as the art allowed, and to dispose them in such a way as to make each step lead onwards, till a circuit was completed by returning to and re-establishing the original starting-point. The first form in which this principle of design is perceptible is the type of ordinary dance tune, which proceeded from a given point to a contrasting point, and laid sufficient stress upon that point to emphasise the contrast, and then worked back again. When this type arrived at any degree of definite organisation, the most noticeable feature was the division into two fairly equal halves, with a close in the key of contrast at the end of the first half. Composers aimed at distributing their materials in such a framework so as to give the strongest emphasis to the most essential points, and to make the ideas lay hold of the mind. The requirements of average human beings were best consulted by making the beginning of the first half coincide in musical material with the beginning of the second half, and the end of the first half coincide with the end of the second half; since the beginnings and ends of phrases are always most easily retained by the mind. The portions between the beginnings and the endings were generally rather vague and indefinite, though composers who had any artistic sense tried to keep the style strictly relevant throughout, and to maintain any rhythm which had presented itself definitely at the outset. The plan of a considerable majority of movements remained on these lines until the end of the polyphonic period of instrumental music; and the movements in the most artistic suites and partitas have very little more in the way of design.

When harmonic principles came to be cultivated in sonatas the same principles were adopted; but, in accordance with harmonic requirements, the passages which coincided in musical material were lengthened, and made more definite, both in respect of melody and rhythm. And at length the passage in the contrasting key, which had originally been little more than a cadence, was expanded to a length fully equal to the passage in the principal key; and it was frequently marked by a second subject or new idea, which became the distinguishing feature of the key of contrast. The ideas presented in the principal contrasting key were repeated in the second half of the movement in positions corresponding to the arrangement of the earlier form; the first idea coming in the key of contrast, and the second in the home key. The part in between the two subjects in the second half began to expand very early; both to widen the scope of the modulations, and because composers' instincts told them that there still was a lack of contrast through the exact regularity and definiteness of the main divisions. They felt that a contrast to this excess of definiteness was wanted, and they found it in the process of breaking up the subjects into their constituent figures and distributing them in progressions which had an appearance of being unsystematic.

By the time the movement had expanded to such proportions, the mere restatement of the second subject at the end was barely sufficient to give a comfortable reassurance of being safe home in the original key. And, moreover, as the progress of music in general was tending to a much more decisive recognition of the musical subjects and ideas themselves as the aim and end of things, it seemed strange that the musical idea, which occupied such prominence by reason of its appearing at the outset, should be so neglected in the latter part of the movement. So it became customary to repeat the first subject as well as the second at the end of all things in the principal key. Then it appeared that there was too much of this first subject, so its formal repetition at the beginning of the second half was dropped, though it still often appears in its old place even in modern works of the sonata order.

The whole process of development may be seen at a glance in a mechanical scheme. Taking the letters to represent the musical material, and the numerals to represent the principal keys, and the double bar to represent the point where the movement is divided into two portions, the process was mainly as follows:—

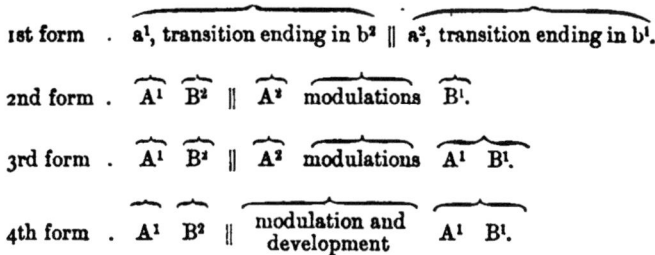

1st form . a^1, transition ending in b^2 ‖ a^2, transition ending in b^1.

2nd form . A^1 B^2 ‖ A^2 modulations B^1.

3rd form . A^1 B^2 ‖ A^2 modulations A^1 B^1.

4th form . A^1 B^2 ‖ modulation and development A^1 B^1.

In the early sonatas both halves of the movement were played twice. As artistic feeling developed, the repetition of the second half was frequently dispensed with, but the repetition of the first half was maintained, mainly to help the mind to grasp firmly the principle of contrast between the two keys. In modern times the repetition of the first half is also commonly dispensed with, because the musical instinct has become so quick to grasp any indication of design that it no longer requires to have such things insisted on; and also because the progress of music towards a more passionately emotional phase makes it noticeably anomalous to go through the same exciting crises twice over. Beethoven's practice illustrates this point very happily; for in the less directly emotional sonatas in which design is particularly emphasised, he gives the usual direction for the repetition of the first half; as in the early sonatas, when the possibility of dispensing with such conventions had not dawned upon him, and in the first movements of such later sonatas as the Waldstein (Opus 53), and the one in F♯ (Opus 78). In movements which are so decisively emotional and expressive as the first movements of the Appassionata (F minor, Opus 57), of the E minor (Opus 90), of the A major (Opus 101), and the E major (Opus 109), the repetition is dispensed with, and the movements are made as continuous as possible from end to end; so as to hide the formal element and guard against the mind being distracted by it.

The prominence which Italian operatic influence gave to melody and to superficial views of art led people to regard the principle of design as consisting of a first tune in one key and a second tune in a contrasting key, and certain developments based on them to follow and complete the scheme. But in fact the musical subject is one thing and the design is another. The "subject," as it is called, had to have a form of its own to begin with; and though some composers, working under operatic influences, did write long continuous passages of melody which successively represent the principal key and the key of contrast, the acuter instinct of true instrumental composers generally aimed at short and incisive figures for their musical ideas, which indicated the spirit and mood of their work, and made it lay hold of the mind quickly; and they completed their musical sentences, which represented each essential key, by repeating such figures in different positions in the scale or with ingenious variations of detail which gave them extra interest. The necessity for making the essential keys clear led to various interesting and probably unconscious devices. The trick of alternating the characteristic harmonies of tonic and dominant in the subject is so familiar that it requires no discussion. More singular is the profusion of examples of different epochs, in which the principal musical idea is conveyed in terms of the tonic chord of the movement, which is the essential point from which the outset is made. A few exampl· s may be noted in the following works. Scarlatti's Sonata in G major—

the principal allegro movement of Tartini's Sonata in minor (Didone Abandonnata)—

Paradisi's Sonata in D major, Mozart's Sonata in C minor, Beethoven's Sonata in F minor (No. 1), the last movement of his Sonata in C♯ minor; the first of his Sonata Appassionata, his Overture Leonora (No. 3), and Weber's Sonata in A♭. The instinctive object of the composer in all cases is to make the whereabouts of his starting-point very definitely understood. Nearly all the finest subjects in existence have some such principle inherent in their structure. But the subject itself is not the form, nor is it itself a part of the form, but the idea which is put into form. It is the musical fact of melody, or rhythm, or harmony which conveys the mood or thought which the composer wishes to express. The mould in which it is cast is a different thing. The idea may be expressed in terms of the tonic chord, but the tonic chord is not the idea. On the other hand, the tonic chord is a part, and a very essential part, of the scheme of design; and upon its being understood the feeling for the design of the movement as a whole depends; but the chord is not an idea till it is vitalised by rhythm or melody. Similarly, the design in a picture does not consist of the subject, but of the way the subject is dealt with. The

design consists of the position the figures or details occupy
in the picture, and of the general disposition of colours
and lines and contours. This point requires to be emphasised, because it is not possible to understand what
Beethoven did for art, or the meaning of all that came
after his time, without realising the distinction between
subject and design.

As a matter of fact, there often are a great number of
subjects in each of the divisions which are generally
spoken of as *the* first or *the* second subject; and in the
most mature form of sonata movement there is almost
always a special third subject whose function and character is strongly illustrative of the harmonic principle of
design. The first key is always easily indicated, because
it comes fresh to the mind ; but the second or contrasting
key requires more management and more establishing,
because the impression of the first has to be obliterated.
For that reason the second principal idea is generally
put into very definite and clear terms of tonality, and
is often followed by numerous passages obviously indi-
cative of the key; and finally, when the period which
represents the contrasting key comes to an end, the
wisest composers confirmed that key strongly by introducing a new subject of slight but often particularly
attractive character, which is entirely modelled upon a
group of chords forming a complete cadence. The function of this subject essentially is to call attention to the
particular point in the design where the division representing the contrasting key comes to an end ; and the harmonic
formula on which it is founded is always peculiarly simple.

The whole scheme of this type of movement, which
was fairly established by the time Haydn and Mozart
began their work, implies the following general purposes.
The first part of the movement aimed at definiteness in
every respect—definiteness of contrast of key, definiteness

of subject, definiteness of regular balancing groups of bars
and rhythms, definiteness of progressions. By the time
this first division is over the mind has had enough of such
definiteness, and wants a change. The second division,
therefore, represents the breaking up of the subjects into
their constituent elements of figure and rhythm, the obli-
teration of the sense of regularity by grouping the bars
irregularly, and by moving constantly from key to key to
give the sense of artistic confusion, which, however, is always
regulated by some inner but disguised principle of order.
When the mind has gone through enough of the pleasing
sense of bewilderment—the sense that has made riddles
attractive to the human creature from time immemorial—
the scheme is completed by resuming the orderly methods
of the first division, and firmly re-establishing the principal key, which has been carefully avoided since the
commencement.

From the point of view of design every moment and
every step from beginning to end should have its own
inherent justification and reason for existence. Each
concord must have its due relation to its context, each
discord must have its resolution, each statement its
counter-statement. From the point of view of the subject or idea every moment is made engrossing by the
distribution and coherent relevancy of the melodies and
rhythms employed, by the variety of the situations and
the lights in which they are placed, and by the development of the climaxes which are inherent in the very
principle of their structure. In the most perfect movements there should be no moment when the principle of
design is lost sight of, or the ideas cease to be articulate.
But it must be confessed that there have been only two
or three composers in the history of the world who have
had such complete hold of their resources as to produce
movements which are entirely perfect from end to end

from every point of view; and even these rarest geniuses sometimes nod.

The opportunities which this peculiar form has offered to composers are so extraordinarily rich that it has been uniformly adopted for sonatas, symphonies, overtures, quartetts, and all forms of chamber music, and sometimes for small lyrical pieces. The development of self-dependent instrumental music almost centres round it, and it gives special character to the long period of art stretching from the second quarter of the eighteenth century till the advent of Schumann and Chopin, and the expressive romanticists of the latter days. It is especially the type of design used for the first movements of sonatas and symphonies; as it is peculiarly suitable for the intellectual and more highly organised kinds of music. It was sometimes used also for the emotional slow movements, but it was more usual to adopt a simpler type of form in them—something similar to the old type of aria, or to the rondo form. And this same rondo form was also found suitable for last movements, as it lends itself happily to light and gay moods; and the constant alternation of definite tunes gives easy animation to the general effect. As a rule, the rondo form is not very suitable to the expression of a very high order of music; but the artistic ingenuity of composers managed to make the form interesting by throwing the various sections into groups, and distributing the subject-matter so as to give enhanced interest to the rather primitive type of structure.

By the time that Haydn and Mozart arrived upon the scene this scheme of instrumental music was fairly established, but it had been used by most composers before them crudely, obviously, and mechanically. While the form was new it was enjoyable as a novelty, and as a mere piece of mechanical ingenuity, and the perverting influence of the predominating operatic taste prevented composers from applying any faculties they might have possessed to the improvement of the details. It was the superior artistic instinct of Mozart and Haydn which led them to give attention to such things, and to develop and organise the system of design to a very high degree of perfection.

The circumstances which gave the two great composers their respective bents were simple and fortunate. Though both were Southern Germans and Roman Catholics in religion, their circumstances and early associations were widely different. Mozart being the child of a professional musician of considerable attainments and musical culture, was surrounded by artistic conditions from his babyhood; and most of the music with which he came into contact was of an artistically organised kind from the first, while his studies were always wisely directed by his very sensible parent. But the circumstances were not favourable to the development of personal character, and as far as his art was concerned he was almost entirely relieved of the individual struggle to ascertain things and make up his mind about them for himself, which has such important results in developing the individuality of the artistic worker. Haydn, on the other hand, was the son of a rustic wheelwright; a real son of the people—whose first musical influences were folk-tunes, whose experience of artistic music came late, and who had, like Bach and Beethoven and many others of the great ones, to work out his own musical salvation. And, to emphasise the difference between the two men, where Mozart had been entirely subject to Italian influences from the first, and found his most congenial model in such a type as John Christian Bach—the Italian Bach—Haydn by good fortune or happy instinct took for his model Philip Emmanuel Bach, the only prominent composer in Europe who retained any touch of the old traditions of Northern Germany, and some of the sincere and noble spirit of his father, which spared not to make everything as characteristic and full of vitality as circumstances allowed. The result is that Haydn is throughout as Teutonic in spirit and manner as it was possible to be in those times, and that most of his work has a high degree of personal characteristic vitality; while Mozart, with more delicate artistic perception, more sense of beauty, a much higher gift of technique and more general facility, is comparatively deficient in individuality, and hardly shows any trace of Teutonism in style from first to last.

The careers of the two composers interlaced very peculiarly, and at different times they exerted influence upon one another. Haydn is commonly held to have exerted some influence upon Mozart at first, and when the latter had progressed rapidly to his highest achievements and had passed away his work undoubtedly influenced Haydn. Though Haydn was twenty-four years older than Mozart, he did not get well into his work much before the younger composer; for the circumstances of his life necessarily delayed him. He appears to have begun writing symphonies at the age of twenty-seven, in 1759, whereas Mozart began at the age of eight, in 1764; so their musical periods really coincide more nearly than the differences of their ages might seem to make probable.

After the severe trials of his youth, Haydn's circumstances changed, and became almost the most favourable ever enjoyed by a composer. After a short engagement to a Bohemian Count Morzin, for whom he wrote his first symphony, he was engaged for many years as Capellmeister to successive princes of the wealthy and ardently musical family of Esterhazy. In their establishment he not only had every encouragement to write the best music he could in every form suitable to instrumental effect, but he also had a complete band always ready to play new symphonies whenever wanted, and an opera-house and an opera company for which he might (and did) write operas. Such favourable circumstances account for the wonderful number of symphonies which he wrote. But it is more to the purpose to note the wonderful growth of his musical powers, and even of the standard of his ideas from youth onwards. His progress is a little epitome of the history of musical evolution. His early quartetts were of the slightest description; short, undeveloped, and not very interesting in detail. His symphonies were exactly of the standard adopted by the average composer of such things all over the musical world; and not notably better in the matter of scoring than John Christian Bach's. There is character and force in them, but the management of the orchestral resources is stiff, and the treatment of the wind instruments mechanical. His development was quite gradual, and he did not arrive at anything particularly notable till after Mozart had achieved his greatest work, and had become in his turn the older man's leader.

Mozart, as above indicated, began writing symphonies as well as operas at the age of eight, and some of his early work is skilful, neat, and artistic. But it was not till after his experiences at Mannheim in 1777 and 1778, so often alluded to, that his full powers in the line of instrumental music were called into play. The musical traditions at Mannheim were at that time probably the best in Europe, and their effect upon Mozart was immediate and salutary. For when he moved on to Paris in 1778, in company with some of the Mannheim instrumentalists, he wrote, for performance there, the first of his symphonies which occupies an important place in musical history. For artistic delicacy in detail, general interest, skilful use of orchestral resources, variety in quality and force of tone, no symphony had ever yet appeared which in any way approached to its standard. But even this by no means

represents his highest achievement in the symphonic
line. The symphony written for Prague in 1786 is a
still further advance, and throws the Parisian one into
the shade in every respect. The general quality of the
musical thoughts is finer, richer, and more interesting;
while the purely orchestral effects, especially in the slow
movement, are among the most successful things of the
kind he ever achieved. And finally the three great symphonies which he wrote in Vienna in 1788 represent his
highest level in idea and in every distinguished quality of
art he ever attained to. They are the crown of his life's
work; for in them he more nearly escapes the traditional
formulas of the Italian opera than in any other form of
instrumental art he employed except the quartetts; and
their general standard is nobler and more genuinely
vigorous than that of any other of his works except
the Requiem. In management of orchestral effect these
latter symphonies must have been a revelation compared
with the standard of the works of his contemporaries and
predecessors. His treatment of design had also become
much more free and interesting. The introduction of
short subtle excursions out of his principal keys in unexpected directions; the variations introduced into his subjects
on repetition, by altering the scoring and the actual melodic
and harmonic details, and many other devices which infuse
new interest into the obviousness of familiar procedure,
show a much greater concentration of artistic faculty than
had been usual with him. The general treatment is harmonic, but of more expressive character than in his operas;
and though the designs are often helped out by conventional formulas which were the common property of all
composers in those days, the general mastery of design is
almost perfect. Haydn commonly receives the credit of
establishing the symphony form on a secure basis; and
no doubt he did a great deal for it. But the first

symphonies which appeared in the world which still justly
keep a hold on the affections of average musical people,
as well as highly educated musicians, are those of Mozart.
Next in importance after his symphonies come his quartetts.
In this form Haydn again was the pioneer, but it fell to
Mozart to produce the first really great and perfect
examples. This most refined and delicate form of art
had come into prominence rather suddenly. It was cultivated with some success by other composers besides
Mozart and Haydn, such as Boccherini and Dittersdorf.
But the quartetts which Mozart produced in 1782 and de-
dicated to Haydn are still among the select few of highest
value in existence. In a form in which the actual possibilities are so limited, and in which the responsibilities towards
each individual solo instrument are so great, where the
handling requires to be so delicate and so neatly adjusted
in every detail, Mozart's artistic skill stood him in good
stead. The great difficulty was the exact ascertainment
of the style of treatment best suited to the group of four
solo instruments. It was easy to write contrapuntal
movements of the old kind for them, but in the new
harmonic style and in form of a sonata order it was
extremely difficult to adjust the balance between one
instrument and another, so that subordination should
not subside into blank dulness, nor independence of inner
parts become obtrusive. Mozart among his many gifts
had a great sense of fitness, and he adapted himself completely to the necessities of the situation; without adopting
a polyphonic manner, and without sacrificing the independence of his instruments.

Instrumental music was at this time branching out into
so many forms that it is not possible to follow his treatment of all kinds of different work. The least important
are his pianoforte works, such as sonatas and variations,
most of which were evidently written without his putting

his heart into them, probably for amateur pupils. There are, of course, very important exceptions, and some interesting experiments which clearly indicate a genuinely earnest humour, such as the two remarkable fantasias in C minor.

Haydn in his turn, without being dependent on Mozart or copying his manner, only came to his finest achievements after Mozart's career was over. Then in the year 1791 began the wonderful series of symphonies which he wrote at the invitation of the violinist and concert-manager Salomon for performance in London. These are as much the crown of his fame as the Prague and Vienna symphonies are of Mozart's. The crudity of his earlier orchestral writing has entirely disappeared; and though he never succeeds in getting such a perfectly mellow equal tone as Mozart's, he treats all his instruments with absolute freedom and fitness. The old traditions sometimes peep out again in rather long solos for wind instruments, and long passages for small groups of instruments in contrast to the "*tuttis;*" but everything is highly characteristic, clear, definite, and mature. On the whole, the treatment inclines to be a little more polyphonic than Mozart's; which accounts for the sound of the instruments not assimilating in the mass of tone quite so well. It was more natural for Mozart to think of the harmonies which supported the melodies in terms of neatly contrived figures of accompaniment, where Haydn, with Teutonic impulse, would incline to think of his mass of tone as divided into various melodic lines. But the shades of difference are so delicate, and each composer is so far alternately harmonic and contrapuntal in turn, that it would be unwise to lay too much stress on this point. Mozart achieves a degree of beauty in his slow movements to which Haydn does not attain; but in the solid allegros Haydn is more genuinely vigorous than Mozart.

In the minuet movements—which form an important addition to their scheme—it is difficult to award the palm. Mozart's are certainly the most popular, but Haydn's dance tunes have some of the ring that comes of his lineage; which indeed is apparent through almost all his work. Even to the last there is a flavour of rusticity about it. His humour and his merriment are those of the simple honest peasant, while Mozart's is the wit of a man of the world.

The crisis which Mozart and Haydn represent is so important that the nature of musical advance made by them in the instrumental line may here be fitly summed up. Before their time, the only two branches in which first-rate and mature work of the harmonic kind had been done were the violin sonatas written chiefly by the great Italian violinists and their pupils in other countries, and the clavier sonatas. The scope of movements was small and without much development; and the ideas even in the best examples were rather indefinite. By the end of their time instrumental art had branched out into a very large number of distinct and complete forms; such as symphonies, concertos, quartetts, trios, and sonatas for violin and clavier. The style appropriate to each had been more or less ascertained, and the schemes of design had been perfectly organised for all self-dependent instrumental music. Both Haydn and Mozart had immensely improved in the power of finding characteristic subjects, and in deciding the type of subject which is best fitted for instrumental music. The difference in that respect between their early and later works is very marked. They improved the range of the symphonic cycle of movements by adding the minuet and trio to the old group of three movements; thereby introducing definite and undisguised dance movements to follow and contrast with the central cantabile slow

movement. Between them they had completely transformed the treatment of the orchestra. They not only
enlarged it and gave it greater capacity of tone and
variety, but they also laid the solid foundations of those
methods of art which have become the most characteristic
and powerful features in the system of modern music.
Even in detail the character of music is altered; all
phraseology is made articulate and definite; and the
minutiæ which lend themselves to refined and artistic
performance are carefully considered, without in any way
diminishing the breadth and freedom of the general
effect. There is hardly any branch or department of art
which does not seem to have been brought to high
technical perfection by them; and if the world could
be satisfied with the ideal of perfectly organised simplicity, without any great force of expression, instrumental art might well have stopped at the point to which
they brought it.

CHAPTER XII.

THE PERFECT BALANCE OF EXPRESSION AND DESIGN.

THE style and intrinsic qualities of music so faithfully reflect the state of human affairs at the time in which it is produced, that it becomes a sort of symbol of the spirit of the world. At the end of the eighteenth century, in things quite independent of art, society in general had arrived at a crisis in secular affairs which inspired men with· a fervour of spirit analogous to the fervour of religious enthusiasm which had sprung up at the time of the Reformation. In certain senses the new ardour was akin to the old. For it was the same protest against the conventions and formalities by which the true spirit of things was hidden, and the development of man's nature and aspirations checked and thwarted. The spirit of the old uprising was illustrated in its highest aspect by the sincerity, depth, and nobility of sentiment of J. S. Bach, and by the best utterances of Handel; and the spirit of the modern uprising found its first adequate musical expression in the work of Beethoven.

As has often been pointed out, a period of art in which rich and powerful expression is possible must necessarily be preceded by a long period in which the resources of design and the methods of artistic treatment are developed. Artistic matters are on no different footing in that respect from the ordinary work of everyday life. Inspiration without means at its disposal will no more enable a man to write a symphony than to build a

ship or a cathedral. No doubt a primeval savage might
be inspired with feelings very much like those of some
modern composers; but the means and the knowledge
how to express these feelings in terms of art are
lacking.   All artistic effort which is worth anything
tends to enlarge such means; and the whole history of
the arts is mainly a continuous effort of artistically
minded human creatures to make the means and the
methods for the expression of the inner impulses richer
and more perfect.   It is a pure accident that when the
means become plentiful and the methods very well understood, many men arise who have a great gift for using these
means and methods without any of that personal impulse
of inner feeling to express themselves which is the primal
motive of all their labour.   The mere management of
design is much easier than the management of expressive
utterance.   Indeed the fact is familiar that the men who
have most to say that is worth saying find the greatest
difficulty in saying anything at all.   A man who has
a genuine impulse to say something beyond common
thought has generally to enlarge the phraseology of the
art or language in which he speaks; and those who cannot
wait for the development of the phraseology required by
the nature of their thoughts, must inevitably remain at
least partially unintelligible to their fellow-creatures.

In music the case is very clearly illustrated by the
results of the many attempts to achieve ideal expression
before the means were adequate.   Human nature is liable
to be impatient of the slow development of resources, and
often breaks out into resentment at having to wait so
many centuries for the consummation of obvious aims.
Monteverde, Purcell, and Gluck are types of those eager
spirits who are impatient of the slow march of things,
and want to find a short cut to their artistic ideals—
just as impatient political enthusiasts long to establish a

millennium before they have organised their human beings
into a fit state to live in it. Such ardent and genuine
composers as they were saw rightly that art is not an
end but a means, and having much more natural feeling
for expression than for the purely artistic side of things,
they tried to make sluggish time move faster, and to
attain their ideal artistic region without the preliminary
of following the long road that led there. The world
nevertheless owes them great thanks; for though men may
be mistaken in hoping too much, progress would be even
slower than it is if no one were capable of heroic mistakes.
Gluck pointed out the danger of accepting conventions
as solutions of artistic problems, and he kept the vital
artistic questions alive. But the slow laws of development had to go on all the same, and in reality it was
just as fortunate that Mozart was by gifts, training,
and circumstances a follower of the old methods, as that
Gluck was consumed with a passionate ardour to have
done with them. At that particular moment in the
history of art the man who was most wanted was not
one with a strong personality or marked individuality of
style and feeling, but one who could look at art mainly·
from the artistic point of view, and with the highest
sense of beauty of effect devote himself to the special
development of technique.

Mozart, in this case, represents the type of man who
is contented with the average progress of things, and finds
no necessity to aim at anything more novel than the doing
of what comes to him to be done in the very best manner
he can. His best manner was the best of its kind, but it
was not final. Even without Gluck and Haydn by his side
the necessary preliminaries would not have been fully complete. They did for characteristic style what he did mainly
for the organisation of melody, colour, and design. And
when those various phases of art which they represented

had been put into practical shape, the resources of the composer who was to come were enormously enlarged.

The superiority of Beethoven's point of vantage to Mozart's is equal to the sum of all the differences between the state of art when Mozart took up his work at the age of eight, and the state at which it had arrived at the end of his career. Besides the difference in opportunities, there were immense differences in the type of man and his circumstances. Beethoven came of the more tenacious northern stock, partly Dutch and partly German; and he had the good fortune to be obliged to cultivate self-dependence very early, and to make acquaintance with J. S. Bach's works at a time when he was sufficiently impressionable to profit by them. His youthful experiences in Bonn were by no means of the smoothest and pleasantest. He had a good deal to endure in his home life that was harsh and unlovely, and he had to endure a good deal of second-rate music while playing in the local opera band. By the former his character was formed; by the latter the most obvious principles of design were strongly impressed into his organisation. Like most artists whose spur is more in themselves than in natural artistic facilities, he was very slow to come to any artistic achievement. It is almost a law of things that men whose artistic personality is very strong, and who touch the world by the greatness and the power of their expression, come to maturity comparatively late, and sometimes grow greater all through their lives. So it was with Bach, Gluck, Beethoven, and Wagner. While men whose aims are more purely artistic, and whose main spur is artistic facility, come to the point of production early, and do not grow much afterwards. Such composers as Mozart and Mendelssohn succeeded in expressing themselves brilliantly at a very early age; but their technical facility was out of proportion to the individuality and force of human nature,

and therefore there is no such surprising difference between the work of their later years and the work of
their childhood as there is in the case of Beethoven and
Wagner.

In Beethoven's nature there was an extraordinarily
keen sense for design, but there was also a very powerful
impulse towards expression. In his earliest days he
seems to waver from one point of view to another.
Most of his early works follow the lines which had
become familiar, and show little change from the artistic
attitude of Mozart or Haydn. But every now and then,
even in the early days at Bonn, the spirit of adventure
possesses him, and then some surprising feat, prefiguring
the achievements of his best days, makes its appearance; such a stroke as the end of the Coda of the Righini
variations, which presents a device which he carried out
more effectually and for more expressive purposes in the
Coriolan Overture. But these sudden revelations of the
spirit that was within him are at first only spasmodic,
and he subsides again after an outbreak of genius into the
grave deportment of the formal period. But from many
indications it can be judged that mere composition as
a purely artistic operation did not come easily to him.
Haydn's want of sympathy with him, and the well-known
verdict of the theorist Albrechtsberger, alike point to the
fact that he was not born to write without an emotional
or intellectual spur. The moment in the history of music
appears to have been reached, when its great resources
were ready to be used for expressive ends of a new type,
and Schubert and Weber were soon due to illustrate the
wide spread of new impulses; but it was allotted to Beethoven to lead the van. And unlike them he was to do his
work within the limits of the old designs of the Sonata
type; by grasping the innermost nature of their principles,
and expanding them to the utmost that they would bear.

It is indeed the most characteristic feature of Beethoven's work that the greater part, and the best of it all, is cast in the form of the sonata, which Haydn and Mozart had organised to so high a degree of perfection as pure design. Beethoven could not have expressed himself adequately within the conditions of perfect design—which his instincts truly told him was an absolute necessity of art—without making use of a form whose principles were fully understood. It was his good fortune that the sonata form had been so perfectly organised, and that the musical public had been made so perfectly familiar with it, that they were ready to follow every suggestion and indication of the principle of form; and even to grasp what he aimed at when he purposely presumed upon their familiarity with it, to build fresh subtleties and new devices upon the well-known lines; and sometimes even to emphasise the points by making progressions in directions which seemed to ignore them. Beethoven had a great gift for extemporisation; and there are many subtle devices in his work that look as if he had tested the power of his audiences to follow his points by actual observation. Like Scarlatti, he often seems to play upon his audience, and to follow the processes that will be going on in their minds; and so well to forecast the very things that they will expect to happen, that he can make sure of having the pleasure of puzzling them by doing something else. But in order to put into practice all the multitudinous possibilities he could foresee, he had to take a form which his audience would thoroughly understand. And this is one of the many reasons for the preponderance of the sonata type in his works.

This preponderance is most marked in the early part of his career. His first period, as it is sometimes called, extends to about Opus 50, and to about the thirty-fourth

year of his life. His first thirty-one works were all of
the sonata order, and the majority of them actually
solo pianoforte sonatas. He did not attempt orchestral
work till he wrote the concertos in C and B♭ which
stand as Opus 15 and 19, but of which the latter was
the earliest. The famous septuor, which is a large
combination of solo instruments, and implies use of
orchestral colour, is Opus 20; and the first symphony
was Opus 21, and was not written till he was twenty-
nine. In this early period there are some very notable
outbreaks of the genuine characteristic Beethoven, as
before mentioned, and they grow more frequent as his
powers grow more mature. The Kreutzer Sonata for violin
and pianoforte has all the traits of the completely great
Beethoven. Its introduction is one of the things that no
one else has approached in its way for both subtlety of
design and expression; and the splendid energy and passion
of the allegro, and the extraordinary beauty of the theme
and variations, are fully up to his best standard of work.
After Opus 50 there comes a sudden flood of works which
are among the greatest treasures of musical art. The brilliant Waldstein Sonata is Opus 53; close upon it comes
the first symphony which is genuinely great in all aspects,
the Eroica, completed in 1804; then one of the most
impulsive and passionate of the sonatas, that in F minor,
Opus 57; then the delicate G major Concerto, with the
extraordinary slow movement, instinct with the dramatic
spirit of the very best moments of Gluck; the Rasou-
moffski Quartetts, Opus 59; the B♭ Symphony; the
Violin Concerto; the rugged Overture to Coriolan; the
C minor Symphony, which is the concentrated essence of
the individual Beethoven of that time; the Pastoral Symphony, which breathes most faithfully his ardent love of
nature and woods and all things health-giving to the
human mind; his one opera, Fidelio; the first Concerto

S

in E♭, justly called the Emperor; the Quartett in E♭; the romantic.Seventh Symphony, and the playful Eighth Symphony, which he called his little one; and the Trio in B♭, Opus 97. But as his Opus numbers pass into the nineties a change begins to be discernible in his style, especially in the Quartett in F minor, Opus 95. The warmth of expression, and the spontaneous flow of energetic thought which marks the middle period, begin to give way before the influx of moods that are at once sadder, more concentrated, and more reflective. By that time—about his fortieth year—troubles of many kinds were beginning to tell upon Beethoven's sensitive disposition. The iron had entered into his soul, and it made him dive deeper into things human. Some of the most divinely and serenely beautiful of all his conceptions belong to this third period, but they are attended by moods which reveal his suffering and his determination to endure. There is more thought and more experience of life in this period; and if less of geniality than in his middle life, an infinitely wider range of feeling, characteristic expression, and style. It seems as if his art had widened out from being the mere expression of his own wonderful personality, and had become the interpreter of the innermost joys and sorrows of all human creatures. In order to find expression for all that he had in his mind, he had to expand his resources of design and expression even further than in his middle period, and the result was that very little of his later music was understood by his contemporaries. Most of it was considered impossible to play. But this was really not because it was more technically difficult than the works of his middle period, but because it was so much more difficult to interpret. And as Beethoven was by this time almost totally deaf, he could not show people how to perform it rightly; and very few people had enough musical intelligence to find out for themselves. In later times the traditions of what is necessary for their adequate interpretation have been so carefully and minutely described, that even people of no intelligence sometimes contrive not to make great artistic conceptions sound like nonsense; and works once thought impracticable are among the most familiar features of everyday concerts.

It is a familiar fact to every one that Beethoven's works sound fuller and richer than those of any composers since Bach. This is partly owing to the warmth and human interest of his ideas, but it is also due to the actual treatment of the instruments. In pianoforte works it is partly owing to the development of genuine pianoforte playing. The manner of playing the harpsichord and clavichord had been to creep over the keys with flat fingers and flat hands. Any attempt to strike the harpsichord as players now do the pianoforte would have the reverse effect from what is intended; for a blow of any sharpness drives the jacks up between the strings, and reduces the instrument to silence. The early pianofortes had but slight fall in the keys, and consequently the traditions of harpsichord playing were transferred to them without much unfitness. But when the keys were deepened to get more tone, new methods became necessary; and though the typical conservative mind regarded any effort to change such things as a species of heresy, the stronger and more practical musicians soon cultivated such heresies with much success. Clementi especially gave much attention to the proper way of dealing with an instrument in which the sound was produced by the blows of little hammers; and Beethoven followed in the same direction. He instantly dissipated the absurd tradition which implied that what was right for the harpsichord was right for the pianoforte. The instrument suited his passionate vigorous temperament; it lent itself to rich harmonisation, to rhythmic variety; and by the aid of the

pedal he managed to produce the floods of tone in which
his soul delighted. His contrivances in the latter direction were especially important, as he not only widened
the capacities of a keyed instrument, but gave the first
impulse to that characteristic softening and clouding of
outlines which is so familiar in the so-called "romantic"
style of recent times. ✓ In the orchestral branches of art
the enrichment of tone by the gradual increase of varieties
of instruments had been going on ever since Scarlatti's
time. The nucleus of strings with two pairs of wind
instruments, and a harpsichord to fill in the harmonies,
which was usually employed for the small symphonies in
the early part of the eighteenth century, was increased by
the end of it to strings, flutes, hautboys, bassoons, two
horns, two trumpets, and drums. Haydn and Mozart
used clarinets sometimes, but not often; it was not till
recent times that the mechanism of the instrument was
sufficiently perfect to make it available, and the tone
of the old clarinets was probably thinner and shriller
than that of modern ones. Beethoven used them from
the first in all his symphonies; in the third symphony
(the Eroica) he added a third horn; in the massive
C minor symphony he added three trombones and a
double bassoon; and in the last, No. 9, he added a fourth
horn as well. His object was not so much to add to the
noise as to increase the opportunities for variety; and to
organise the actual and relative possibilities of instrumental tone to the utmost.

The constitution of the orchestra has remained as he
established it ever since. The aspirations of modern sensational composers have not managed to improve upon the
actual order of the instruments, though they have often
increased the numbers; and the wood wind being now
somewhat overbalanced by the great number of stringed
instruments used for large concert-rooms, the only balance

in "forte" passages is between strings and brass instruments. And this, combined with the growing taste for brilliancy of colour, has led to a slight increase in the latter department. Beethoven enjoyed the advantage, over Haydn and Mozart, that the actual powers of performance on orchestral instruments had greatly improved. He could afford to write more difficult passages, and to use a wider range of sounds. Even in his first two symphonies he has advanced beyond the earlier masters in variety of effect and in a certain solemn depth which is very characteristic of some of his moods; and he uses his instruments with more and more distinctness of purpose as he goes on. He knows exactly where the bright sparkling tone of the flute will serve his turn, and where the pathetic tenderness of the hautboy; the liquid fulness of the clarinet had a place in his scheme, and the extraordinary varieties of the bassoon's tones are most familiar to him, in all its grotesque, humorous, plaintive, and even pathetic aspects. The curious human-like uncertainty and mystery of the horns, and their powers of enriching the softer harmonies, are most especially congenial to him. He knows the majestic force of the trombones in the loud passages, and their impressive solemnity in soft passages; and, unlike many later writers, he never makes them odious with vulgar brutish blatancy. He sees all the varieties in their true light. For the tone qualities of the various instruments serve not only for contrast, but like colours, to excite sensibilities. Mozart occasionally used special instruments to enforce situations, as in the wonderful accompaniment of soft swelling trombones and horns to the voice of the oracle in Idomeneo; and in the familiar passages for the brass instruments in Don Giovanni and Zauberflöte. But a large majority of his special effects are for the mere purpose of pure beauty or contrast; and his variety is not very great. For there is a great family likeness about his various uses of thirds in double octaves for bassoons and flutes or hautboys, though the effect is quite beautiful enough to be borne very often. Beethoven's use of his resources in this respect is very much more full of variety, and in a very large number of cases it is so absolutely to the purpose, that it seems the necessary outcome of the mood which his particular melody, rhythm, or harmony, or the sum of all three of them, conveys at the particular moment.

But, in truth, design, colour, and expression are so closely wedded in his best work that it is difficult to disintegrate them. The expression is great because it comes exactly in the true place in the scheme of design to tell. The colour exerts its full influence mainly because the expression and the design put the mind exactly in the receptive condition to be fully impressed by it. Even the most limited of instruments can be made to produce an astounding effect through its relation to its context. The whole of the scherzo of the C minor symphony is as near being miraculous as human work can be; but one of its most absorbing moments is the part where for fifteen bars there is nothing going on but an insignificant chord continuously held by low strings, and a pianissimo rhythmic beat of the drum. Taken out of its context it would be perfectly meaningless. As Beethoven has used it, it is infinitely more impressive than the greatest noise Meyerbeer and his fellows ever succeeded in making.

Beethoven's attitude in relation to art and expression naturally led him by degrees to modify the average scheme of the design of instrumental works in accordance with the ideas which he felt he could artistically express. This was one of the features which indicated the direction in which art was destined to travel after his time. But the changes he made were mainly in respect of the general order and grouping of the movements, and not often in the disposal or ordering of their contents. The form of the principal movement (which is commonly known by the unhappy name of " binary ") is so wonderfully elastic that he found little occasion to alter it except by strengthening the main pillars of the structure, and widening its general scope, wherever possible; as in the Codas. His early solo sonatas were on the usual plan, but increased to four movements, like Mozart's and Haydn's symphonies. But in later times, when he had attained a more comprehensive view of the situation, he varied the number and order of the movements in all classes of instrumental works, sometimes increasing to five, and sometimes reducing to two. Sometimes beginning with a slow movement, sometimes omitting it altogether. His most important alteration in the general scheme was the introduction of the scherzo in place of the old minuet. The virtue of introducing the minuet after the slow movement lay in the decisive contrast the rhythmic principle of the dance afforded to the cantabile character of the slow movement. But the choice was not really a happy one, because the minuet was not naturally a vigorous rhythmic dance, but graceful, flowing, and rather slow and sedate. Mozart and Haydn were both led correctly by their instincts to give their minuets a far more animated and vigorous character than the actual dance motions warranted; and composers ultimately gave up all attempts to pay attention to the relation of the music to hypothetical dance motions, and took it *presto*, and called it by a new name, the scherzo.

The fact that the scherzo had been known long before does not lessen the importance of Beethoven's systematic adoption of it, which gave it its place in modern music. For both by implication and in fact it is one of the most important of the features which made their appearance in the early part of this century. The fact that it made

such a much better contrast to the slow movement is
really of secondary importance, though from the purely
artistic point of view that is considerable. Very much
more important is its meaning in respect of expression.
Many people have unfortunately got into the habit of
taking "expression" to mean only sentimental expression;
and convention has deprived the language of a comprehensive word in order to give it a special bearing
In reference to music, it must be taken in its widest
sense; and at this moment it is particularly important
to take note of the fact; as the essence of musical
progress from Beethoven onwards lies in the development of infinite varieties of expression. Beethoven's
adoption of the scherzo was like a manifesto on that
point. The scherzo has become one of the most valuable
types for the conveyance of all those kinds of expression
which are not sentimental.; and require to be described in
terms of action rather than terms of vocal utterance. In
this its primal dance origin confirms the gesticulatory
meaning of the rhythmic element in music. With
Beethoven the scherzo became the most free of all the
movements in the sonata group. He did not restrict it
to the characteristic triple time of the minuet, but took
any time that the situation required; and so far dispensed
with the systematic orderliness of the harmonic type that
the plan of a movement is often as difficult to unravel as
that of any of Bach's merriest and lightest fugues. In
ranging wide and free among human characteristics this
apparent independence of regularity and rule was just
perfectly apposite; and it is interesting to note that Mendelssohn's keen insight divined this point, and that he
struck out an equally informal line in his scherzos with
much success; for the genuine "scherzo" impulse had a
very happy and wholesome effect upon his disposition.
But of course he cannot be compared with Beethoven

either for variety or scope; for nowhere is the subtlety of Beethoven's imagination or the keenness of his insight more conspicuous; and no form shows more clearly or variously the character of the man. His love of every-thing that concerned the human creature, without re-spect of persons or classes, comes out. Other movements supplied him with the opportunities for uttering graver sentiments and emotions, here he dealt with mischief, raillery, humour, fun of every description, in the terms that are like the healthy honest spirits of a child. In-deed the analogies are generally most likely to be found in the spontaneous merriment of children, for the veneer of respectability in people of mature years buries most of the natural expansion in such directions out of sight.

The resources of the pianoforte were hardly adequate to his purposes in this line; and though he wrote some very successful and graphic examples for the instrument, his most brilliant achievements are in the symphonies, quartetts, and trios, where either variety of colour or the crystalline clearness of violin tone afforded him better opportunities.

The matter of design is of such pre-eminent importance in his works that it must inevitably be discussed in some detail; since the effect of his work depends so much upon his marvellous concentration and self-control in that respect. Very few people realise the importance of management of design, and the extent to which it can be carried; and though they cannot fail to see how important it is in small things, they do not follow out their observa-tion to its logical consequences, and see that it is equally important in great. Even people of little intelligence can perceive that when one chord or figure has been going on for a long while, it is a relief to have it changed; and it does not take any great powers of mind to realise that there is a right place and a wrong for the change to come. But

even when that much is seen, and it is realised that the
proper management of the successions of chords is the basis
of modern instrumental design, people still seem to forget
that what applies to one little part applies to the whole;
and that in a highly organised work of art there is a right
place and a wrong for every change of harmony, and for
every rise and fall of the melody throughout a long piece
of music. The full effect of every great stroke of art in
such cases depends upon the perfect control of the motion,
direction, and even the colour of every successive moment
in the work. Beethoven often makes a stroke which is
only intelligible by its relation to some other passage
that is some hundreds of bars away in another part of
the movement; but he manages it so perfectly that an
auditor over whom he has cast his spell can instantly
seize his drift. The extraordinary degree of concentration in this respect is such as no other composer has ever
approached. With all Mozart's skill in design his work
is very loose in texture compared with that of his successor. A short discussion of minutiæ may help to make
this clearer. It so happens that both Beethoven and
Mozart used the same root idea—the former in his first
sonata, and the latter in the last movement of his G
minor symphony. The spirit of the idea is an energetic
upward leap through a rhythmic arpeggio to a strongly
emotional high note.

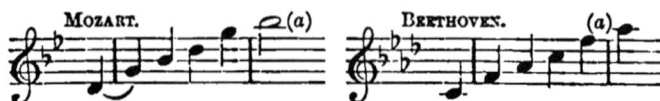

The high note, as the crisis, naturally requires something
to round it off Mozart makes the emphatic point subside into a sentimental harmony; Beethoven cuts it off
sharply by an emphatic turn.

Mozart then simply breaks off and continues the proceedings by a new phrase, which from an emotional point
of view would be quite trivial.

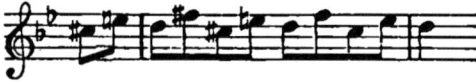

Beethoven, on the contrary, keeps firm hold of his text;
and enforces it by repeating it in another position in the
scale, which makes his emotional point rise a step higher.

Then taking his emotional point and its characteristic
appendage, he drives it home by repeating it with strong
accent, rising higher each time to give it extra intensity.[1]

And only when the highest point of the crisis is reached
does he relax the tension, and a softer and more yielding
version of the turn is moulded on to the cadence which
concludes his sentence; which therefore stands in its
entirety :—

---

[1] Compare the Irish folk-tune on page 85 for the principle.

Thus the whole of Beethoven's first sentence is knit together in the closest bonds by insistence upon his emotional
point. Mozart, having given his root idea and its counter
idea to balance it, repeats them in the same order, but
with the order of the harmony reversed, taking dominant
first and tonic to finish with, and so concludes :—

Beethoven, over and above the close consistency with
which he uses his idea, unifies the whole passage of eight
bars by the skilful use of his bass, which marches up step
by step from the leading note below the tonic starting-
point to the dominant above it; thereby helping the
mind to grasp the principle of design and to feel the close
unity of the whole sentence. In Mozart's passage the
alternation of tonic and dominant is very obvious, and is
the means whereby the tonality of the passage is made
clear. In Beethoven's passage the alternation of tonic and
dominant is equally present and equally regular, but the
bass happily disguises it, while it also serves as an additional indication of the structure of the passage. To show
the whole artistic purpose and skill of the first twelve
bars would require a chapter to itself, for with Beethoven
nearly every progression has several aspects. All that can
be attempted here is to show how the process is carried
on, in such a manner that each step becomes the necessary
outcome of the impulse which is expressed at the moment
of starting. The end of the first sentence above quoted
in full leaves the hearer in the air, as it were; for it ends
only on a relatively final chord, the dominant. Further
proceedings are therefore necessarily expected; and Beet-

hoven resumes his subject in the bass by way of contrast,
and in a position of the scale which for the moment is
purposely obscure. He does not wish to reveal his intentions all at once; so the key seems to be C minor, when it
is intended to lead to A♭. When the emotional point is
reached it is immediately pushed on, together with the
turn which makes it identifiable, by an unexpected discord. This of course requires its resolution, which is
made in. such a way as to produce another discord; and
so by the necessities of each resolution the music is
pushed on step by step till the dominant of the new and
contrasting key is reached, and the circuit of this first
division of the movement is completed. The root idea
has never for a moment been lost sight of; so from both
points of view—idea and design alike—no step is without
its significance and its bearing. And all the rest of the
movement is carried out on the same principles.

To avoid misconception, it is as well to point out that
Mozart, in the parallel case above quoted, also uses his
materials very consistently, and develops them into new
phases; but not with the close concentration even of
Beethoven's earliest work.

Of the almost endless devices and subtleties Beethoven
uses to make his design intelligible, the most familiar is a
steady progress of the bass by tones or semitones up or
down in accordance with the spirit which the moment
requires. Where subsidence from a crisis is wanted, it
goes down, where extra animation is wanted it rises; and
always so as to direct the mind towards the point which it
is essential to realise. One of the most remarkable instances is in the middle of the first movement of the great
Appassionata Sonata. The course of events has brought
about a point of repose in the key of D♭; and for the purposes of design it is necessary to modulate back to the
principal key, F minor, and concentrate all the attention

upon the chord immediately before the chord which finally
announces that the rambling and voyaging division of the
movement is over, and the principal key reached again.
To do this Beethoven makes his bass rise slowly step by
step for fifteen bars—from the D♭ below the bass stave
to the D♭ next under the treble stave. The whole mass
of the harmony rises with it, with increasing excitement,
so that the crisis of the emotional aspect of the progression exactly coincides with the point which it is most
essential that the mind should grasp firmly as the last
before one of the most important points in the scheme—
the return to the original key and subject. And, by way
of contrast to the long-continued motion, the penultimate
chord, when arrived at, continues unchanged for eleven
bars, the mind being fully occupied with the rattling
brilliancy of figured arpeggios. The same kind of sequence
transferred to the treble part is to be found in the development portion of the first movement of the sonata in A♭,
Opus 110, where the progression drops down step by step
for a whole octave; thereby completely unifying the whole
of the "development" portion of the movement.

Another device of the same kind is that which makes
the whole mass of the harmony move upon a bass constantly shifting by steps of thirds. The most remarkable
instance is the introductory movement to the fugue in the
sonata in B♭, Opus 106, where the dropping steps of the
thirds continue through the whole movement without
intermission; supplying an underlying principle of order
to all the varieties of mood and expression which occur in
it. Another very remarkable instance of the same device
is in the middle of the first movement of the sonata in E
minor, Opus 90. Some such sequence or principle of order,
either on a small or a wide ranging basis, gives coherence
and sense of orderliness even in his most elaborately
contrived effects of harmonic motion.

His ways of insisting upon his key, without letting it be seen that he is doing so, are many and various. As has been pointed out, he often casts his leading idea in terms of the tonic chord. But he is very fond of suggesting and bewildering at the same time. Thus the principal part of the Eroica subject is made out of the tonic chord of E♭,

but then the whole aspect of things becomes perplexing for a moment by its passing straight out of the key with

; and the mind is for a moment

in doubt of its whereabouts. And then Beethoven slips back into his key again as quickly as he went out, as if he made light of his own device. Whereas he has no intention of making light of it. For when the same passage comes back some five minutes later he knows quite well that his audience will remember it, and thereupon he turns the progression inside out; leaving them even more perplexed and interested than before. Similarly he sometimes begins quite out of the key in order to make the safe arrival at the true starting-point the more striking. Again he sometimes casts his subject in the form of a sequence, which leads out of the key immediately, as in the sonata in E minor, Opus 90; but the progressions move by such a logical process that when the circuit is complete the impression of the key is a great deal stronger and more vital than if he had contented himself with tonic and dominant all the while. Both Brahms and Wagner have followed him in this device. Brahms in the Second Rhapsody, and Wagner in the Vorspiel to Tristan. Another way of insisting on the key is the obvious one of emphasising in succession all the principal chords which represent it—tonic, dominant, subdominant,

supertonic, &c. Of this there are two exactly parallel
cases in works as different as the little G major sonata,
Opus 14, No. 2, and the first movement of the Waldstein ;
where they occur exactly in analogous positions, in the
section representing the second key.

His subjects themselves very often have some wide
principle of general effect besides the mere interest of
the details. It may be a systematic rise of a characteristic figure, as in the subject of the A♭ sonata, Opus 110;
or the persistence of a rhythmic nucleus which underlies a more general melodic outline—as in the first sentence
of the C minor symphony, or it may be the recurrence
of some very striking feature, such as the two fierce
blows at the end of the rushing arpeggio in the last
movement of the C♯ minor sonata (commonly called
Moonlight). And when there are phases like this he
generally extends them, in the development of the subjects, into new situations and aspects. A happy instance
of this is the treatment of the second subject in the
last movement of the C♯ minor sonata :—

Here at the asterisks the accented note successively rises
and gains in warmth; and thus it becomes the most striking feature of the subject. So at the end of the movement Beethoven enhances the passion of it (with great
effect also for the purpose of design) by extending the rise
and pressing the emotional points closer :—

His power of presenting the same subject in different aspects has very important bearing on the progress of art. In his case it is particularly valuable in the development of a movement, as it enabled him to keep true to his initial idea without sameness, and at the same time to add to its interest. He showed this faculty in the highest degree in his variations, a form of which he was quite the greatest master. His treatment indeed makes it one of the most interesting forms of art, while in the hands of composers of· less power it is one of the most detestable. With him the theme is a sort of chameleon thought which is capable of undergoing all kinds of mysterious changes; and of being expressed sometimes gaily, sometimes sadly, sometimes fiercely. He groups variations together in accordance with their affinities, and distributes the different moods so as to illustrate one another, and to make a complete composite design.

The texture of his work as a whole is far more polyphonic than that of his predecessors, and illustrates the tendency of the time to revert to the methods of Bach, in the free motion of the bass and the internal organisation of the harmony—adapting the methods at the same time to the system of harmonic form. The case is parallel to the reversion to the methods of the old ecclesiastical music after the Florentine revolution of Peri and Monteverde. But the counterpoint is by no means that of Bach; it is less ostensible, and the various inner parts and figures that move are kept in relative subordination in accordance with their relative degrees of importance. Music by this means regained an immensely enhanced power of expression of the highest kind. The harmony not only became more interesting and rich, but very much more powerful at the moments when powerful discord was required; and at the same time it afforded much more delicate gradations of degrees of harshness.

The tendency to use the art for expression naturally led Beethoven to identify his work occasionally with some definite idea or subject. As in the Eroica Symphony, which was intended for his ideal of Napoleon (so soon shattered); the Pastoral Symphony, which embodied his feelings about the fields, and brooks, and woods, and birds he loved so well; the "Lebewohl" Sonata, which embodied his ideal musical sense of friends parting, of absence, and of the joyous coming together again. But with him, for almost the first time, the true principle of programme music is found, and he indicates it with absolute insight into the situation in his remark on the Pastoral Symphony. That it was "mehr Ausdruck der Empfindung, als Malerei"—"More the expression of inner feeling than picturing." The most common failing of minds less keen than Beethoven's is to try and make people see with their ears. Beethoven goes to the root of the matter. For, as pointed out in the first chapter, it is not the business of music to depict the external, but to convey the inner impressions which are the result of the external. And music is true in spiritual design only when it is consistent in the use of the resources of expression to the possible workings of the mind in special moods or under the influence of special external impressions. With Beethoven and Bach the consistency of the harmonic, melodic, and rhythmic elements of expression is so perfect, that with all the infinity of change and the variety that is necessary for design's sake, the possible working of a mind affected by some special exciting cause is consistently represented by the kind of treatment that is used. That people often can feel this for themselves is shown by the general adoption of such a name as "the Appassionata," which was not given by Beethoven, but which is eminently justified in every particular by the contents of that wonderful sonata.

Beethoven's opportunity lay in the enormous development of the resources of art, and in the fact that the principles of a singularly malleable type of design were ready to his hand when he came upon the scene. His imagination and his powers of concentration were equal to his responsibilities. The resources of art were as yet not so great as to tempt him to extravagance. Indeed he himself had to collect and systematise much of them, and enlarged them more than any other man except Bach. The sonata form, moreover, was new enough to afford him scope without forcing him either to risk commonplace, or to resort to hyper-intellectual devices to hide its familiarities. In his hands alone the forces of design and of expression were completely controlled. Self-dependent instrumental art on the grandest and broadest lines found its first perfect revelation in his hands, not in a formal sense alone, but as the highest phase of true and noble characteristic expression.

CHAPTER XIII.

MODERN TENDENCIES.

BEETHOVEN stands just at the turning-point of the ways
of modern art, and combines the sum of past human
effort in the direction of musical design with the first
ripe utterance of the modern impulse—made possible by
the great accumulation of artistic resources—in the direction of human expression. After him the course of things
naturally changed. In the art of the century before him
formality was prominent and expression very restrained;
in the times after him the conditions were reversed, and
the instinct of man was propelled to resent the conventions
of form which seemed to fetter his imagination, and began
his wanderings and experiments anew in the irrepressible
conviction that every road must lead somewhere. A new
artistic crisis had been passed, similar to the crises of
Palestrina and Bach, but implying a still greater organisation and a richer accumulation of actual resources than
was available for either of the earlier masters. All three
crises represent a relatively perfect formulation of human
feeling. Palestrina without emotion embodies the most
perfect presentation of contemplative religious devotion.
Bach, more touched by the secular spirit, and fully capable
of strong emotion, formulates a more liberal and energetic
type of religious sentiment, and foreshadows, by his new
combination of rhythm and polyphony, the musical expression of every sort of human feeling. Beethoven expresses
the complete emancipation of human emotion and mind,
and attempts to give expression to every kind of inner

sensibility which is capable and worthy of being brought into the circuit of an artistic scheme of design.

But only at particular moments in the history of art are such crises possible. For it needs not only the grandeur of a man's nature to think of things worthy of being grandly said; but it requires a condition of mankind which shall be as appreciative of artistic considerations as of expression. There may be nobility, truth, and greatness in art at all times; but the perfect adjustment of things which is necessary to make a grand scheme of art, and to render possible examples of it which are nearly perfect from every point of view, is only to be found at rare moments in the history of human effort. The love of art for art's sake is generally a mere love of orderliness in things which require a great deal of ingenuity to get into order; at best it is a love of beauty for itself. At one stage in art's history this attitude in relation to it is inevitable, but humanity as it grows older instinctively feels that the adoration of mere beauty is sometimes childish and sometimes thoroughly unwholesome; and men want to be more sure ʻthat the human energies are not sapped by art instead of being fostered by it. The natural result is that a crisis follows in which the worshippers of abstract beauty and the worshippers of expression both find almost complete satisfaction; but after that things tend to leave the grand lines which imply a steadfast reverence for the highest phase of abstract beauty, and men seek a new field wherein to develop effects of strong characterisation. Art comes down from its lofty region and becomes the handmaid of everyday life. It seems to be so in most of the arts; for they each have their time of special glory, and are then turned to the more practical purposes of illustration. The greater portion of the arts of painting and drawing in modern times is devoted to illustration of the most definite kind; and even the pictures which aim at special artistic value, and are exhibited in important galleries, are of infinite range in subject, and endeavour to realise within the conditions of artistic presentation almost anything which has impressed an artist as worthy of permanent record. The instinct for beauty and the feeling for design may still have plenty of scope in accordance with the disposition of the artist, but they are by no means so prominent a part of art as they were; and many pictures have had immense fame which have been nothing but the baldest presentations of totally uninteresting everyday occurrences, without a trace of anything that shows a sense of either beauty or design.

It is much the same in literature. Nothing is more conspicuously characteristic of the present age than the immense increase of short characteristic stories which make vividly alive for all men the varieties of human circumstances and character, from the remotest districts of India and the steppes of Russia, to the islands of Galway Bay and the backwoods of Australia. The few men that still have the instincts of great art cling to the great traditions and deal as much as they can with great subjects, but the preponderant tendency in all arts is towards variety and closeness of characterisation.

As has before been pointed out, the premonitions of this tendency are already discernible in Beethoven; and many other external facts in his time and soon after show in what direction the mind of man was moving. A characteristic point is the much more frequent adoption by composers of names for their works; which evidently implies taking a definite idea and endeavouring to make the music express it. No one emphasises this fact more than Spohr. By natural musical organisation and habit of mind he was the last composer of whom one might expect unclassical procedure. Mozart was his model, and Beethoven was barely intelligible to him except in his least characteristic moods. But Spohr set himself in a very marked way to emphasise illustration. To many of his symphonies he gave definite names, and made it his endeavour to carry out his programme consistently. The well-known "Weihe der Töne" is a case in point. He meant originally to set a poem of that title by Pfeiffer as a cantata, but finding it unsuitable he wrote the symphony as an illustration of the poem, and directed that the poem was to be read whenever the symphony was performed. Moreover, he endeavoured to widen the scope and design of the symphony to carry out his scheme, with eminently unsatisfactory results, as far as all the latter part of it is concerned. His "Historical Symphony" has a similarly definite object, though not so close an application; as it was merely a very strange attempt to imitate the styles of Bach and Handel, Mozart and Beethoven in successive movements. More decisively to the point is his symphony called "The Worldly and Heavenly Influences in the Life of Man," in which the heavenly influences are represented by a solo orchestra, and the worldly by an ordinary full orchestra. The general idea is very carefully carried out, and the heavenly influences are made particularly prominent in the early part, and apparently succumb to the power of the worldly orchestra towards the end. Another symphony of Spohr's is called "The Seasons," which is a very favourite subject, and also a very suitable one, for true musical treatment. Weber was naturally on the same side, both on account of his romantic disposition and the deficiencies of his artistic education. His one successful instrumental work, on a large scale, the Concertstück for pianoforte and orchestra, deliberately represents a story of a knight and a lady in crusading times. The inference suggested is even stronger in the case of Mendelssohn, who was ultra-classical by nature, but gave names and indicated a purpose or a reason for the particular character of all his best symphonies—The Reformation, the Italian, and the Scotch. Even the symphony to the Lobgesang has a very definite and intelligible relation to the cantata which follows; while as far as musical characterisation is concerned, the overture and scherzo in the Midsummer Night's Dream music are among the most vivid things of modern times.

To all appearance the line which Berlioz took is even more decisive. But important as it is, the fact of his being a Frenchman reduces its significance a little. The French have never shown any talent for self-dependent instrumental music. From the first their musical utterance required to be put in motion by some definite idea external to music. The great Parisian lute-players wrote most of their neat little pieces to a definite subject; Couperin developed considerable skill in contriving little picture-tunes, and Rameau followed in the same line later. The kernel of the Gallic view of things is, moreover, persistently theatrical, and all the music in which they have been successful has had either direct or secondary connection with the stage. Berlioz was so typical a Frenchman in this respect that he could hardly see even the events of his own life as they actually were; but generally in the light of a sort of fevered frenzy, which made everything— both ups and downs—look several times larger than the reality. Some of his most exciting experiences as related by himself are conceived in the spirit of melodrama, and could hardly have happened as he tells them except on the stage. This was not the type of human creature of whom self-dependent instrumental music could be expected; and it is no wonder that when he took to experimenting in that line of art he made it even more theatrical than ordinary theatrical music; because he had to supply

the effect of the stage and the footlights and all the
machinery, as well as the evolutions and gesticulations of
the performers, by the music alone. His enormous skill
and mastery of resource, brilliant intelligence, and fiery
energy were all concentrated in the endeavour to make
people see in their minds the histrionic presentation of
such fit histrionic subjects as dances of sylphs, processions
of pilgrims, and orgies of brigands. Even the colossal
dimensions of his orchestra, with its many square yards
of drum surface, and its crowds of shining yellow brass
instruments, is mainly the product of his insatiable
theatrical thirst. It imposes upon the composer himself
as much as it imposes upon his audience, by looking so
very big and bristling to the imagination. But though
it makes a great noise, and works on the raw impressionable side of human creatures, and excites them to an
abnormal degree, the effect it produces is not really so
imposing as that of things which make much less show—
for instance the opening of Beethoven's B♭ Symphony,
which requires only seven different instruments to play it,
and is all pianissimo. The means are in excess of the
requirements; or rather what should be means become
requirements, because the effect is made by the actual
sound of the instruments, and often not at all by the
music which they are the means of expressing. And
this aspect of Berlioz's work is even more noteworthy
in relation to modern musical development than the fact
that he uniformly adopted a programme for his instrumental works. He was a man of unusually excitable
sensibility, and the tone of instruments, like colour,
appealed to him more than any other feature in music.
He was also a man of literary tastes, and had no inconsider-
able gifts in that line, and was more excited by the notion
of what music might be brought to express than by the
music itself. The result of such influences and predis-

positions, was to impel him to endeavour to express literary
or theatrical ideas in terms of colour and rhythm. He
was the first composer who emphasised the element of
colour to such an extent; and so strong was his predis-
position in this direction that it can easily be seen that he
often speculated in effects of colour quite independently
of the musical ideas; which he afterwards evolved to fit
into the colours. As a painter might cover his canvas
with the strangest tints he could devise, and work them
up into a subject-picture or a landscape afterwards. But
quite independent of these very marked peculiarities in his
character, his genius and originality are incontestable.
When the spirit of a situation like the opening scene of
Faust, or Margaret's meditation in the prison, inspired
him wholesomely, he was capable of rising to very high
and genuinely musical conceptions.

The sum total of his work is one of the wonders of the
art—unique in its weirdness and picturesqueness; and
notable for the intense care with which every detail that
ministers to effect is thought out. Not only are the scores
very complicated in respect of the figures and rhythms of
the actual music; but they are full of minute directions as
to the manner of performance; extending to the putting of
wind instruments in bags and playing drums with sticks
with sponge at the end, and many other original contrivances. The tendency to exaggeration is all of a piece with
the high tension of his nervous organisation; but inasmuch
as the whole object is to intensify characteristic expression
in every conceivable manner, his work is very noteworthy
as an illustration of the general tendencies of modern art
since Beethoven. His methods have not found any very
conspicuous imitators, though some very successful French
composers have learnt a great deal from him in many ways.
Indeed the modern French have more natural gift for
colour and a greater love for it than for any other depart-

ment of art. It appears to express most exactly their
peculiarly lively sensibility; and their passion for it, and
for what they call *chic*, has enabled them to develop in
recent times a style of orchestration which is quite their
own, and is generally very neat, graceful, finished, and
telling, especially for lighter kinds of music and for opera.

Even that very serious and reserved branch of art, the
oratorio, was influenced by the tendencies of modern art,
and gained a new lease of life through the development of
richer means of effective expression. The oratorio had
almost collapsed after the time of Handel and Bach, for
the universal domination of Italian operatic style affected
it more vitally than any other branch of art. The growth
of the singularly perverted taste for having church music
in the same style as opera, with set arias for " prima
donnas " at what might be expected to be extremely
solemn moments, and the emptiest and baldest commonplace harmonisation in place of the old polyphonic choral
music, affected oratorio almost fatally. For though oratorio was not necessarily a part of any ecclesiastical
function, its associations were of a religious order, and the
style was closely assimilated to that of the various works
written for church use. But it could not afford to be
as empty as either church music or opera, for it stands
mainly òn its own footing; and if the music is not interesting in itself, there is neither scenic effect, nor action,
nor the glamour of an ancient ceremonial to help it
out. Other conditions told in the same direction; for it
is probable that people did not use performances of oratorios quite so much as operas for fashionable gatherings
and gossip; and if the music was tiresome they were
bound to become aware of it. So the formality of the
arias which were introduced, and the graceful futility of
the Italian style in general, had full effect, and oratorios
fell completely into the background. People would not

U

listen to things in the lofty style of Bach's Passions,
and so composers were driven to write things that
were not worth listening to at all. Composers like Philip
Emmanuel Bach, who tried to put good work into their
oratorios, wasted their efforts; for even they had to put
in some of the usual arias, and the conventional stiffness
of that form counterbalanced the parts of their works
which were of superior quality.

It was not until operatic art had had the benefit of
Gluck's reforms and Mozart's improvements, and the arts
of orchestration had been substantially founded upon
definitely modern lines, that a revival became possible.
Quite at the end of the eighteenth century the appearance of Haydn's Creation serves as a sort of landmark of the new departure. It is full of obvious traces
of operatic influence in the forms of the movements and
the style. But the sincere peasant-nature of the great
composer gave a special flavour even to the florid and conventional airs, which distinguishes them from the ordinary
types, and gives them a characteristic ring which the
world was not slow to recognise. Moreover, his experience
of Handel's choral work while in London inspired him to
treat his choruses in a more animated style than usual, and
his great skill and experience in orchestration enabled
him to make the most of that important element of effect;
and so, after a long period of coma, the oratorio form was
felt to have come to life again. The traces of operatic
style are equally apparent in Beethoven's Engedi, but the
dramatic character and picturesqueness of some of the
details quite distinguish it from earlier works, though it
is by no means among the great master's most happy
productions. The emancipation from Italian operatic
influence becomes more complete in Spohr's works of
this kind. Being a Protestant, he escaped the influence of
the Italianised music of the Roman Church, and learned

to see things in the same sort of light as J. S. Bach. His treatment of the choral portions of his works is much more like what such work ought to be; and there was just sufficient dramatic sense and sentiment in his disposition to enable him to deal with his subjects characteristically and consistently; while his very exceptional gifts as a master of orchestral effect placed in his hands one at least of the most prominent of the new resources which brought about the revival of this form of art. The impulse to cultivate oratorio took special hold of Protestant countries, and those which were the homes of the higher orders of instrumental music—such as the symphony and various forms of chamber music; and the first important crisis in the modern story of oratorio is undoubtedly centred in the work of Mendelssohn in that department. He was one of the earliest of modern musicians to become intimate with J. S. Bach's work, and to a certain extent to understand it. His insight was keen enough to see the wonderful interest of the Passion-music type, and the possibility of adapting it to modern conditions; while Bach's intensely earnest style served him as an inspiring example. His critical feeling was subtle enough to hit the true standard of style, just poised half-way between the strict clearness and reserve of instrumental music and the loose texture of the dramatic style; and his scheme proved so generally successful that it has served most composers as a model ever since the appearance of Elijah and St. Paul. The works are so well known that it is hardly necessary to point out the degree in which they make for expression rather than for mere technical effect. To many people they have long formed the ideal of what such expression ought to be. Mendelssohn undoubtedly emphasised melody, but by no means to the exclusion of other means of expression. He was one of the few composers to whom, in his best

moments, all the resources of art were equally available.
His choral writing was the best that had been seen
since Handel and Bach, and for mastery of orchestral
effect he had no real superior in his time. His harmony
is full of variety and sufficiently forcible; and his facility
in melody quite unlimited. He applied his resources
almost to the highest degree of which he was capable in
this line of art, and it naturally followed that his solution of the problem of oratorio has satisfied the constant
and exacting scrutiny of most musicians ever since.

To make this the better understood it will be as well to
consider shortly what are the conditions which govern
the style and scheme of oratorio. The essence of the
situation is the object to present a dramatic story in
musical setting without action. The absence of scenic
accessories and of all such things as are conveyed to the
mind and feelings through the eyes, has drawn the form
in the same direction as abstract instrumental music;
for people are more critical about details when their
whole attention is concentrated on the music than when
it is distracted by other elements of effect. So that
oratorio has been found to require more definite and
clear forms and more distinct articulation in minutiæ
than opera. In opera slovenly workmanship has generally been preferred by the public to artistic finish which
bores and distracts them from the play. In oratorio
slovenly workmanship or faulty designing cannot long pass
without being observed. And moreover the conditions
are more favourable for careful and scrupulous artistic
work. The absence of action relieves the stress of
necessity to keep the music continuously going. In opera
the action is impeded and weakened by breaking up the
music into disconnected pieces, however finished and
beautiful they may be in detail; but in oratorio it is a
distinct advantage to have breaks that rest the mind, and

even to emphasise points in the movements themselves
by occasional and discreet repetition. So that it is not
only necessary to make design clear and artistic workmanship thorough, but the situation actually gains by the use
of set forms which render such treatment possible. On
the other hand, in point of style and dramatic force
oratorio is much more limited than opera. Even positively vulgar music is sometimes defensible in connection
with the stage when a character is presented in the
drama who would not be completely represented in the
music associated with him without some suggestion of his
vulgar side. And a much more undisguised use of frank
appeals to the unsophisticated animal side in man has
always been tolerated, even generally welcomed, in operatic
matters. But in oratorio such things would soon betray
their artistic falseness. The ignoble has very often to be
dealt with on the stage, but in the music of the concert-
room the responsibilities of a great and serious form like
oratorio cut composers off from everything that is not in
a high sense dignified and elevated. But as a compensa-
tion the resources of oratorio are much more elastic. In
opera the attention is centred upon the individual singers
and their stage fortunes; and the chorus, who cannot
learn anything at all complicated by heart, are little
better than lay figures. But in oratorio the prominence
of the soloists is immensely toned down, and is more on a
level with the other elements of effect; and this form of
art is in no respect more strongly distinguished from all
other branches of music than by the inevitable prominence
of that democratic element the chorus.[1]

In the oratorio of the eighteenth century the chorus
generally had a very perfunctory share in the work.

---

[1] It is perhaps worth while to remark in passing that the element of
the chorus has always thriven best in societies and branches of society
with very strong democratic energies; while music of the soloists is the
delight of the courtly, fashionable, and plutocratic branches of society.

They had to sing things which were intended to be inspiring, but were in reality quite mechanical—such things as formal theorists' fugues, and movements consisting of mere succession of chords, with a great deal of dull note-repetition to fit the syllables, and no individuality in the parts at all—such as the passage "Jam plebis devote canentis una est vox, exaudi precantes exaudi," &c., in Mozart's "Splendente te." The comprehensive change of the whole aspect of the chorus is one of the most significant features of modern art; and nothing emphasises more signally the change from the formal to the spiritual. Composers did not always take a perfunctory view of the possibilities of chorus in the formal age, as Mozart's splendid conception of "Rex tremendæ majestatis" testifies; but as a rule the choral body was a mere heavy aggregate of figures with lungs and throats whose humanity was merged in a submissive crowd. The modern chorus becomes more and more like an organised group of human beings with human passions and feelings, and with collective ways of expressing them, which are as near as the circumstances allow to what human beings might be expected to adopt in the dramatic situations in the oratorios. The choruses of Baal's priests behave and sing in a way which conveys the impression that they are meant for Baal's priests and not for lay figures; and in one of the finest of recent modern oratorios the choruses of angels and of devils sing passages which express the characteristic impulses of angelic and diabolic natures to a nicety. This recognition of the personal nature of the constituents of a chorus was prefigured very strongly in Bach's choral works, and also frequently in Handel's; but the development of orchestral music and of the resources of general dramatic effect have so enhanced the opportunities of composers that the chorus tends more and more to be the centre of interest

in such works—and as choral singing is the department of
music in which the largest number of people can take
an active share, it is all of a piece with the interlacing
of the endless phases of cause and effect which conduce
towards important results, that the development of the
methods of art which make chorus singing interesting in
detail, and identify those who sing in them as human
beings should coincide with the great growth of democratic energy which marks the present age. And in such
respects the forms of secular choral music, such as odes
and cantatas, which are cast on the same general lines as
oratorios, and are controlled by absolutely the same conditions of presentation, tend to become even more important and comprehensive than oratorio itself. There is
nothing more ideally suited to the inward nature of music
than the presentation, in the closest and most characteristic terms, of great reflective and dramatic poems and
odes by genuine poets; and for such purposes the chorus
is ideally suited. The declamatory method which is growing up and increasing makes every member of the chorus
take a share in the recital of the poem; and the practice
of choral singing may yet become a happier means for the
diffusion of real refinement of mind and character among
large sections of the people than the world has hitherto
ever had the fortune to contrive. For a composer who
has enough cultivation and refinement of mind to appreciate great poems, and commensurate mastery of the arts
of choral music and instrumentation, may emphasise the
beauties of a poem and bring out its meaning far more
effectually than any amount of commentary and explanation. This is eminently a case which illustrates the value
of the rich accumulation of resources of various kinds, and
the wide facilities which they offer to modern composers;
for till comparatively lately the range of design and the
power of composers to wield varieties of means so as to

make the form intelligible was so limited, that unless
poems were constructed purposely to fit into conventional
types of musical form, they could not be effectively set.
But since Beethoven has shown how various are the means
of making a work of musical art coherent, systematic and
intelligible, and other composers of the modern school
have discovered how to adapt various means of expression
to the requirements of musical form, there need be but
few poems which are in a mood adapted for music that
will not admit of an effectual treatment. And the advantages composers now enjoy are so copious that there is
little excuse for their adopting the feeble resource which
once was so universal, of repeating words and sentences
without reference to their importance; for with increased
range of means of expression and design poems can perfectly well be presented in conformity with the poet's
intentions.

The same conditions which make possible the treatment of poems on a grand scale of this kind, with all
the splendid resources of orchestration and choral effect,
have brought about the profuse cultivation and diffusion
of the typical modern song; in which the music is brought
into close relation to the poems set to an extent which was
altogether unknown, and indeed impossible, in any less
elaborately organised artistic system. Songs there have
been at all periods in history. Solo song is the thread
that runs from end to end of the story; but it is only
in late years that a system has been devised which is
elastic enough to follow every turn of the poet's thought,
every change of his mood, every subtlety of his wit, and
every beauty of his diction. Till comparatively recent
times the scheme of song as a setting of poetry was tune
and tune only. Tune can be admirable, and can express
a good deal when properly dealt with; but it is not very
comprehensive, and the same tune cannot adequately

represent different moods unless the performer has great. skill in putting extra expression into it which is not necessarily there. A genuine singer of folk-tunes takes unlimited liberties with them. He makes them fast or slow at will—agitated or quiet—loud or soft—alters the accents and the rhythms, and even the length of the notes. There are still in modern times many public singers who like to have their songs as empty as possible, in order that they may put in all the expression for themselves. But a composer cannot be satisfied with such conditions, and wants to put in for himself the expression which the words convey to him; and to have singers who can fall in with his feeling and make their art serve to interpret what is worth expressing, instead of making what does not want any interpretation at all seem to be worth it by their art.

In old days composers did not trouble themselves much about the poems which they set. They regarded them as a collection of syllables which admitted of being used for a catchy tune. When the poet for expressive, or structural, or rhythmic reasons slightly altered the disposition of the accents, the musician rode roughshod over the difficulty it presented to him, and presuming that his tune was of more importance than the poet's intentions, set short syllables to long notes, and accented syllables to unaccented notes with equal impartiality. Similarly with any change in the mood of the words. The relation of the poem to the music was almost ignored, except in a very general sense. This was especially the case in respectable artistic circles. In the music of the people the words counted for a good deal, and plebeians liked to hear them. But in respectable circles the situation was much the same in songs as in operas of the formal period. There were exceptional occasions now and then when composers paid close attention to the words, but as a rule the object was to make a nice piece of melodious music rather than to make it characteristic, or in any way to represent the intention of the poet. The Italian domination was a little in fault here also; for people who did not understand the language, but liked the music the great singers sang, got into the habit of thinking that the words were of no consequence in other things as well as Italian arias. Songs had a better chance out of the range of that sort of civilisation, and in quarters where democratic conditions or national predispositions prevailed, the means for adequately interpreting poems as solo songs improved. Composers saw how to make the harmonisation of a tune alter its character, and how to make their accompaniments characteristic of the mood of the poem or of the situation it expressed, instead of adopting purely mechanical formulas like an Alberti bass for all sentiments alike. The excessive prominence of the element of mere melody was thereby reduced; while its capacity for expression was enhanced by the circumstances with which it was surrounded. Then, as harmony was more richly developed and tonality better understood, modulation came in as an additional means of effect. And so, little by little, under various influences, the final blossoming of the form was approached.

The culmination was rather sudden when it came, and was favoured by singular circumstances. Schubert is conspicuous among great composers for the insufficiency of his musical education. His extraordinary gifts and his passion for composing were from the first allowed to luxuriate untrained. He had no great talent for self-criticism, and the least possible feeling for abstract design, and balance, and order; but the profusion of his ideas was only limited by lack of time for writing them down. And these ideas were instinct with genuine individual life, not mechanical artificial products like opera

arias. They had a form and a character which meant
something above mere adaptation to formulas of design.
In instrumental music he was liable to plunge recklessly,
and to let design take its chance. The thirst in him was
for expression. And when he looked at a manuscript
of Beethoven's, and saw the infinite labour of rewriting
again and again to get all the climaxes and changes of
harmony and progressions of all sorts exactly in their
right places from every point of view, he shook his
head and doubted whether such labour was worth while.
With him, perhaps, it would not have been worth while,
for he is hardly likely to have developed enough perception in that direction to know where to stop or where
to press on. But this was the ideal nature for modern
song writing. That form of art did not require any great
scope of intellect or self-control. The poems he set had to
supply him with the design, and his receptive mind, as it
were, spontaneously reproduced in musical terms the impression which they made upon him. The wonder is that
he could find such varieties of characteristic expression so
soon after the formal period. "Gretchen am Spinnrade"
was written in 1814, and the Erl König in 1815, within
six years after the death of Haydn, and even before Beethoven's Ninth Symphony. But they are both instinct
with the full measure of vitality in every part; and are
absolutely complete representatives of the modern spirit
of musical expression. Harmony, rhythm, colour, tonality
—all minister to the full utterance of the poems as well
as melody. In the Erl König the vivid portrayal by the
accompaniment of the rage of the storm is familiar to
every one. But the subtlety of instinct is even more
remarkable in less obvious directions. For instance, if
people's sense of tonality had not become so developed
by his time the skilful device of beginning the question
"Wer reitet so spät durch Nacht und Wind?" upon a

secondary harmony would have been merely obscure; and
the modulation to a different key from the opening in the
second line of the song would have been yet more so.
Here a highly developed feeling for key is made use of for
purposes of expression. The question and answer which
give the clue to the spirit of the song are isolated, so as to
make them stand out from the context. Then again, instead of having a tune for the solo voice like earlier songs,
the vocal part is so exactly a reproduction of what a good
reciter might do in declaiming, that each rise and fall
seems to belong inherently to the words. Its melodic
significance is much more the result of its accompaniment than of the solo part itself. When a more definitely
tuneful phrase makes its appearance, it comes because it
is so particularly suitable to the moment; as when the
Erlking is made to wheedle the child with promises of
flowers and pretty games. The characters of the several
speakers are perfectly identifiable throughout, notwithstanding the ceaseless rush and turmoil; and the changes
of moods are perfectly conveyed without any break in
its continuity. The musical portrayal gains in intensity
as the song proceeds, and is finally concentrated into the
characteristic passage in the bass just at the end, where it
goes stamping upwards till it arrives at a point that is
purposely obscure in relation to the key of the song, so
as to accentuate the cadence and isolate the dénouement.
The rush and turmoil suddenly cease, and the consummation of the tragedy is conveyed in the mood of awe which
is as near as possible to silence. And, just as in the
passage quoted (on p. 292) from Beethoven's Appassionata,
the very tension of the situation gives the cadence all the
requisite degree of impressiveness to round off the design
into completeness. This is indeed one of the most significant instances of the relation between expression and
design in modern art.

The wonderful " Gretchen am Spinnrade" is dealt with in precisely the same manner. It is unified by the suggestion of the spinning-wheel in the accompaniment, and the perfect management of the harmonic scheme of the music gives perfect freedom to the treatment of the words. How vivid such a situation can be made in musical terms may be illustrated from the treatment of the words " Und ach, sein Kuss ! "

The rise to the highest emotional point, with the acutely sensitive harmonies enforcing the complicated mood of the moment; the pause in the spinning and then the sudden drop to the silence of reflection—the broken fragments of the characteristic spinning accompaniment —which might from one point of view suggest the sobs and the difficulty of getting back to the spinning again; and the exact adjustment of the harmony to the desperate sadness of the mood. Every resource is thus made use of to emphasise the expression. And so it is with numbers of other songs which will bear the closest analysis; especially when the poems happen to be fine enough to inspire fine music and close and consistent treatment.

In the gigantic mass of Schubert's songs there is necessarily a large quantity that is of no great value—that is even flat and pointless. But this is all of a piece with the spirit of the new age which he prefigured so ripely. His aims were in a sense speculative. He had no preconceived idea of the form in which to put his utterances; he only felt that he had to start from a given point of tonality and get back to it. If the thought of the poet suggested modulations which were not too copious or too ill distributed to be intelligible, the result was a success; if the poet's imagery was too flat and his thought too mechanical, or on the other hand too turgid and too indefinite, the chances were in favour of a failure. Schubert had the good fortune to have some truly superb poems to inspire him; and even in lower standards, whenever any "local colour" or strong human characteristics can be associated with the words, his mind would fasten on them and make them the cue for his manner and the matter he gave to his instrument.

It is very significant that with a divine gift of melody he rarely condescends to rely upon that alone. The greater number of his melodies gain their very expressive character through his harmonisation. He instinctively understood the relation of harmony to melody, and its power of emphasising definite expression at a moment; where melody would have to express a thing—if it could do it at all—by a long phrase. It is also characteristic of the time that his melodies are often constructed of figures which are very definite and decisive in themselves. The articulation is sometimes almost as clear as in Beethoven's subjects. Mozart, and the Italians among whom

he represents the highest type, usually made long meandering passages of melody with no very definite articulation.
The true Teuton aiming at concentration of expression
compresses his thought into figures which are specially
definite and telling. They become the nuclei by which he
indicates the spirit of his work. The process of figure
development is especially characteristic of instrumental
music, because in it rhythm helps the concentration and
definition; and the use of such characteristic figures in
the instrumental part of songs is a very conspicuous
feature in Schubert's work and that of all other great
song-writers; but it is also characteristic in a lesser degree
of the finest vocal melody.

The development of song art after Schubert's time
is mainly notable in respect of the application of new
resources as they come into being; and the special attitude towards poetry taken by the composer. Schumann,
as a man of exceptional cultivation, highly imaginative, and
closely in sympathy with poetry, was of the ideal type
to follow in Schubert's steps. He was gifted with more
of the familiar Teutonic disposition to reflect and look
inward than Schubert, whose gaiety of the Viennese
type generally kept him in touch with the outward aspect
of things. There is more passion and depth and sensibility in Schumann, but less of the gift of portrayal.
Schumann excelled in the things that are direct utterances of inner feeling. Many phases of the impulses of
love find most vivid expression with him, which Schubert
could not have touched. "Du meine Seele," "Ich grolle
nicht," are moods which are eminently characteristic of a
later phase of human musical sensibility than Schubert's,
and help to fill up the whole circuit of song types; which
is still further enriched by the remaining great German
song-writer of the present day, Johannes Brahms. The
three between them fill up almost the whole range of the

higher type of song-writing. Numbers of other successful
song-writers there are—and unsuccessful ones—who fully
understand what an opportunity the association of a solo
voice with an instrumental accompaniment affords for
definite and close characterisation. And composers of
different nations impart the flavours of Slav, English,
Norwegian, and French to their songs, but make them, if
they have any sense, on the same general terms as the great
Germans. Each national flavour lends a special interest
to the product, if the product is a sincere and genuine
musical utterance; but the methods upon which they
are constructed remain as they were with Schubert and
Schumann.

The advantage of the song branch of art is that
the expressive resources of music are applied for purposes which the words make plain. Where the words
are thoroughly musical, and the composer particularly
sensitive and skilful, the music fits every instant of the
lyric, and makes the words glow with intensified meaning.
In some ways the other principal branch of domestic
music labours under the apparent disadvantage that its
exact meaning is often left obscure. Even when pianoforte pieces are identified with ideal subjects by titles,
composers do not very often attempt to emphasise the
details of their working in the mind; and such realistic
devices as were popular in former days to depict "The
Battle of Prague," and similarly exciting events, are recognised by all the world as laughable. Unconsciously
the development of the musical world's sense of criti-
cism tends to arrive at the truth, that though realism is
admissible as a source of suggestion, the object of the
expressive power of music is not to represent the outward semblance of anything, but to express the moods
which it produces, and the workings of the mind that
are associated with them. When Beethoven calls a

movement "Am Bach," he justifiably uses the ripple of the water as his accompaniment. But the ripple does not make the sum total of the effect, and is not the aim of the movement; it only forms the musical atmosphere or medium in which the expressive material is embodied. The little disjointed fragments of figure which float on the rustling sound of the water are, as it were, broken ejaculations of happy contentment, which gather into volume at length with the full sweep of pure delight expressed in the melody :—

In such a movement, indeed, Beethoven's power of giving utterance to human feeling seems even to be intensified by associating it with a little realism. And it may at once be granted that a little of such realism is sometimes a help to the composer, for it keeps his moods in tune; but it is also a dangerous weapon to handle, and every one is conscious in a moment if the subordinate relation of realistic to inward presentation is exceeded.

These conditions help to explain the peculiarities of the course of one important department of modern music. The pianoforte has become one of the most familiar objects of domestic life, and occupies the position at one time held by the lute, at another by the harpsichord and clavichord. It is eminently a practical instrument, and can be made to serve for the wildest excesses of vulgarity as well as for a very tolerable amount of fine and noble music; which gives it a great advantage over previous instruments from a purely practical point of view. The lute was slow moving, soft and delicate; it could neither rage nor rattle. The harpsichord could rattle, and tinkle counterpoint, and present fine effects of harmony, and give a picturesque sound; but it was only moderately efficient for rhythm

x

and *cantabile*. The pianoforte, lacking certain beauties
which both the earlier instruments possessed, is infinitely
more efficient for every kind of characterisation. It combines common sense with a very tolerable capacity for
becoming poetical. It puts a wide range of musical
expression into the hands of one performer, and enables
him to present music in all the phases of harmony, polyphony, colour, melody and rhythm which have become
necessities of modern music. It is the compendium of
musical performance, and as such is most apt for domestic
use. Its sphere of public activity, the great concert
room, is secondary to this; and is the mere outcome of
the need for giving a large general public the opportunity
of hearing celebrated performers. It is rather its position
as the chosen instrument of intimate home life which has
induced composers to write so much for it; and the consciousness that its real function is to deal with things
intimately has had considerable influence upon the style
of music written for it; especially in the earlier stages of
pianoforte music. The intimate music of home life is
that which people like to have always with them. It is
the music that they like to dwell upon, and to hear again
and again as the true presentation of human feeling, and
as finished and refined works of art. The purest conceivable ideal of such intimate music is to be found in Bach's
"Wohltemperirte Clavier." But that lacks the modern
sensibility, the modern luxury of tone, and the phases
which represent those developments of harmonic design
and colour which have become part of modern musical
life. Later composers have aimed at supplying all varieties
of tastes with pianoforte music which is for home con-
sumption; and, inasmuch as this implies dealing with
characteristics at close quarters, and addressing themselves to an infinite variety of small groups of individuals,
the circumstances have produced a wider range of char-

acteristics in pianoforte music than in any other branch
of the art. What people like to have at home is the
true test of their standard of refinement. The diversity
is obviously immense; ranging from Bach and Beethoven
to mere arrangements of popular items from the latest
Italian opera, or the buffoonery of nigger minstrels. But
this only emphasises the theory of constant differentiation, and growth of diversity of character in such things.
For in these days nearly every taste can be satisfied.

To come finally to the working of the influences which
have made modern pianoforte music what it is under these
circumstances. In Beethoven's work the world felt that
the high water mark of art and expression in sonata form
had been reached. Certain expansions of it, no doubt,
were possible; and in such branches as quartetts, trios,
and other forms of pianoforte chamber music, there still
is vitality. But in essentially pianoforte music it was not
worth while to do again what had been done as well as
seems humanly possible. Moreover, composers have become conscious that the sonata form is spread rather wide,
and is best suited for rather special occasions; and further,
that it is not quite perfectly suited to many types of thought
which are quite fit to be treated musically, though not at
such great length. And so there has grown up a common
consensus of opinion to explore new possibilities. And here
men of various types have necessarily taken various lines.
There were all sorts of ways in which new departures
might be made. Some men delight in neatness of design,
some in ardent expression, some in ingenuity, and some
in display. All types found their exponents. Schubert
left many beautiful little movements in very characteristic
vein; Field made an important mark with his nocturnes;
and Mendelssohn came very prominently before the world
in a similar line with his "Lieder ohne Worte," which
rightly took a very comprehensive hold upon the artistic

public through their thoroughly refined character and the finished qualities of their art. It is patent to all the world that these last are totally different in form as much as expression from sonatas. Their title admirably expresses them, and the more so if it be remembered that "Song" was coming to mean something vastly different from the old conception; and implied a work of art in which all the factors—melody, harmony, figure, rhythm—combined to the common end. Under such conditions, when the name Song has become almost inappropriate, a "Song without words" was not such an anomaly as it would have been in less developed stages of art. Mendelssohn, however, as was natural in his days, rather emphasised the melody which is the counterpart of the absent voice, and thereby somewhat restricted his resources of expression; so his work may be said to lean in the formal direction more than many later productions.

Of conspicuously different type were the wild theories of a certain group of enthusiasts, whose eagerness to solve artistic problems was in excess of their hold upon the possibilities and resources of art. They emphasised unduly the expressive aims of Beethoven, and thought it possible to follow him in that respect without regard to his principles of design; and sought to develop a new line of art by the use of clearly marked musical figures, which were to be presented in an endless variety of guises in accordance with some supposed programme. The scheme recognised the expressive aims of music to the fullest possible extent, and might have come to a more successful issue but for two circumstances. One of these was that through taking the superficial theorists' view of sonata form to represent all the facts, they entirely overlooked the deeper principles, and rejected those deeper principles along with some of the superficial conventions of the theorists. And this rendered the failure of their scheme inevitable until they arrived at a better understanding of the situation. The second circumstance was the accident that they were closely connected with the most advanced school of technicians; indeed, one of the foremost representatives of their views was the greatest pianoforte virtuoso of modern times; and the outcome of this connection was that their reforming efforts were completely drowned and extinguished by the flood of ornamental rhetoric to which the abnormal development of pure technical facility in performance gave rise. Nearly all the energy of composers of this section of humanity was expended in finding ways to make scales and arpeggios sound more astonishing than they used to do when they were played in the old-fashioned ways; and further, of finding opportunities for showing off such futile dexterities. It so happens that their root theory of working up figures and bits of tune into programme movements adapts itself well to the requirements of display. It is only people of inferior organisation who are taken in by such empty extravagance of barren ornament; and for people of that type tunes out of operas which they already know, or familiar popular tunes, are the most intelligible forms of musical material. So, when a composer of this school addressed himself to his task of showing off the new kinds of scales and arpeggios, he had only to collect a few familiar tunes and intersperse them with all the ornamental resources of which he was master, and the scheme was complete. Curiously enough, though works of such kind are totally worthless intrinsically, the skill which the composers developed in technique materially widened the resources of effect which thereby became available for better composers to use. In that sense the development of technique, and of the effect which comes of it, is of great historical importance; and his achievements in that direction give Liszt a noteworthy position quite apart from the actual quality of his musical effusions. He, indeed, summed up a great period of development of pianoforte technique, and put the crown on that branch of music.

However, the result of technical development has not been all gain. It has been carried to such an excessive extent that pianoforte music has been rather overburdened. A faulty tradition has got into the very marrow of this branch of art, and a composer has to address himself so much to technical effect that there is little vigour left over for genuine expression.

But by the side of the school of virtuosi, and in touch with it, the spirit of Chopin has laid a spell upon musical people all the world over, and. has coloured a singularly wide range of musical activity in all countries. His circumstances were specially suited to the necessities of the moment. The Poles are peculiarly different from the more happily regulated races of the western part of Europe; and the fact of having been unfortunate in their relations with their most powerful neighbours has intensified nationalist feeling. Such feeling, when repressed, generally bursts into song, and very often into very expressive song; and in Chopin's time everything combined to enhance the vividness and individuality of Polish music. Chopin, with Polish blood in his veins, and brought up in pure Polish surroundings, absorbed the national influences from his early years. Under such circumstances a national dance becomes a vital reality of more than ordinary calibre. A mazurka was a rhythmic expression of the national fervour. A polonaise symbolised the exaggerated glories of the Polish chivalric aristocracy. Music which was so vivid and direct, and had such a touch of savage fervour, was not of the kind to go satisfactorily into sonatas. There needed to be very little intellectuality about it, but a great deal of the rhythmic element and of poetic

feeling, and these things Chopin was eminently fitted to
supply. On the other hand, his sensitiveness was acute
even to morbidity; and being less gifted with force and
energy than with excitability, he applied himself instinctively to the more delicate possibilities of his instrument.
With him ornamental profusion was a necessity; but,
more than with any other composer except Bach, it
formed a part of his poetical thought. With most of
the player-composers who cultivate virtuoso effects the
brilliant passages are purely mechanical, and have little
relation to the musical matter in hand. With Chopin
the very idea is often stated in terms of most graceful
and finished ornamentation, such as is most peculiarly
suited to the genius of the instrument. Beethoven had
grown more and more conscious of the suitableness of
very rapid notes to the pianoforte as his experience increased, and he had tried (in a different manner from
Chopin) to achieve the same end. But the reserve and
grandeur of his style did not admit of the sort of ornaments that Chopin used; for these are made peculiarly
vivid by profuse use of semitones and accessory notes of
all kinds, which do not form part either of the harmony or
the diatonic scale in which the passages occur. It gives
a peculiarly dazzling, oriental flavour to the whole, which,
joined with a certain luxurious indolence, a dreaminess of
sentiment, and a subtlety of tone, makes Chopin's the ideal
music for the drawing-rooms of fairly refined and pros-
perous people. But there is enough of genuine humanity
and dramatic feeling to make his works last. There are
even passages of savagery, such as those in the polonaises
in A♭ and F♯ minor, which sound like some echo from a
distant country, and serve to rouse people just enough in
relation to the rest of those fine and stirring works. The
"Ballades" and so-called Sonatas and Scherzos convey a
rich variety of moods and effects on a considerable scale,

while the nocturnes, and some of the preludes and mazurkas, exactly hit the sensuous side which is so highly developed in modern life. Fortunately with Chopin the general departure from sonata lines was no result of theory, but the spontaneous action of his nature. His music was the spontaneous utterance of a poetic and sensitive disposition, in the terms ideally suited to the instrument whose innermost capacities he understood more thoroughly than any one else in the world. Design of a classical kind was comparatively unimportant to him. He did not know much about it. But he most frequently cast his thoughts in simple forms, such as that of the nocturne—which Field had brought successfully before the world just before his time—or the ordinary forms of the dance. When he struck out a form for himself, as in some of the best preludes and studies, it was like a poem on new lines. But the methods by which they were unified were usually the same as those employed by J. S. Bach. Only in respect of their much more vivid colour, and intensity of feeling for modern expression, do they differ from the far more austere master. Of the degree in which expression is emphasised rather than form there can hardly be question. But when the form is original it is extraordinarily well adapted to the style of the expression; as, for instance, in the preludes in E minor and D minor, where the form and expression are as closely wedded as in the most skilful and condensed poetical lyric. But such types of thought could not be expanded into great schemes of design. His largest works in original forms are the Ballades, and these are as unlike sonatas as any. The whole collection of his works is an illustration of the wide spread of possible variety which the new departure in the direction of expression, after the formal age, made inevitable.

Utterly different as was the nature of Schumann, his work in general tends in the same direction; and, as it

were, fills up the other half of the circle which Chopin
left comparatively vacant. Schumann was a typical Teuton
in his introspective disposition, his mystic imaginings, his
depth of earnestness. The rhythmic side of music did not
appeal to him with anything like the elastic, nervous
intensity with which it excited a Pole, but rather with
the solemnity and orderliness of a German waltz. His
department was rather the type of music which belongs
to the reflective mind; and the types of thought, both
emotional and noble, which appeal to a cultivated in-
tellectualist. As it was not intended to make music his
life's occupation, his education in his art was not as complete and thorough as that of many other composers; but
it brought him into closer contact with the expression
of human feeling in poetic forms and in general literature, and forced him to take an unconventional view of
his art. He saw from the first that something different
from sonatas was wanted; and though he did write a few
sonatas, the one that is most like the old sonatas is rather
weak in design though brilliant in effect; while the sonata
in F♯ minor is a deliberate attempt to distribute the
ideas in a manner totally different from the old sonata
order. In forms which afforded some fresh opportunities
for treatment and effect, as in the quintett and quartett
in E♭, he is very much more successful in contriving
something like the old sonata forms; but in the main
his works for the pianoforte are attempts to open up a
new path, and to increase the variety of types of form and
expression in music. To a great many of his epigrammatic
musical poems he affixes names—such as the familiar
"Warum," "Träumeswirren," "Grillen;" the numbers
of Carnival figures, the beautifully finished and neatly
expressive Kinderscenen; in some cases he gives no names
to individual numbers, but makes it very clearly felt that
he has a decided poetic purpose, as in the Kreisleriana

and the Davids-bündler. Moreover, the general names he gave to these sets supply the clues to those who know his particular lines of reading, and his special enthusiasms at particular times in his life, which indicate what he meant to express by them. In other cases he gives general names, such as Novelletten, to imply new experiments in form without so much of an acknowledged poetic purpose. In the case of the fantasia in C, he tried to develop a work on a scale fully equal to sonatas, but totally different in character and principle of design. In most of these works his idea seems to be to give the full sense of design by the juxtaposition of ideas which illustrate one another in a poetical sense, and to contrive their connection by means which are in consonance with the spirit of the ideas, and sometimes by making some characteristic musical figure into a sort of text. The experiments are so far novel that it is almost too much to expect of them to be always entirely successful. But at least in the last movement of the fantasia, the principle of design and the development of the whole scheme is as successful as the ideas themselves are beautiful and poetical.

Schumann, like Beethoven, revels in a mass of sound. But his sound is far more sensuous and chromatic. He loved all the pedal it was possible to use; and had but little objection to hearing all the notes of the scale sounding at once. He is said to have liked dreaming to himself, by rambling through all sorts of harmonies with the pedal down; and the glamour of crossing rhythms and the sounding of clashing and antagonistic notes was most thoroughly adapted to his nature. A certain confusion of many factors, a luxury of conflicting elements which somehow make a unity in the end, serve admirably to express the complicated nature of the feelings and sensibilities and thoughts of highly organised beings in modern times. Chopin's style has coloured almost all pianoforte music since his time, in respect of the manner and treatment of the instrument; and many successful composers are content merely to reproduce his individualities in a diluted form. But Schumann has exerted more influence in respect of matter and treatment of design. With him the substance is of much greater significance, and he reaches to much greater depths of genuine feeling. There must necessarily be varieties of music to suit all sorts of different types of mind and organisation, and Chopin and Schumann are both better adapted to cultivated and poetic natures than to simple unsophisticated dispositions. That is one of the necessities of differentiation; and music which is concentrated in some especial direction can only meet with response from those who possess the sensitive chord that the music is intended to touch. There are natures copious enough to have full sympathy with the dreamers as well as the workers; but as a rule the world is divided between the two. People who love much imagery and luxury of sensation do not want to listen to Cherubini's best counterpoint, and those who only love energy and vital force do not want to listen to the love scenes in the Walküre. But as illustrating the profusion of sensations, the poetic sensibility, and even the luxury and intellectuality, the passion and the eagerness of modern life, Chopin and Schumann between them cover the ground more completely than all the rest of modern pianoforte composers put together.

For greatness of expression and novelty of treatment Johannes Brahms stands out absolutely alone since their time. Disdaining the ornamental aspects of pianoforte music, he has had to find out a special technique of his own; and in order to find means to express the very original and powerful thoughts that are in him, he resorts to devices which tax the resources of the most capable pianists to the utmost. Moreover, he taxes the power of the interpreter also; which is a thing all virtuosi pianists are not prepared for. There is something austerely noble about his methods, which makes thought and manner perfectly consistent; and though it cannot be said that his line of work is so easily identifiable with the general tendency towards definite expression, he has produced many works that are decidedly not on the line of sonatas—such as his Rhapsodies and Clavier-Stücke; all instinct with the definiteness and decisiveness of individuality which mark him as an out-lying representative of the great family of Teutonic musical giants.

The aspect of pianoforte music in general seems to indicate that composers are agreed that the day for writing sonatas is past, and that forms of instrumental music must be more closely identified with the thoughts which are expressed in them. The resources of harmonic and poly-phonic effect, combined with rhythm and melody, are much richer than the resources of simple accompanied melody; and the growth of fresh resources is by no means at an end. There is plenty of room for characteristic work. Composers have begun to import national traits into their pianoforte compositions with perfect success; and the identifying of a nation's essential character with its music can be aptly and very considerably extended in pianoforte music as in other branches of art. The field for characteristic musical expression is certainly not exhausted; and composers who have any gift for de-vising consistent and compact forms which are perfectly adapted to the mood of their ideas, have still room to achieve something new in the most interesting modern phases of art. The sonata type was no doubt adapted to the highest and noblest kind of musical expression; and it is not likely that anything so noble and so perfect in design as Beethoven's work will be seen in the world for a long while. But even if illustrations have not so elevated a dignity as the works of a great artistic period, they may serve excellent purposes, and be in every way admirable, and permanently interesting and enjoyable, if they are carried out with fair understanding of the true necessities of the situation, and with the sincerity of the true artistic spirit.

One of the most obvious features of the modern condition of music is the extraordinary diversity of forms which have become perfectly distinct, from symphony, symphonic poem, and opera, down to the sentimental ballad of the drawing-rooms. And in all of them it is not only the type of design which has become distinctive, but the style as well. For instance, one of the branches of music which is still most vigorously alive is chamber music, which consists mainly of combinations of varieties of solo, stringed, or wind instruments, with pianoforte, in works written on the lines of sonatas. Its present activity is partly owing to the fact that it has rather changed its status from being real chamber music, and is becoming essentially concert music. The instruments are treated with less delicacy of detail than they were by Beethoven, with a view to obtain the sonority suitable to large rooms. The style has therefore necessarily changed to a great extent; but nevertheless it is as closely differentiated from the style of all other branches of art as ever. A touch of the operatic manner instantly betrays itself as unsuitable, and so do many of the devices of orchestration. Thus there is an average mood and style of idea which composers have instinctively adopted for each branch of art, so that they are distinct not only in technical details but in spirit. And even in the highest branches of art, represented by the noble symphonies of Brahms, which illustrate the loftiest standard of style of the day, the significant change from the old ideals is noticeable. For the aim is but rarely after what is equivalent to external beauty in music. What beauty is aimed at is beauty of thought, the beauty of nobleness, and high musical intelligence. Even beauty of colour is but rarely present; but the colours are always characteristic, and confirm the reality of the powerful and expressive ideas. So the rule holds good, even in the most austere lines, that the latest phase of art is characterisation.

CHAPTER XIV.

MODERN PHASES OF OPERA.

GLUCK's theories of reform had strangely little effect upon
the course of opera for a long while. The resources of
art were not sufficiently developed to make them fully
practicable, and even if they had been, it is quite clear
that in many quarters they would not have been adopted.
The problem to be solved in fitting intelligible music to
intelligible drama is one of the most complicated and
delicate ever undertaken by man; and the solution is
made all the more difficult through the fact that the
kind of public who frequent operas do not in the least care
to have it solved. Operatic audiences have always had
the lowest standard of taste of any section of human
beings calling themselves musical. They generally have
a gross appetite for anything, so long as it is not intrinsically good. If the music is good they have to be forced
to accept it by various forms of persuasion; and a composer who attempts any kind of artistic thoroughness has
to look forward either to failure, or to the disagreeable
task of insisting on being heard. It follows that progress
towards any ideal assimilation of the various factors of
operatic effect has to be achieved in spite of the taste of
the audiences, and by the will and determination which
is the outcome of a composer's conviction. Nations vary
very much in their capacity to take sensible views of
things, as they do in their capacity for enjoying shams
and taking base metal for gold; so a composer's opportunities of emancipating himself from convention, and of

solving the problems he sees to be worth solving, are much better in one country than another. It is conspicuously true in operatic matters that the public decide what they will have, unless a man is strong enough to force them to listen to what they have at first no mind for; and even then the public have, as it were, a casting vote.

It cannot be pretended that all the causes of the different aspects of opera in different countries can be conclusively shown; but the general and familiar facts are strangely in accordance with the general traits of national character which are commonly observed. The Italians appear to have been the most spontaneously gifted with artistic capabilities of any nation in Europe. In painting they occupy almost the whole field of the greatest and most perfect art; especially of the art produced in the times when simple beauty of form and colour was the main object of artists. In music too they started every form of modern art. Opera, oratorio, cantata, symphony, organ music, violin music, all sprang into life under their auspices. But in every branch they stopped half way, when the possibilities of art were but half explored, and left it to other nations to gather the fruit of the tree which they had planted. Numbers of causes combine to make this invariable result. One of the most prominent is curiously illustrated by the history of opera. The Italians are generally reputed to be on the average very receptive and quickly excitable. The eagerness of composers for sympathetic response is found in the same quarters as quick receptiveness of audiences to the music that suits them. The impressions which are quickly produced do not always spring from the most artistic qualities, but the Italian composer cannot take note of that; he is passionately eager for sympathy and applause, and is impelled to use all the most obvious incitements to obtain them, without consideration of their fitness. The

way in which Italian opera composers resort to the most
direct means to excite their audiences is a commonplace
of everyday observation. The type of opera aria, which
was polished and made more and more perfectly adapted
to the requirements of the singer from Scarlatti's time
to Mozart's, was ultimately degraded under the influence
of this eagerness for applause into the obvious, catchy
opera tunes which are the most characteristic features
of the works of the early part of this century. The good
artistic work which used to be put into the accompaniment, and was often written in a contrapuntal form by the
composers of the best time, degenerated into worthless
jigging formulas, like the accompaniments to dance tunes,
which have neither artistic purpose nor characteristic relevancy to the situation. The blustering and raging of
brass instruments when there is no excuse for it in the
dramatic situation, and such tricks as the whirling Ros-
sinian crescendo (which is like a dance of dervishes all
about nothing), produce physical excitement without any
simultaneous exaltation of higher faculties. These and
many more features of the same calibre are the fruits of the
excessive eagerness in the composer for immediate sympathetic response from his audience. He has no power to
be self-dependent, or take his own view of what is worthy
of art or what is not, or of what represents his own identity. The thirst for the passionate joy of a popular
triumph must have its satisfaction. What men constantly
set themselves to obtain they generally succeed in obtaining; and the objects of Italian opera composers have
been abundantly achieved. The furore of Italian operatic
triumphs, such as the Rossini fever after Tancredi, sur-
passes anything recorded or conceivable in connection
with any other branch of art. The opera tunes of Bellini,
Donizetti, and the early works of Verdi have appealed to
the largest public ever addressed by a musician; and that

Y

is the sum of their contribution towards the modern development of their art. In respect of the details of workmanship of which their public were not likely to take much notice, such as the orchestration, they were careless and coarse; and the advance made from the standard of Mozart all round until recent times has been made backwards.

The Italians emphasised the musical means of appealing to their audiences from the first; the French, on the other hand, always had more feeling for the drama, and stage effect, and ballet. Though the stories of Roland, Armide, Phaeton, and the other subjects Lulli used are somewhat formal in their method of presentation, they are made quite intelligible, and the situations are often very good, and very well treated. In that sense, indeed, Lulli's work is more genuine than Scarlatti's. The same aspect of things continues throughout the history of French opera. French audiences seem to have been capable of being impressed by the pathos, tragedy, and human interest and beauty of the situations. Their minds seem to have been projected more towards the subject than the music. Gluck's dramatic purpose found a response in Paris that he failed to find even in Vienna, where Italian traditions prevailed. Things would seem to have bid fair in the end for French opera. When Italians came under French influence they did good work. French influence helped Cherubini to achieve his great operatic successes. Perhaps the enigmatical relation between his reputed character and his actual work may have been somewhat owing to Parisian influence. Personally he appeared to be endowed with all the pride, reserve, and narrowness of a pedant, yet his Overture to Anacreon is as genial as the ancient poet himself may be supposed to have been, and expresses all the fragrance and sparkle of the wine of which he sang with such enthusiasm. He

was cold and hard and devoid of sympathetic human
nature, but nevertheless he devised the tragic intensity
of his opera Medea with unquestionable success.

In later days the influence exerted by French taste
upon Rossini is even more notable and pregnant with
meaning.   After his wild triumphs in Italy he came into
contact with the French operatic traditions, and they
at once brought out whatever there was of real dramatic
sincerity in his constitution.   William Tell, the one work
which he wrote for a Parisian audience, puts him in quite
a new light; for under the influence of a more genuinely
dramatic impulse even his artistic work improved; the
orchestration becomes quite interesting, the type of
musical ideas is better, and they are better expressed,
and the general feeling of the whole is more sincere and
rich in feeling.

In light comic operettas and operatic comedies the acute
sympathy of the French with the stage produced the happiest results of all.   In this line the French took their cue
from the Italian opera buffa, which had been introduced a
little before Gluck's time, and became very noticeable by
reason of the ferment of controversy that it produced.
Once rooted in the soil and cultivated by French composers,
it was found to be even more at home than in Italy.   The
quick wit, and the sense of finish—even the element of
the superficial which the French cultivate with so much
interest and care—all told to make the product peculiarly
happy.   A special style was developed, which in the
hands of many composers was singularly refined, neat,
and perfectly artistic.   The music is merry, and in the
true comedy vein without descending to buffoonery:
carelessly gay, without being inartistic in detail.   In the
early days no doubt the resources of art were not very
carefully used, and however excellent the spirit and wit
of Grétry, it cannot be pretended that he attempted to

deal with the inner and less obvious phases of his work
with any artistic completeness. He professedly contemned
musicianship, and in a sense he was right. The typical
pedant never shows more truly the inherent stupidity
of his nature than when he obtrudes conscious artistic
contrivance into light subjects. But the perfect mastery
of artistic resource does not obtrude its artistic contrivances. It uses them so well that they are perfectly
merged in the general ensemble. The fact that Bach
was the most perfect master of artistic contrivance did
not prevent his writing perfectly gay dance tunes; and
Mozart's careful education in the mysteries of his craft
enabled him to write his comic scenes in a fully artistic
manner, without putting up sign-posts to tell people
when to look out for a piece of artistic skill. In that
respect Grétry was wrong, and his successors much
wiser. For men like Auber and Gounod, and other still
living representatives of this branch of art, use the resources of their orchestra with most consummate skill
at the lightest moments; just hitting the balance of
art and gaiety to a nicety; while the rounding and
articulation of their phraseology, the variety and clearness of their ideas, and the excellence of their design,
up to the point required in such work, is truly admirable.
In no other branch of music is the French genius so
completely at home and happy. Even in the coarser
types of the same family of operetta, which have become
rather popular in recent times, the composers who set
the licentious and unwholesomely suggestive dialogue at
least caught something of the spirit of their more refined brethren, and showed a skill of instrumental resource
and a neatness of musical expression and treatment which
are surprising in relation to such subjects. Whenever the
play aims at real human interest, and the capacity of the
composer for looking at it as human interest is equal to the

demand, French effort, even in the more serious branch of
opera, produces eminently sincere and artistic results. But
in the more serious subjects it has been generally happiest in
very reserved phases like those illustrated by Cherubini and
Méhul. The dangerous susceptibility of the French nature
to specious show and mere external effect seems peculiarly
liable to mislead them when it comes to great or imposing occasions. The French are so devoted to " style " that
they omit to notice that it is a thing which may be very
successfully cultivated to disguise inherent depravity and
falseness. It seems to be chiefly owing to this weakness
that the result of their enthusiasm for musical drama does
not come nearer the complete solution of the problem of
opera. At all events, the most imposing result obtained
in the direction of French opera is strictly in accordance
with those characteristics of the nation which have persisted so long that they were even noticed by the conquer-
ing Romans.

The influence is apparent even in Lulli's and Rameau's
work. The spectacular side is carefully attended to, and
forms a conspicuous element in the sum total. Gluck
had to submit, and to satisfy the taste to a certain
extent, and its effect is even more noticeable in the
works of his successor, Spontini. In many ways, however, French influence had an excellent effect upon the
latter composer. His operas are singularly full of true
dramatic expression; the details of orchestral effect are
worked out with marvellous care, and are extremely rich
and full of variety for the time when he wrote. The
scores are marked almost as fully and carefully as Wagner's, and the inner and outer phrases are thoroughly
articulate, and well suited to the instruments used.
He wielded all his resources with power and skill—
chorus, soloists, and orchestra alike. He saw his dramatic points clearly, and often rose to a degree of real

warmth and nobility of expression. But with all these excellencies the tendency to pomp and circumstance of display is unmistakable. The situations are often really fine, but many of them are rather weakened by being overdone. The coruscations of the long ballets, the processions, the crowds of various nationalities, and even the very tone and style of much of the music, show clearly which way things are tending. The same specious element of show peeps out now and then in the works of other composers, such as Halévy; and when ultimately the type of man arrived who knew how to play upon the weak side of French society's susceptibility to display, the true portent arose; and the crown which was put upon the long development of French grand opera, and embodied most of the results of French operatic aspiration, proved to be very imposing, but not of the most perfect metal.

Meyerbeer was of the brilliantly clever type of humanity. His gifts were various, and of a very high order. At first he was known as a brilliant pianist, and was famous for his quickness in reading from score. Then, a pianist's career not appearing imposing enough for his aspirations, he conceived the notion of becoming an opera composer. He tried several styles in succession. First he wrote German operas, without success. Then he went to Italy, and wrote operas in the Italian style, and met with a good deal of success. But as even this did not satisfy his aspirations, he inspected the situation in Paris, and seems to have made up his mind that the audience there was just suited for him. Indeed the Oriental love of display which is so frequently found still subsisting in people of Jewish descent marked out Meyerbeer as essentially the man for the occasion. He is said to have studied things French with minute care—both history and manners—and he made his first experiment upon the Parisians in 1831 with Robert le Diable, and achieved full measure of success.

At long intervals he followed it up with further experiments—The Huguenots in 1836, Le Prophète in 1849, and so on—till he had built himself a monument so large that if size were any guarantee of durability he would be as secure of perennial honour as Horace himself.

The fact which is conspicuously emphasised by these works is the gigantic development and variety of the resources of effect in modern times. Meyerbeer thoroughly understood the theatre, and he took infinite pains to carry out every detail which served for theatrical effect. He tried and tested his orchestral experiments again and again with tireless patience. He had L'Africaine by him for at least twenty years, and never got it up to the point of satisfying him, and finally died before it was performed. He was so painfully anxious that his effects should tell that his existence at the time when any new work was in preparation for performance is described as a perfect martyrdom. Beethoven, too, took infinite pains, and wrote and rewrote constantly. But his object was to get his ideas themselves as fine and as far from commonplace expression as possible; and to get the balance and design as perfect as his own critical instinct demanded. Meyerbeer's object was to make the mere externals tell. He did not care in the least whether his details were commonplace or not. His scores look elaborate and full of work, but the details are the commonest arpeggios, familiar and hackneyed types of figures of accompaniment, scales, and obvious rhythms. Musically it is a huge pile of commonplaces, infinitely ingenious, and barren. There is little cohesion between the scenes, and no attempt at consistency to the situations in style and expression. No doubt Meyerbeer had a great sense of general effect. The music glitters and roars and warbles in well-disposed contrasts, but the inner life is wanting. It is the same with his treatment of his characters. They metaphorically strut and pose

and gesticulate, but express next to nothing; they get
into frenzies, but are for the most part incapable of
human passion. The element of wholesome musical
sincerity is wanting in him, but the power of astonishing and bewildering is almost unlimited. His cleverness
is equal to any emergency. For instance, when a situation requires something impressive, and he has nothing
musical to supply, he takes refuge in a cadenza for a
clarinet or some other instrument, and the attention of
the public is engaged by their interest in the skill of the
performer, and forgets to notice that it has no possible
relation to the significance of the situation. The scenes
are collections of the most elaborate artifices carefully contrived and eminently effective from the baldest theatrical
point of view. But for continuity, development, real feeling, nobility of expression, greatness of thought, anything
that may be truly honoured in the observance, there is
but the rarest trace. He studied his audience carefully,
developed his machinery with infinite pains, carried out
his aims, and succeeded in the way he desired. No doubt
his works are worth the amusement of getting up, and of
seeing also, because of the extraordinary dexterity with
which the immense resources are wielded; but it cannot
be said that he attempted to face the problem of musical
drama at all. In that respect Faust and Carmen are
much nearer the mark. In both the types of expression are infinitely more sincere, there is more artistic work
in the details, more genuine sense of characterisation, and
a much higher gift both of harmony and melody. Even
the feeling for instrumental effect is really much finer; for
there is more of real beauty of sound and more indication
of ability to use colour to intensify situations. But in the
end, neither of these approaches the complete solution of
the problem. The traditional formulas of cheap accompaniment, the laxness in the treatment of inner minutiæ,

the set forms of arias, and the detachable items that only hang together and are not intrinsically continuous, and many other features of convention and habit, prevent their being a completely satisfactory type of musical drama from the highest standpoint.

Germans were much slower than other nations in finding a national type of opera. They learnt very early how to succeed in writing operas for other nations, and surpassed the Italians in their own lines when it was worth doing it. But the discovery of the style and method suited to their more critical aspirations took many centuries. Mozart had done something for the cause in Seraglio and the Zauber-flöte. Then there was a pause of many years, till Beethoven at last found a subject which he thought worthy of musical treatment, and gave the world Fidelio. In the interval musical art had advanced a good deal, chiefly through Beethoven's own efforts. He had written his first three symphonies, and got to the end of his "first period;" which implies a considerable development of the resources of real expression. As is natural, it is in the scenes where human circumstances become deeply interesting, and deep emotions are brought into play, that Beethoven is at his best. In the lighter scenes between Marcellina and Jacquino, in Rocco's song, he is less like himself; and even Pizarro's fierce song rings a little hollow. Beethoven could hardly bring such things within the range of his particular type of expression. But for the more truly emotional situations, especially in the prison scene, he wrote the finest and truest music that exists in the whole range of opera. In fact, the whole work is too reserved and lofty to be fit for any but extremely musical audiences, and it has never been a genuine success with the public. Moreover, though the language of the play was German, and the serious spirit in which the music was written is worthy of the great German's attitude towards music, it was not essentially a German subject, and traces of old Italian influence through Mozart are still apparent. It was reserved for a man of far less personality to satisfy the aspirations after true Teutonic music drama.

The chief advantages of Weber's early years were the opportunities he obtained for getting into touch with the theatre, through his father's eagerness to possess an opera-producing prodigy after the Mozart pattern. He was not especially identified with national sentiments till after Napoleon's failure in the expedition to Moscow. Then, in common with many patriotic enthusiasts, the hope for independence inspired him, and he became the mouth-piece of national feeling in his superb settings of patriotic songs by Körner. These gave him a position which was emphasised by his being appointed successively at Prague and Dresden to organise a genuine German operatic establishment. Dresden had long been under the domi-nation of the Italians, headed by the conductor Morlacchi, and the constant plotting and opposition which went on even after his appointment only served to intensify his patriotic feeling. This at last found its full expression in "Der Freischütz," which was brought out at Berlin in 1821, and was immediately taken by the Germans to their hearts. It was indeed the first successful fruit of their aspirations, and its out and out German character in every respect gives it a great prominence in the history of the art. The style is consistently German almost throughout; the tunes are the quintessence of German national tunes and folk songs; the story is full of the mystery and romance which the Germans love, and is about real German people with thoroughly German habits and German characters. Apart from that, the musical material and the actual workmanship are Teutonically ad-mirable. Weber's sense of instrumental effect was always very great, but in this work he rose to a higher point than usual. The tones and characteristics of the various instruments are used with unerring certainty to strengthen the emotional impression. The score is alive in all its parts, not full of dummy formulas and fragments of scales and arpeggios that have no relation to the situation. The various characters are also perfectly identified with the music that they have to sing. Kaspar, the reckless meddler in dangerous magic, was easily drawn; but the heroine Agathe, and the lighter-spirited Aennchen, both also keep their musical identity quite well, even when they are singing together. The scenes are separate, but the final transition to the continuous music of later times is happily illustrated in such a case as Agathe's famous scena, in which a great variety of moods and changes of rhythm and speed and melody are all closely welded into a perfectly complete and well-designed unity.

In Freischütz the German tradition of spoken dialogue is still maintained; the music being reserved for the intenser moments. In Euryanthe Weber set the whole of the dialogue, and thereby approached nearer to the ideal which the first originators of the form had conceived. The work in other respects keeps the same consistently German style, and possibly contains finer individual passages than its forerunner; but the desperate foolishness of the libretto makes the whole almost unendurable, except to people who have the capacity to attend to the music alone and to ignore what is going on on the stage. Weber had a curious inclination for stories of a romantic and chivalric cast, as well as delight in the supernatural, which is probably to be explained by the instinct of a composer for finding things out of the hackneyed range of common everyday experience. For light and comic music the familiar dress of everyday life answers perfectly well. It may even accentuate the funniness of things.

But when there are highly emotional, serious, heartfelt things to be dealt with, the association of the familiarities of everyday life with dialogue passionately sung, becomes too conspicuously anomalous. Thoughts that have any genuine greatness about them do not fit quite easily into commonplace terms. At any rate, Weber tried to escape from such familiarities in his librettos, and had the ill luck to fall into extremes of childish unreality which prevent his two later works being acceptable in more matter of fact times. But the excellence of the musical material, the freedom and breadth with which the scenes are developed without the requirements of musical design interfering in the least with the action, the complete achievement of a genuinely Teutonic theatrical style, quite different from the style of classical quartetts and symphonies and such self-dependent music, give Weber a position among the great representatives of musical achievement. Wagner fitly characterised him as most German of the Germans; and he himself was not a little indebted to him for mastering one of the last points of vantage necessary for the full attainment of the ideal of pure dramatic music.

Weber's style powerfully influenced his successors, even in domains outside opera; his supernatural line was followed in something of the same style by Marschner and others, while Spohr plodded on by the side of them writing operas with very little dramatic style about them, but with good feeling for artistic finish and refined effect. But Germans are slow moving as well as tenacious, and act as if they meant to do great things, and knew that great things took time to mature. It was many years before another great stroke for essentially German opera was achieved. German energy was not entirely relaxed, but it was concentrated in the person of Meyerbeer, who was busy writing French grand operas, and was best fitted for that occupation. Wagner, though born in Weber's life-time, did not begin to put his singular powers to any definite use till nearly twenty years after Weber had passed out of the world. Born of a family of actors, brought up in constant contact with the stage, inspired with dramatic fervour from early years, and passionately devoted to Beethoven and Weber, he had sufficient to impel him to the career of an opera composer. But at first he struck out at random. The impulse in him was mainly dramatic, and only experience could reveal to him what line and style of composition would serve him. His musical education was extremely defective, and his first experiments in opera contained things that were at once feeble and feebly expressed. Many were his changes of position. First he was chorus-master at a theatre at Wurzburg, then conductor at various places; he wrote several works which were inevitable failures; and finally with the ardent conviction of his mission, characteristic of his curious personality, he made up his mind to take by storm the central home of the art in the Grand Opera in Paris. Meyerbeer was then in the full plenitude of his glory, and the need of propitiating Meyerbeer's own particular audience probably prompted him to write his grand opera Rienzi in Meyerbeer's style, with all the glitter, blaze of brass, and scenic splendour he could think of. But as far as Paris was concerned his journey there was a failure. His importunities were in vain, and after many weary months he returned to Germany. But meanwhile he had been busy with a new work, Der fliegende Holländer, which, when completed, marked the definite commencement of his real career. The essence of the situation is that Wagner is throughout as much dramatist and master of theatrical requirements as musician. In fact, at first the spontaneous musical gift was comparatively small; but the intensity of his dramatic and poetic feeling produced musical figures and musical moods in his mind which he found out by degrees how to express in more and more powerful and artistic musical terms. The vitality of the Flying Dutchman lies more in the superbly dramatic story than in the music. But at the same time there are movements when the music rises to an extraordinary pitch of vivid picturesqueness and expressiveness. The whole of the overture is as masterly a musical expression of omens and the wild hurly-burly of the elements as possible, and carries out Gluck's conception of an overture completely; Senta's ballad is one of the most characteristic things of its kind in existence, and hits the mood of the situation in a way that only a man born with high dramatic faculty could achieve; and the duet between Senta and the Holländer is as full of life and as fine in respect of the exact expression of the moods of the situation and as broad in melody as could well be desired. Rienzi looks back to the past of Meyerbeer, and is comparatively worthless; Der fliegende Holländer looks forward along the way in which Wagner is going to travel, and already embodies traits of melody and particular devices of modulation and colour which become conspicuous, with more experienced treatment, in his maturer works.

His progress from this point was steady and steadfast in direction. Having struck on the vein of old world myths, and found their suitableness for musical treatment, he soon saw the further advantage of using stories which were essentially Teutonic in their source and interest. He wisely chose such as symbolised a great deal more than the mere stories convey, and so have a deep root in human nature and a wider scope. The story of Tannhäuser and the hill of Venus, and of Lohengrin the knight of the Holy Grail, each in their way show the growth of his powers of musical resource. Lohengrin is not so vigorous as its predecessor, but there are fewer crudities and formalities in it, and fewer traces of an unwholesome influence which made some parts of Tannhäuser run very near to vulgarity —splendid as the whole work is. A long time intervened between Lohengrin and Rheingold, the preface to the great mythic cycle—and the step in point of style and artistic management is as wide as the interval of time. He seems to have thought out his scheme more thoroughly. Indeed it may well be doubted if he had any scheme or method at all in the earlier works. In the Flying Dutchman the traces of the old operatic traditions are extremely common. The complete set movements merely holding together only by their ends, the musical isolation of scene from scene, the disconnection of the overture from the opening of the drama, and many other points, show that he had as yet by no means made up his mind to break away from the conventional traditions. In Tannhäuser and Lohengrin he made the musical texture of the scenes much more continuous, but the long operatic tunes still make their appearance along with many other familiar signs of the old genealogy. The use of the same characteristic musical figures in various parts of the works wherever some special personality or characteristic thought or situation recurs, is frequently met with, but the figures are not used with the systematic persistence that is so conspicuous in the later works. It seems extremely probable that it was reflection upon the earlier works, and writing about his artistic theories at the time of his exile, that led him to the uncompromising attitude of the later ones. The impulse which led to the new features in his earlier works was simply his dramatic feeling. He had no theoretic idea of replacing the principles of the old operatic formulas of design by "Leit motive." They were the result of the accident that he was trying to illustrate a dramatic subject in musical terms; and when any one so essential to the story as the Holländer or

Lohengrin or Elsa came prominently forward, it was
natural to repeat a figure which best expressed their
character. It conduced to unity as well as to characterisation. But it was done unsystematically in the earlier
works; and "Leit motive" only began to pervade the
whole texture of his musical material at last in the cycle
of "Der Ring des Nibelungen."

The change from the earlier works even to Rheingold,
the first drama of "The Ring," is as great as the change
from Beethoven's earliest symphonies to his C minor; and
apart from style and materials, the changes are the same
in principle. In the Symphony in D No. 2, the manner of
expressing the ideas is often very much like that of the
earlier generation. Even in the presentation of the first
idea there is a certain stiffness and formality, which is not
quite like the full-grown Beethoven. It seems to utter
the same kind of complacent attitude as is implied in
the work of John Christian Bach or Galuppi. But in the
C minor the first four
notes are quite enough
to give the mind the
impression that music has passed into a different region
from that of the formal politeness of the previous century.

Analogously in Tannhäuser there are many passages
which have the flavour of Italian opera about them—
many that even suggest the influence of Meyerbeer and the
Grand Opera. Long passages of melody of the formal
type, and frequent traces of things like the relics of rudi-
mentary organs, that have not perfectly merged into the
rest of the organism. But the first dozen bars of Rheingold give indication of quite a different spirit. The object
clearly is to express the situation at the beginning of the
first act. The depths of the Rhine are there, the swaying
waters, darkness. The music is the exact equivalent of
the central idea of the situation; and at the same time it

supplies a principle of design without having to fall back
on familiar formulas to make that design appreciable. The
dramatic conception is formed first, and is then expressed
in terms of art which follow every phase and change
of mood without having to stop to make the music intelligible apart from the drama. The principle of treatment is the same as in Schubert's great songs, the " Junge
Nonne," or the " Erl König ; " only the scale is larger
and the style different. Wagner wrote his own dramas,
always with a clear feeling of what was fit to be expressed
musically; and as he grew more experienced, he was
able to hold all the forces he had to use for dramatic
ends more surely in hand, and to control their relations
to one another with more certainty. While writing the
poems he probably had a general feeling of what the
actual music was going to be, just as a dramatist keeps
in his mind a fairly clear idea of the scene and the
action of the play he is writing; and as certain general
principles of design are quite indispensable in musical
works of this kind, he evidently controlled the development of his stories so as to admit of due spreading of
groundwork, and of variety of mood; and devised situations that admitted of plain and more or less diatonic
treatment, and crises which would demand the use of
energetic modulation, and so forth. But in reality this
requires less restriction than might be imagined; for the
working and changing of moods in a good poem is almost
identical with the working and changing of moods adapted
for good music. They both spring from the same emotional source, only they are different ways of expressing
the ideas. As poetry and music approach nearer to one
another, it becomes more apparent that the sequence of
moods which makes a good design in poetry will also
make a good design in music.

One thing which strikes the attention at once from the

z

commencement of "The Ring" is the difference in the treatment of the musical material. As has been pointed out before, there is a constant tendency in music to make the details more distinct and definite. The instinctive aim of the most highly gifted composers is to arrive at that articulation of minutiæ which makes every part of the organism alive. The type of vague meandering melodies which formed the arias of Hasse and Porpora became far more definite in organisation in Mozart's hands; the contrast is even greater between their treatment of orchestral resources and Mozart's. The very look of the score of Idomeneo is busier than any earlier score; and Mozart made his details more finished and more definite as his view of instrumental music matured. In the next generation the process of defining details progressed very fast in Beethoven's hands. Even in his first sonata the tendency to concentrate his thoughts into concise and emphatic figures is noticeable, and the habit grew more decisive with him as his mastery of his resources improved. The same tendency is shown in almost every department of art. Schubert's accompaniments to songs are often made up of little *nuclei* which express in the closest terms the spirit of the situation, and the way in which he knits them together is a perfect counterpart, in little, of Wagner's ultimate method. The advantages of the plan are obvious. It not only lays hold of the mind more decisively, but it enables the musical movement to be knit into closer unity by the reiteration of the figures. Wagner, in his earlier works, appears to have realised the importance of condensing the thought into an emphatic figure, as every one knows who has heard the overture to the "Fliegende Holländer," though he did not make much use of such figures in the actual texture of the earlier music. But from the beginning of the Rheingold he seems to have clearly made up his mind not only to condense his

representative musical ideas into the forms which serve
to fix them in the mind, but to weave them throughout
into the texture of the music itself, to dispense with the
old formulas of accompaniment, and to use next to nothing
except what was consistent and definite. The result is
that in the main the texture of the music is something of
the same nature as a fugue of Bach. Wagner often uses
harmony as a special means of effect, but in a great
measure the harmony is the result of polyphony, often of
several distinct subjects going on at once, as they used
to do in the ancient fugues. This immensely enlarges
the range of direct expression, as it is possible by the use
of familiar devices, such as accented passing notes and
grace notes, occurring simultaneously in different parts, to
produce transient artificial chords of the most extraordinary description.

Wagner notoriously rejected the conventional rules of
the theorists about resolving chords and keeping strictly
within the lines of keys, and many other familiar phases of
doctrine. He tried to get to the root of things, instead of
abiding by the rules that are given to help people to spell
and to frame sentences intelligibly. But he by no means
adopts purely licentious methods in treatment of chords,
nor does he forego the use of tonality—the sense of key
which is the basis of modern music—as a source of effect.
He did not attempt to define his design by the means
required in sonatas and symphonies, because the situation

did not warrant it; neither would he submit to the conventions which prevented his using certain progressions
which he thought the situation required because they happen to mix up tonalities. Many of the progressions which
Beethoven used outraged the tender feelings of theorists
of his day who did not understand them, and thought he
was violating the orthodox principles of tonality. Yet
Beethoven's whole system was founded on his very acute
feeling for it. He expanded the range of the key as much
as he could, and Wagner went further in the same direction. But he is so far from abandoning tonality as an
element of design and effect, that he uses it with quite
remarkable skill and perception of its functions. When
he wants to give the sense of solid foundation to a scene,
he often keeps to the same key, even to the same harmony, for a very long time. The Introductions to Rheingold and Siegfried are parallels in this respect, the first
almost all on one chord, the second almost all in one key;
and the principle of design is the same in both cases;
consisting in laying a solid foundation to the whole work
by rising from the lowest pitch, and gradually bringing
the full range of sounds into operation. In the accompaniment of the ordinary dialogue he is often very obscure in tonality, just as J. S. Bach is in recitative; some
instinct prompting them both to avoid the conditions
which make the music that approaches nearest to ordinary speech seem too definite in regular design. When
he wants to express something very straightforward and
direct, like the character of Siegfried, he uses the most
simple diatonic figures; but when he wants to express
something specially mysterious, he literally makes use of
the very fact that human creatures understand modern
music through their feeling for tonality, to obtain the
weird and supernatural effect he wants. For in that case
he almost invariably makes his musical idea combine

chords which belong to two or more unassimilable tonalities, on purpose to create the sense of bewilderment, and a kind of dizziness and helplessness, which exactly meets the requirements of the case. If people's sense of tonality were not by this time so highly developed, such passages would be merely hideous gibberish; and they often seem so at first. It is just on a parallel with language. A man may often say a thing that is most copiously true which his audience does not see at once, and everybody has experienced the puzzled, displeased look that the audience gives—till, as the meaning dawns upon them, a cloud seems to pass away, and the look of pleasure is all the brighter for the transition from bewilderment to understanding. Wagner's device stands in the same relation to the musical organisation of the present day as Beethoven's employment of enharmonic transition to that of his time. Men judge such things instinctively in relation to the context. The transition from the first key to the second in Beethoven's great Leonora Overture produces the same sort of feeling of momentary dizziness, in relation to the simpler diatonic style of the rest of the music, that Wagner's subtle obscurities do in relation to his far more chromatic and highly-coloured style. It need not be supposed that he deliberately adopted such a device. True composers very rarely work up to a theory consciously, in the act of production; but they may afterwards try to justify anything very much out of the common on some broad principles in which they believe. It is much more likely to have been the fruit of highly-trained instinct that caused Wagner to adopt the same procedure so invariably. A familiar example is the musical expression of that really marvellous poetic conception, the magic kiss of the god which expels the godhead from the Valkyrie and makes her mortal.

Even more conspicuous is the figure associated with
the "Tarnhelm," the helm of invisibility. But in that
case the effect often depends a good deal upon the way in
which the figure is taken in relation to a context in an
obscurely related key. The motive of the magic ring *
is condensed very closely, and is much to the point.

The death-figure in Tristan is constructed on similar
principles, but curiously enough the figure used for the
magic love potion, which pervades the whole musical work
of that drama, is not of mixed tonality, but only made
to seem so by the use of chromatic accessory notes. The
opening passage of Tristan is, indeed, peculiarly interesting in respect of clearness of tonality, for Wagner uses
the same device of sequence (which is the repetition of
an identical phrase at different levels) which is familiar in
ancient folk-song, in the opening movements of several of
Corelli's Sonatas (in just the same position in the scheme
of design), at the beginning of Beethoven's E minor
Sonata (Opus 91), and in Brahms' Rhapsody, No. 2,

where the device is carried to even greater lengths
than by Wagner. The subject of the love potion is
necessarily puzzling to the mind; but the use of the
sequence gives a sense of orderliness and stability which
is clearly essential at the beginning of a great work.
The sequence is perfectly familiar in its order, and
turns on nearly related keys—first A minor, then its
relative major C; then, taking the same step of a third
as the cue, E major, which is the dominant of A, and
therefore completes the circuit. And the process keeps
things in the right place too, for despite the very close
involutions of subordinate secondary tonalities, the system
of design in that wonderful Vorspiel is mainly centralised
on the relationships of A minor and C, and its general
scheme is the same as that of the introduction to Rheingold, Siegfried, and Parsifal; and in Parsifal, moreover,
he uses precisely the same device of sequence at the beginning, only developing it on a very much wider scale, as
suits the solemnity of the subject. It may be concluded,
therefore, that Wagner is very far from ignoring tonality.
His use of it is different from that of composers of sonatas
and symphonies, but he shows a very clear understanding
of the various opportunities that it affords for the purposes of effect.

In the use of the effects of tone producible by various
instruments (which people for want of a better word seem
to have agreed to call colour) he is clearly the most comprehensive of masters. Instinctively he adopted the true
view for his particular work. In old days colours were
disposed in relation to one another principally in order to
look beautiful. Perugino and Mozart seem much alike in
that respect. Gluck used the moderate variety of colours
at his disposal to add to the vividness of his situations.
Beethoven used colour to the extreme of conceivable perfection; and all to the ends of expression, as far as the

conditions of abstract self-dependent instrumental music admitted.

Wagner took the uncompromising position of using every colour, whether pure or composite, to emphasise and intensify each dramatic moment, and to complete the measure of expression which is only half conveyed by the outline and rhythmic movement of the musical ideas themselves. The great development of instrumental resources gave him enormous advantages over earlier composers. The improvement of instruments, the general improvement in the skill and intelligence of players, both served his turn. From the first his excitable nature was particularly susceptible to colour; but the more his powers matured, the more he used his colours with absolute aptness to the end in view. The composite vividness of the cellos, hautboys, corno inglese, horns, and bassoons at the beginning of the Vorspiel of Tristan, is not more absolutely to the point than the wonderful quietude and depth of solemnity of the tone of the strings alone at the opening of the third act. The magic sound of the horns in the music of the Tarnhelm is not more nor less suggestive than the merry cackle of the wood-wind in the music of the apprentices in "Die Meistersinger," or the vivid combination of various arpeggios for strings, with the solemn brass below, and the tinkling of the Glockenspiel at the top, which represent the rising of Loge's flames that shut out Brunnhilde from the world. Even with regard to the honourable old-world devices which have not much place in opera, the requirements of the situations brought out the requisite skill. The art of combining many subjects together, of which theoretic composers make so much, is carried by Wagner to a truly marvellous extent. The texture of the music is often made of nothing but a network of the various melodies and figures which are called "Leit motive," each associated with some definite idea in the drama. The extent to which this subtle elaboration is carried on escapes the hearer, because it is done so skilfully that it passes unperceived. But it is one of those respects in which the work of art bears constant close scrutiny, as a work of art should, without ceasing to be wonderful. It makes all the difference between the earlier types, when the figures of accompaniment had been only so many tiresome formulas, and the later work in which everything means something, and yet is not obtrusive. The elaboration of all the detail is still subordinate to the general design and the general effect. When a work is faulty in such respects it is because the composer tries to produce all his effect by the multiplicity and ingenuity of his details alone. The importunity of minutiæ soon makes works on a large scale insupportable. But Wagner's minutiæ are not importunate, because the effect in general is proportionately great. The wide sweeps of his sequences, the long and intricate growth towards some supreme climax, the width and clearness of the main contrasts, the immense sweep of his basses, the true grandeur of many of his poetic conceptions, keep the mind occupied enough with the larger aspects of the matter. And though, as in human life, all the little moments are realities, their prominence is merged in the greater events which form the sum of them.

Wagner's use of the voice part illustrates musical tendencies in the same way as every other part of his work. The traditions of solo singing which still persist in some quarters imply that the human voice is to be used for effects of beauty only. The old Italian masters subordinated everything to pure vocal effect; they made the utmost of pure singing, and singing only. Occasional reactions against so limited a view, and in favour of using the human voice for human expression, came up at various

points in history. Purcell is often a pure embodiment
of ill-regulated instinct for expression. John Sebastian
Bach's recitatives and ariosos are still stronger in that respect. The Italian reaction that followed him was all in
favour of beautiful vocal sound and simple intrinsic beauty
of melody; but in Schubert the claims of expression again
found an extremely powerful advocate. He appealed to
human creatures a good deal by means of melody, but much
more by his power of general expression. He often produces
much more effect by a kind of recitative than by tune.
He uses tune when it is suitable, otherwise musical declamation. He appeals to intelligent human beings who
want music to mean something worthy of human intelligence; and Schumann does eminently the same, though
he too knows full well how to express a noble sentiment
in a noble melodic phrase. Wagner again takes an attitude of "no compromise." The voice has an infinity of
functions in music. It may be necessarily reduced to the
standard of mere narrative, it may have to utter dialogue
which in detail is near the level of everyday talk; it must
rise in drama to the higher levels of dramatic intensity,
and it may rise, at times to the highest pitch of human
ecstasy. For each its appropriate use. The art is not
limited to obvious tune on one side, and chaotic recitative
on the other, but is capable of endless shades of difference.
Wagner makes Mime sing melody because he is a
sneaking impostor who pretends to have any amount of
beautiful feelings, and has none; that no doubt is a
subtlety of satire; but otherwise he generally reserves
vocal melody for characteristic moments of special exaltation. That is to say, the actor becomes specially prominent when the development of the drama brings his
personality specially forward. The human personality is
an element in the great network of circumstances and
causes and consequences which make a drama interesting

and no doubt it is the most interesting element; but there is no need that the actor should always be insisting upon his own importance, and the importance of his ability to produce beautiful sounds. The human voice is for use, and not only for ornament. People must no doubt learn to sing in a special way in order to do justice to the beautiful old-world artistic creations; and art would be very much the poorer if the power to give them due effect was lost. But the expression of things that are worth uttering because they express something humanly interesting is much more difficult, and implies a much higher aim. Both objects require a great deal of education, but the old-fashioned singer's education concerns chiefly mechanical powers; the singer of the genuine music of Bach, Schubert, Schumann, Brahms, and Wagner requires education of the mind as well.

Of Wagner's general reforms in connection with music-drama this is not the place to speak in detail. His hiding away the unsightly fussy motions of the orchestra under the stage, and his alteration of the arrangements of the theatre, are accessories which do not immediately bear on the musical question here under discussion. His aim in all is to control the multitudinous factors and elements, from small minutiæ up to the largest massing of combined powers to the ends of perfect expression of his dramatic and poetic conceptions. His personality, and the particular subjects that he chooses, and the manner in which he looks at them, affect people in different ways; that is a matter apart from the development of resources or the method of applying them. Of the method itself it may be said that it is the logical outcome of the efforts of the long line of previous composers, and the most completely organised system for the purposes of musical expression that the world has ever yet seen.

SUMMARY AND CONCLUSION.

THE long story of music is a continuous and unbroken record of human effort to extend and enhance the possibilities of effects of sound upon human sensibilities, as representing in a formal or a direct manner the expression of man's inner being. The efforts resolve themselves mainly into impulses to find means to produce the effect of design, and to contrive types of expression which are capable of being adapted to such designs. And as the difficulty of coping with two things at once is considerable, men have generally concentrated their efforts on design at one time, and on expression at another. So that some periods are characterised by special cultivation of principles of form, and others by special efforts in the direction of expression; and owing to the interlacing of various causes in human affairs, these conditions have generally coincided with conditions of society which are adapted to them. The formal character of the music of Mozart's and Haydn's time agrees very well with the character of society in their time; and when a more vehement type of expression became possible the style agreed well with the character of the time, which was specially marked by that impulse to shake off the old conventions which found its most violent expression in the French Revolution.

The first steps in the direction of the essentially modern type of music were made when men attempted to improve upon pure melodic music by singing melodies simultaneously at different pitches. It took an immense time to produce a satisfactory result in part singing; but by degrees men found out how to vary their bald successions of fifths and fourths by ornamental notes, and to make their various simultaneous tunes move without too hideous a cacophony. They found out how to systematise the result at least so far as to make the closing point bear some relation to the beginning, and to contrive something which had the effect of a cadence. And in the course of some centuries, without making the inner organisation of their movements at all definite in design, they succeeded in stringing harmonies together by means of independent voice parts in such a way as to produce the most purely beautiful sound possible. Things arrived at the first crisis under the influence of the Roman Church, and almost all music was then written in the same contrapuntal style used in the Church services.

Then, having apparently exhausted the possibilities in this direction, a new impulse seized upon composers, to apply music more decisively to secular uses, and to find a method of treatment better adapted to secular ideas. They began to employ some of the devices which had been mastered in the way of chord effects in a new way, and gave a solo voice something like musical talking to do. It was like going back to chaos at first; but they had something to build upon, and as the solo voice-part grew more definite, so did the order of the chord successions. They found out that a chord with one definite set of notes afforded an excellent contrast to another chord made up of a different set of notes, and that certain chords were more nearly allied to one another than others. They also found that the old scales that they had used in ecclesiastical music were not accommodating enough for the successions of chords they wanted; and under the influence of their growing feeling for systematisation of these chords they modified these old modes till they had got the tones and semitones in better order for harmonic purposes, and a fair quantity of extra chromatic notes to give variety to their progressions. Music began to expand into a variety of types. Instrumental music began to take a different character from choral music, and secular from sacred vocal music. And by degrees, as the various resources made available by the new arrangement of the scales became better understood, and the devices of the old counterpoint were adapted to the new system, the second great crisis was achieved, in the great works of Bach and Handel, who gave utterance to the new vigour of the Protestant impulses.

Here again men seemed to have arrived at the highest point possible without another change of method; and they applied themselves to developing new types of design, in which melody and harmony were combined in new ways. Their feeling for the relationships of harmony enabled them to spread their bases of structure over wider areas, and to obtain effects of contrast by making one long passage represent one key, and another represent a contrasting one; and by combining various types of contrast into one complete design. The ease with which such a type of design could be handled, enabled them to make use of other elements of effect. The element of colour began to come in very noticeably, and a new climax was reached when all the resources so far attained were combined in symphonies and operas. Art had by this time branched out into a very considerable number of forms, but their actual style was not very distinct. The respective styles of opera and of symphony, of sonata and of Church music, were all very much alike. The principles on which the various forms were constructed were the same; and their internal organisation, as far as minutiæ were concerned, was rather indefinite and conventional.

But in the next age things began to move at a very much increased speed. It was the age of revolutionary ideas; and men were bent on getting rid of conventions, and on seeing things as they are. The art began branching out right and left; symphony style began to differ more intrinsically from opera style; song style from sonata style; oratorio style from the style of Church services, and all from one another. Men found that different objects entailed different treatment; and the subtleties of style had their full measure of attention from men gifted at last with a fine critical sense of relevancy and appropriateness. Again, the internal organisation of works began to be much more definite and articulate. Ideas were put into compact and vivid forms, and the various inner and secondary parts gained more distinct vitality.

Then came the time when men, having many resources at their disposal, sought to use them more decisively for the purposes of expression. The differentiation of forms went on faster than ever. Each large group was subdivided into subordinate groups, and each different item received different treatment. Pianoforte music came to comprise dances of various kinds and calibres, nocturnes, lyrics of all sorts, sonatas, scherzos, capriccios, fugues, and endless other varieties. Operas came to comprise the grand, the comic, the buffa, the seria, and various other national and distinctive types. And each form that had vitality showed a still further advance in effects of colour, articulation of detail, and close approximation to dramatic or expressive consistency. The principle of tonality was expanded to the utmost limits both for design and effect; and with all the resources of harmony and polyphony for form and direct expression; with melody—both inward and outward—for general tone and all that corresponds to vocal utterance, and with rhythm to convey the impression of gesticulatory expression and colour to intensify meaning, mankind seems finally to have full measure of almost unlimited materials available to illustrate anything he will.

But the resources are so immense, that none but composers gifted with special vital energy, and power to grasp many factors at once, seem likely to use them to the full. There are plenty of indications that men are tired of the long journey, and find the rich variety of resource rather overwhelming, and long for things a little less copious in meaning and artistic fulness. Those who aim highest must have command of all resources; but there must be music for all types of mind and all varieties of nature; and there is no necessity that because a thing employs only the minutest fraction of the available resources of art, that it need be bad. The song from the Music Hall may be excellent and characteristic, and often is; the music of people who have every opportunity to be refined and cultivated may be detestably bad, and often is. There is an infinite variety of moods which admit of being expressed, from the noble, aspiring, human sincerity of a great nature like Brahms', to the rank, impudent, false sentimentality of impostors who shall be nameless. The unfortunate art may be made to grovel and wallow as well as to soar. A man may use slender resources to very good ends, and great resources to very bad ones. It rests with a very wide public now to decide what the future of the art shall be; and if they can understand a little of what music means, and how it came to be what it is, perhaps it may help the world to encourage sincerity in the composer, and not to lay itself open to be imposed upon by those who have other ends in view than honouring their art.

If the art is worthy of the dignity of human devotion, it is worth considering a little seriously, without depreciating in the least the lighter pleasures to which it may minister. If it is to be a mere toy and trifle, it would be better to have no more to do with it. But what the spirit of man has laboured at for so many centuries cannot only be a mere plaything. The marvellous concentration of faculties towards the achievement of such ends as actually exist, must of itself be enough to give the product human interest. Moreover, though a man's life may not be prolonged, it may be widened and deepened by what he puts into it; and any possibility of bringing people into touch with those highest moments in art in which great ideals were realised, in music in which noble aspirations and noble sentiments were successfully embodied, is a chance of enriching human experience in the noblest manner; and the humanising influences which democracy may hereafter have at its disposal may thereby be infinitely enlarged.

INDEX.

THE END.

PRINTED BY BALLANTYNE, HANSON AND CO
EDINBURGH AND LONDON